BLIND IN ONE EAR

BLIND IN ONE EAR

THE AVENGER RETURNS

Patrick Macnee

and

Marie Cameron

MERCURY HOUSE, INCORPORATED

San Francisco

To Thea

Copyright © 1989 by Patrick Macnee and Marie Cameron. Originally published in Great Britain by Harrap, London, copyright © 1988 by Patrick Macnee and Marie Cameron.

Published in the United States by
Mercury House
San Francisco, California

Distributed to the trade by
Consortium Book Sales & Distribution, Inc.
St. Paul, Minnesota

Mercury House and colophon are registered trademarks of
Mercury House, Incorporated

Manufactured in the United States of America

Library of Congress Cataloging-in-Publication Data

Macnee, Patrick, 1922–
    Blind in one ear : the avenger returns / Patrick Macnee and Marie Cameron.
        p.   cm.
    Includes index.
    ISBN 0–916515–58–3 : $19.95
    1. Macnee, Patrick, 1922– . 2. Actors—Great Britain—Biography. I. Cameron, Marie, 1936– . II. Title.
PN2598.M27A3   1989
791.45'028'092—dc20
[B]   89–32147
                                                                        CIP

PREFACE

'I'm so sorry,' murmured Erishka, the wife of one of my favourite restaurant owners. 'We don't like her disturbing our guests, but we're very indulgent. You see, she's blind in one ear.'

I looked down at the mother duck who, followed by her tiny fluffy ducklings, waddled in stately fashion among the tables, devouring scraps of food tossed to her by the diners. 'Blind in one ear,' I thought. 'Surely she means deaf in one ear.' And she probably did, but I hesitated to correct the lady as I didn't like to say.

I mused upon Erishka's remark that evening as I worked in the garden of my home in Palm Springs. A simple confusion of words, and my failure to speak out, revived an early childhood memory.

When I was five years old I was packed off to my first school. I hadn't wanted to leave my parents and nanny, and I hadn't believed their assurances that it was for my own good. My doubts were confirmed when I was beaten for the first time, from which moment I declared war on the adult world. My fury was mixed with self-reproach, however, for I had not uttered a word of protest. I had been brought up not to question parental decisions, however outrageous they might appear. This unquestioning acceptance of the odd or incongruous has stayed with me throughout a strange life. And my genius for misunderstanding has led to some very close scrapes. Perhaps I too was blind in one ear.

On my next visit to England I asked Mama about my being sent away to school all those years ago.

'If you didn't want to be sent away,' she replied, 'then why didn't you say?'

'Because you taught me not to say. And besides, I'm blind in one ear.'

Mama assumed her 'the boy's mad' expression and thought for a moment. 'Blind in one ear,' she said eventually. 'Hmm. It certainly doesn't run in the family. At least, not on my side.'

I leave readers of this book to come to their own conclusions about that!

Patrick Macnee
Palm Springs, California
1988

— 1 —

'I think I'm going to have a baby,' said Mama to Pa one day.

'Boy or gel?'

'Won't know until it makes its debut.'

A pair of alarmed eyes peeped over the top of *The Sporting Life* and blinked at Mama, who was seated at the far end of the refectory table sipping champagne for breakfast.

'Damn rum business, this breedin' lark,' Pa snorted. 'Horses or women, the mountin' of either always ruptures me balls.' And with that, he returned his attention to the runners at Newmarket.

Nicknamed 'Shrimp' on account of his size, Pa was a bustling leprechaun who'd spent most of his youth racing road coaches out of London and across the Home Counties. The son of a Scottish engineer, he was encouraged to join the family firm. Having watched his own father screw half the nuts and bolts into the Forth Bridge, various prison gates and an odd lunatic asylum, Pa yawned, turned his back on crowbars and opted for a life of training horses.

Great-Grandpapa had enjoyed a more 'genteel' way of scratching for his daily crust. Named Daniel, and hell-bent on becoming an artist, he'd encountered fierce parental opposition in the pursuit of his ambition. This opposition crumbled only after he'd run away from home for the fourth time. It was not that the family objected to life's Van Goghs. If these fellows wished to snip off their ears then why shouldn't they? But no gentleman painted a lady without her clothes.

Apprenticed to one John Knox, whose namesake and distant ancestor had conspired to kick Mary, Queen of Scots, off her throne, the young Daniel Macnee showed early promise in painting and pleasure. He became the ringleader of a nineteenth-century gang of rakes, which included the genial Robert Macgeorge, later to become Dean of Argyll, and a certain Mr Macnish, author of the best-selling book, *The Anatomy of Drunkenness*. In spite of his youthful abandon, the artist was always impeccably behaved towards ladies, whatever their social station. No doubt he took the view that courtesy is one of the most persuasive ways of talking ladies into doing what they protest they don't usually do. Passionately fond of the theatre, Macnee was banned from Mason's Circus and other playhouses for chasing chorus girls. Being a practical boy, he shrugged off this prohibition and formed his own theatrical company, for which he painted the scenery and acted. Within weeks the takings exceeded those of his rivals.

At this time, the young Daniel Macnee was tall, dark, slim and aristocratically handsome. He also sang well, was amiable, and was described by a contemporary as being 'possessed of the most agreeable and buoyant faculty of imagination, imitation and invention'. Some of these qualities have been inherited by his descendants, but singing is not one of them.

As Macnee's career progressed, he was commissioned to draw anatomical sketches. The family's most sinister fears were confirmed. Their son was not only drawing naked ladies but also showing what amounted to a fetish for their bottoms. He once vowed that during a coach journey to London he would seduce a girl at each stop. Shortly afterwards, Macnee married for the first time and was tamed – temporarily.

He graduated to portrait painting, whereupon his abilities were commented upon favourably by Sir Walter Scott. It was a noble compliment from the author of *Rob Roy*, whose clan, the Macgregors, had signed a peace treaty with the Macnees in 1613 after centuries of thieving each others' cattle and wives. Now 'the' fashionable painter in Scotland, Macnee had half the Scottish nobility tripping their way into his studio. Such good luck couldn't last and didn't. One day, having partaken too liberally of a fine malt, the artist overbooked and arrived at work to find Lord Chancellor Brougham, the Marquis of Lorne and a couple of dukes squabbling over a sitting. After some quick thinking, Macnee suggested a group portrait. With clan rivalries on the boil, this idea was not well received. A row broke out, and an aristocratic punch-up seemed inevitable. Macnee passed his malt, tempers cooled, and everyone got drunk and swore eternal friendship. Lord Brougham was last seen clambering up towards Edinburgh Castle, his wig crooked, his accent slurred, but his dignity, in his Chancellor's robes, almost intact.

Daniel Macnee became a popular figure in Edinburgh society, and his work was likened to that of Gainsborough. Such praise came from the unsociable Turner, Macnee being one of possibly only three people this introverted artist ever invited to dinner. It was said that Macnee could tell the same story many times but never in the same way. Convulsed with mirth over one of these tales, William Makepeace Thackeray pronounced Macnee 'The Prince of Raconteurs'.

Following the death of his first wife, the painter married a great beauty who called herself Mary Buchanan. She was in fact a Macnee, but both she and her husband remained noticeably discreet as to the exact proximity of their blood relationship.

With many of his works now hanging in Scotland's major galleries and stately heaps, the artist was elected President of The Scottish Royal Academy, received numerous academic and civic honours and he was knighted by Queen Victoria in 1877. Sir Daniel must have been loved, for after his death a succession of friends quickly followed him to the grave; but Lady Macnee survived for another fifty years!

In contrast to Pa's family, whose money was 'new', Mama came from what was quaintly, if satirically, termed 'The Quality'. As clubs go, the British aristocracy is arguably the most exclusive in the world. Being a niece of the Earl of

Huntingdon, Mama qualified for membership at the moment of conception. If the Huntingdon family are to be believed, she was descended from Robin Hood. The Huntingdons, whose family surname was Hastings, were ambitious. Robert de Hastings was a toady of William the Conqueror, and years of grovelling paid off. Robert's son became keeper of Henry the First's napery, a grand way of saying he kept an eye on the royal table-cloths.

A century later, another Hastings married a great-great-grand-daughter of King David the Seventh of Scotland. Consequently, the family spent a fortune and several centuries trying to prove they owned the country. When this con trick failed they resumed their sucking up to the English monarchy, and, once again, it paid off. The Hastings were showered with manors, dowries and lands. A Hastings was made keeper of the lions in the Tower of London, while another was appointed Keeper of the Royal Mint.

Dark clouds loomed when the first Lord Hastings got tangled up with the luscious Jane Shore, Edward the Fourth's live-in girl-friend. A sensual man, Edward wasn't one to pontificate on sexual proclivities, but his successor, Richard the Third, was more conservative in outlook. Accusing Hastings and Jane of witchcraft, he held them responsible for his physical deformities. Wanting rid of my ancestor, Richard listened to bent lawyers, got the charge of witchcraft upgraded to one of treason, and Hastings was executed. At least he was awarded the posthumous consolation of having his death immortalized by William Shakespeare.

The family were finally granted the Earldom of Huntingdon by Henry the Eighth, but from this time their finances began to slide. The main offender was the Fifth Earl of Huntingdon, who squandered thousands upon entertainment. Already encumbered by his ancestor's debts, the Seventh Earl incurred a prison sentence and vast fines for telling the Royal Family they weren't the kind of people he'd include on his guest list. The

Ninth Earl died from a fit of apoplexy in Downing Street, possibly having regrets about the family motto, which was 'Victory is the truth'.

So much for my ancestors. But what about my parents themselves? By the age of twenty-two, Mama had shown no interest in marriage. While other girls all but devoted their lives to making a good match, her desperate parents lined up the more eligible remnants of the First World War and ordered their daughter to make a choice. In a scene surely reminiscent of an identity parade, the wayward girl inspected ranks of shell-shocked bachelors before tapping Pa on the shoulder.

'Him,' she all but accused.

My parents' union of 'new' money to old blood was not unusual. Lawyers had been drawing up similar contracts for years. Such arrangements were highly popular at the turn of the century when a swarm of Croesus-rich American heiresses bought their way into Britain's ducal houses. Given such an unromantic start and an eighteen year age difference, my parents were remarkably polite to each other and agreed to appear together in public. They were nevertheless a monument to matrimonial disaster. Pa was immersed in his horses, gin and country life, while Mama, a radiant creature of stunning wit and physical beauty, had an appetite for high living and preferably in London.

After the First World War, there existed what J.B. Priestley called 'The Three Englands', those of Shakespeare, Victorian industrialization and twentieth-century shapelessness. As a courageous officer in the Yorkshire Dragoons, Pa had nevertheless been shaken badly by the holocaust of the trenches. Having survived a conflict which had all but destroyed a generation of men, he faced an uncertain future in 'The Three Englands'.

It would be a future that brought a social upheaval greater than the Reformation. With some ten million acres of land changing hands, a major break up of many great estates began. My parents watched with sadness and apprehension as friends and social acquaintances sold out. But the British upper class possesses the ability to cope with changing social, political and economic trends, and to absorb itself into any new world such transformations may bring. Some families did 'go to the wall', but most did not. Taking a deep breath, I blinked and stumbled my way into such a world on 6 February 1922. Within weeks, I'd been christened Daniel Patrick Macnee in honour of my paternal great-grandpapa. Even at such an early age, I'm told that a physical likeness was already recognizable. The more sensual side of my character had yet to develop.

All but anaesthetizing himself against the nation's ills, Pa hibernated in the country with his horses and gin, but not Mama. Always able to sniff out a wild party in London, New York or Paris, she bounced on to that giddy roundabout, 'The Roaring Twenties'. With only the vaguest understanding of her nuptial vows, she could dedicate herself to fun with saintly devotion. Possibly overlooking the fact that she was nine months pregnant, one day Mama crammed several parties into one evening. Leaving a great house in Piccadilly, she tossed a coin to a boy employed to clean up after the horses and ordered her carriage to Park Lane. Within minutes she was creaking with labour pains and she screamed at the coachman to head for the nearest hospital. Scattering obstacles, mostly of a pedestrian nature, a couple of foaming horses sprinted towards Bayswater. At that point, Mama's memory blanked. Although subjected to numerous interrogations over the years, she could never be sure whether she'd produced her first son in a carriage, a hospital bed or the gutter. On seeing his son for the first time, Pa sniffed and nodded with conventional approval before grumbling, 'Good loins. Pity he's only got two legs.' He then returned to Wiltshire at once.

Mama's hectic socializing had already incurred the wrath of

her in-laws. These included Pa's formidable trio of sisters, my Aunts Aggie, May and Tibby, otherwise known as the Kilkenny Cats. With the surprise of childbirth scarcely behind her, Mama felt unable to cope with 'The Cats', and remained in London under the pretext of resting. Within days she was back on the party circuit, however, where she dined with Lord Northcliffe, chatted with the newly engaged Lord Mountbatten, and danced with the Duke of Leinster, a man who made more appearances in the bankruptcy courts than he did at parties. She even found time to drop in on Rosa Lewis, an aged ex-girl-friend of Edward the Seventh. Her mind going, Rosa still believed that the King visited her every night. No one had the heart to say the old boy had been dead some twelve years.

At the murkier but far more fascinating end of the social scale, Mama had chummed up with a Mrs Meyrick, whose handsome Chinese boy-friend, one 'Brilliant Chang', was London's undisputed dope king. While Mama puffed reefers, courtesy of Chang, Mrs Meyrick unfolded her life story. The wife of a Brighton doctor, she'd graduated from night club hostess to opening her own establishment. As she explained tearfully, 'How could I otherwise afford to educate my girls?'

Among Mama's many talents was an ability to spend money at a rate which would have even alarmed the Duke of Leinster. She'd always worn couturier clothes and handmade accessories, squandered vast sums on riotous entertainment, and was a sucker for any down and out who begged for a shilling and expected a guinea. By now, it must have occurred to Pa that his wife had 'gone missing'. A few months after my birth, Mama received a telephone call from Wiltshire.

'How considerate of you to telephone.'
'Can't find me gelding irons.'
'And how are the horses?'
'Eating their bloody heads off.'
'Such expense.'

'That boy, Patrick. What's he up to these days?'

'According to nanny, he's still incontinent.'

'Filthy little bugger.' This compliment was followed by a positively revolting rasp which suggested a clearing of the throat. 'Er, will we be seeing anything of yer?'

'Oh, I think it's time I looked in.'

'Capital.'

'Oh, and when you do find the gelding irons, have a care. They've been the cause of so many accidents.'

Mama headed for Wiltshire with eighteen pieces of luggage and me. My parents shook hands, sat down to dinner and made stilted noises at each other.

During Mama's absence, Pa's clientele expanded. The new owners for whom he was training included Lord Porchester, whose father, the Earl of Carnarvon, had taken up residence in the Valley of the Kings to excavate Tutankhamun's tomb. As Mrs Meyrick confided to Mama, 'When he was in my club only the other week, the King of Egypt's brother complained about his Lordship fiddling with the dead.' Lord Carnarvon died. All in all, a dozen or so other people connected with the excavation followed suit. For weeks, the world's press was obsessed with lurid tales of Pharoahs' curses and phantom mummies haunting the Nile Delta. The rumours circulating London's clubland were of a more exotic nature. Monocles popped and moustachios quivered as tales of Luxor's teenage Cleo's steamed their way through White's and Boodle's. The way these girls reputedly contorted their anatomy while belly dancing inspired subalterns and revived war veterans. With visions of pelvic thrusts and body snake rolls, there was an immediate stampede to Thomas Cook's for one-way tickets to Egypt. If the girls didn't come up to scratch, one could always fall back on a trip around the pyramids.

Pa's only concern was that the Pharoah's curse wouldn't stretch a grisly smile over the new Earl of Carnarvon's horses, some of whom were now stabled at Badon Hole. This was

Pa's recently acquired home and training establishment, set high on the Wiltshire Downs near Marlborough. It was also my first home; until I was three years old, I lived there deep in the country, rarely meeting other children. One of my godfathers, Henry Young, not only stabled his horses at Badon Hole, but proved to be a roistering drinking companion for Pa. He also owned a brewery. For over three hundred years, the Youngs have brewed their excellent beer at the Ram brewery in southern London.

Henry Young often lent his country home to Edward the Seventh for discreet assignations but was soon besieged with complaints from his sovereign. The royal bedroom was over the stables, where the clip clop of horses' hooves distracted the king from his love making. Rather than inconvenience his royal guest by moving him to another room, Henry solved the problem by carpeting the stables. With Henry standing at six feet seven inches, and Pa at a mere five feet, the two men made an odd looking couple. When they weren't tearing around the track at Brooklands in early Vauxhalls, Pa and Henry patronized their favourite country inns around the Froxfield, Avebury and Bishop's Canning triangle down in Wiltshire.

Mama observed these activities through the bubbly blurr of Dom Perignon. Deciding that she wouldn't be missed, she planned a series of furtive trips back to London. Before leaving, she had to find a replacement for my nanny, who'd fled the house some months previously. After auditioning several hopefuls, Mama settled for a veritable carthorse of a girl who oozed affection through her plump breasts and plumper buttocks. Once in the care of this side of prime fillet I must have felt instinctively that my luck was on the turn.

Through her socializing, Mama had become acquainted with the divine Tallulah Bankhead, who'd just arrived in town to open in her first West End play. The daughter of an American senator, Tallulah's pouting good looks and huskey voice, added to her smoking, drinking, swearing and lively enthusiasm for affairs with both sexes, endeared her greatly to the twilight side of society.

Upon her return to Wiltshire, Mama discovered she had been missed! She was all but scratched to ribbons by the Kilkenny Cats. Devoted to their baby brother, who'd been something of a mother's boy, the trio accused Mama of desertion and worse. As their accusations were vague and invariably trailed off in mid-sentence, the 'worse' could only be assumed. Not a quarrelsome lady, Mama decided to lie low, affecting an interest in country life for the time being. When my parents were seen together in public, it was either at race meetings or out riding with hunts, their favourites being The Old Berks and The Craven. There was some amusement when the Earl of Craven made a run for South Africa with the Countess of Cathcart, forty trunks of family heirlooms and two suits of armour. Indeed, the Earl's run even aroused grudging admiration, as he had only one leg. But given the heat of Capetown, what the devil would he do with two suits of armour?

Down in the country, occasional conversations did take place, but they were not encouraged. Opinions, along with books, were regarded with grave suspicion, being thought of generally as the pursuits of liberals, foreigners and Roman Catholics.

By now, Pa was hitting the gin at breakfast. Mama joined in and quickly showed talent as a promising young lush. During one of her furtive trips to London for what she now termed 'shopping', Mama received an hysterical telephone call from Mrs Meyrick. The police had at last caught up with 'Brilliant Chang', who'd just been sent down on dope charges. Before she knew it, poor Mrs Meyrick herself was bundled off to prison for selling alcohol without a licence. The court seemed unimpressed that her clients had included The Prince of Wales.

With Pa spending most of the time well in his cups, pleasant though this undoubtedly was, it did lead him into making rash promises. Always the gentleman, Pa never went back on his word, but his undertakings were then carried out with much regret and mumbled cursing. Having promised Mama a visit to the London theatre, he found himself dragged off to see Noel Coward in *The Vortex*. Notwithstanding Sir Gerald du Maurier's remark that 'All the public want is perverted filth,' the play was a smash. After the show, Pa was dragged off yet again, this time to a theatrical party where the guest of honour was the septuagenarian George Bernard Shaw. Coached by Mama and a couple of enticing flappers, the old boy tried dancing the Charleston. Towards the end of the evening, an onlooker remarked, 'He kicked and leapt with gusto.'

1925 was one of the most important years of my life, for it was then that I discovered sex. Nanny, whose affection would have compensated for fifty sets of neglectful parents, had no inhibitions about allowing me to peep at the globular swell of her *décolletage*. Come Christmas and birthdays, I was even allowed a squeeze. Such wanton lust in a three-year-old could not go unpunished, and my retribution was the glowering face of a sulky young man. A chauffeur by profession, he was Nanny's 'intended'. As he was also the owner of a row of terraced cottages in Lambourn, such a marriage would be one step up the social scale for Nanny. Possibly feeling broody, Nanny began treating me as her own child. The chauffeur's glowers deepened.

Mama's forced enthusiasm for country life waned quickly. Back on the rounds in London, she discovered an establishment in the King's Road, named The Pheasantry. Always on the look out for a new adventure, she'd wandered in, ordered drinks for all and introduced herself to The Pheasantry's members. One of these members was to have a calamitous effect upon my upbringing.

The club was a popular meeting place for ladies who were, in many respects, pioneers of what has come to be known as the Feminist Movement. These ladies included Evelyn, an heiress and courageous explorer, Elaine Erowa, a noted Swiss writer, Nesta de Robeck, who divided her time between palatial homes in Venice and Assisi, Dolly Wilde, a niece of Oscar, half the Sackville-Wests, Mrs Tyndell, a formidable Australian lady with feet that resembled flippers, and the incredible 'Toupie' Lowther. The eldest daughter of the Earl of Lonsdale, Toupie had founded and driven bravely in an ambulance unit during the First World War with her close friend, Miss 'Desmond' Hackett, and was later arrested in Spain for 'masquerading as a woman'.

Out of this hotch-potch of eccentrics who frequented The Pheasantry, it was Evelyn who caught Mama's ever-roving eye. The admiration was reciprocated. A fine-looking woman with an aquiline nose and large eyes set in a face which seemed sculptured from lily-white marble, Evelyn bore a startling resemblance to the young Franklin D. Roosevelt. Evelyn's excellent deportment accentuated her broad shoulders, which were covered either in tweeds or a vividly coloured smoking jacket. A chain-smoker and a heavy drinker of Scotch whisky, Evelyn was always accompanied by several dogs of varying breeds. All in all, she must have oozed smouldering, macho virility.

The two women discovered they were near neighbours, Evelyn being the owner of Rooksnest, a vast Tudor mansion just outside Lambourn. Quickly accepting Evelyn's invitation to drive over and take afternoon tea, Mama must have seen Rooksnest and its obvious attractions as a refuge from the tedium of her own home and marriage.

By now apparently inseparable, Mama and Evelyn chased off to see Tallulah Bankhead, who'd just opened at The Globe in Noel Coward's *Fallen Angels*. Perhaps predictably, the play became a success when the critics described it as obscene.

After the show, Mama and Evelyn went to Mrs Meyrick's. Since her release from jail, this enterprising lady had expanded her commercial interests and now owned a string of night clubs. Such business acumen was not appreciated in every quarter. Mrs Meyrick's arch-enemy was the then Home Secretary, Sir William Joyson-Hicks, known to London's whores, as 'High Kicks Hicks'. Such was the Minister's determination to rid London of Mrs Meyrick and what he'd convinced himself was her bad influence that he suffered permanent migraines. This, coupled with overwork, mostly on a file labelled 'Meyrick', caused him to collapse at a Buckingham Palace garden party.

Yet again, it must have occurred to Pa that his wife had 'gone missing'. This time there was no telephone call to summon her back to the country. Instead, he bolted down a bottle of gin and stormed up to London. After a stiff exchange of words, Mama agreed to leave Evelyn and follow her husband back to Wiltshire. Such acquiesence was possibly encouraged by the knowledge that the welcoming portals of Rooksnest were so deliciously nearby.

It was probably around this time that Pa first considered leaving England. During his trip to London, he'd met the Maharajah of Patiala, who'd taken over an entire floor of the Savoy Hotel for his stay. One of the fantastically wealthy Indian rulers, the Maharajah reputedly paid upwards of one hundred and fifty pounds for specially upholstered under-pants. In what form this scaffolding came and at what point it was erected, society could only guess at, but the dusky voluptuary certainly enjoyed notable success with women. Having promised to find Pa a position in the horse racing world should he ever settle in India, the potentate then plied him with an aromatic tobacco from the East, and suddenly the little man's world seemed very much rosier.

Before returning to the country, Pa was dragged off to the theatre again. So impressed had she been by *Fallen Angels*, that Mama not only wished to see the play a second time, but had decided her theatre-loathing husband couldn't possibly fail to enjoy the show. In the event, he adored the performance, if not the advertised programme. As Pa snored his way through the first act, he was awoken by a commotion. The nineteen twenties' answer to Mrs Mary Whitehouse, one Mrs Charles Hornibrook, was in Row A of the stalls. A supporter of 'The Council for the Protection of Public Morality', she leapt to her feet and scrambled up on the stage. Brandishing an umbrella, this worthy soul lambasted a stunned house with a stern lecture on the play's supposed immoral content. Two minutes into her address, Mrs Hornibrook was interrupted by a raucous Billingsgate accent which roared, 'Go on. Git 'er, lads.'

A riot broke out, and with a howling mob threatening to lynch her, Mrs Hornibrook and most of the cast got themselves caught up in the safety curtain, which some stagehands had mistakenly let down. The police were called, and still ranting about adulterers and sodomists incurring the wrath of God, a kicking Mrs Hornibrook was carried to safety by four sturdy constables. In an effort to cool tempers, the conductor calmly raised his baton and the orchestra struck up, 'I Want To Be Happy'.

Pa realized that his marriage was not a success. Assisted by his old friend the gin bottle, he contemplated Mama's unpredictable conduct and the possible means of keeping her out of London. Egged on by the Kilkenny Cats, he even toyed with the idea of having her legally detained by the Master in Lunacy, but in the event couldn't bring himself to start an action. Behind that gruff exterior lay a kindly little man whose upbringing had also taught him that one did not publicize one's private life before the great unwashed. Pretending the situation didn't exist, he took to tearing around the countryside in his old coach.

For some months, I'd noticed Pa eyeing me up and down. Eventually he ordered a local vet to measure me and give an opinion as to what my eventual weight and height might be. When this had been done, the two men clustered in a corner of the stable yard, where they muttered conspiratorially. As I attempted to make a run for it, Pa yanked me back by the scruff of the neck and, spraying me with an Eau de Cologne of stale gin, hissed, 'We'll have you winning the Derby, boy.' Ignoring my screams, he plonked me on the top of a racehorse measuring seventeen hands, beamed with what might have passed for parental pride, and announced I was going to be a jockey.

'Think you'll look well in Lord Rosebery's,' he roared. He did not specify whether he was referring to the Earl's racing colours or his truss.

Realizing that home was a dangerous place, I took to vanishing with my Collie dog. No one seemed to notice I'd gone. In a rare moment of agreement Pa and Mama had christened my canine chum Buckingham Palace. I called him Stinker. Together we'd run off and hide on the Downs where we lay together for hours hugging each other while I conjured up fantasies. I longed to dress up in wigs and lace ruffles and look like the gentlemen whose portraits hung from the walls of my parents' reception rooms. As I continued to hug Stinker, I realized this affectionate rug of silken fur was my only friend, apart from Nanny. Heading for home, I was more apprehensive than unhappy. I could never be sure what might happen next.

We moved from Badon Hole and went to live at College House in Lambourn which, after Newmarket, is probably the most important horse-racing town in the British Isles. Pa acquired even more horses and seemed cheerful, although he was now dropping wistful hints about the glories of the British Raj in India. Taking the view that her husband was hallucinating, Mama paid fewer visits to London, preferring to take tea with Evelyn at Rooksnest. With my parents so otherwise occupied, Nanny was effectively my surrogate mother, although by now the feelings of her 'intended' towards me were all but verging on the homicidal.

The climate worsened when Nanny announced she'd never

marry until Master Patrick was old enough to look after himself. As my background would have retarded the most balanced child, it looked as though Nanny might have a long wait. Shortly afterwards, I clambered into my toy car and peddled off down a hill. Along the way, a couple of wheels mysteriously fell off. As I screamed for help the car over-turned, depositing itself and its driver in a ditch. Nothing was ever proved, but I did wonder about Nanny's intended.

It was decided that 'the boy Patrick' should get to know other members of the family, and come the following summer holidays, I was sent to stay with Uncle Joe and Aunt Peggy. I was well used to lunatics by now, and this unlikely couple didn't surprise me. Aunt Peggy was a cold, dominating woman, but she liked me, regarding me as the son she'd never had. What remained of her reserves of affection was rationed between her horses and dogs. She spent much of her time stomping about in riding boots, enjoyed cracking whips, and was embroiled in a steamy affair with a man called 'Tiger'. In spite of his ferocious nickname, 'Tiger' was very obedient. Aunt Peggy's first husband had tried to shoot her. Of course, the scandal was hushed up, but the marriage was annulled when the poor man went mad.

My Aunt's second husband, Uncle Joe, was a sweet man, but his wife couldn't speak to him. He was quite deaf, and shouting was her only successful means of communication. With my own ear drums effectively ruined by the noise, I examined the extraordinary collection of ear trumpets and other hearing aids littering the house, and imagined what it was like living with Beethoven.

The result of this marriage was my cousin Josephine. A pretty, apple-cheeked girl, she was loved by her father and loathed by her mother, whose sole ambition for Josephine was to make her the finest horsewoman in Great Britain. On my first night with these relations, Josephine and I looked out from our bedroom window at the cemetery Aunt Peggy had built for her dogs. The two of us didn't say very much, but I certainly wondered about the strange world of adults.

After the holiday, my parents sent me to a small kindergarten in Lambourn, to 'keep the boy out of mischief'. Up to their own necks in mischief, Mama and Evelyn chased back to London to see Tallulah Bankhead open in her latest play, *Scotch Mist*. Another burst of moral outrage, this time spearheaded by the unmarried Bishop of London, ensured the play's success. By now Tallulah had bought a fabulous West End mansion where she devoted herself to throwing a series of outrageous parties. Eagerly accepting an invitation to one of these jamborees, Mama and Evelyn were greeted by a naked Tallulah who directed them to the bathroom, which had been decked out as the cocktail bar. The actress's boy friend, a pleasant young twit called Sir Francis Laking, added to the entertainment by dressing up as a woman, before performing a spectacular striptease.

Pa, meanwhile, was becoming somewhat agitated over the General Strike. Seeing the Britain he loved crashing around him, he exploded over a family dinner. The evening hadn't gone well, with a dozen or so relatives glaring at each other when they weren't chomping or grunting. What conversation there was had been confined to horses until some drunk suggested that perhaps we'd been harsh over German war reparations. Remembering the holocaust of the trenches, Pa grabbed a shot gun, leapt on to the table and began his own onslaught. Kicking silver into startled laps, he threatened to shoot the pacifist Marquis of Tavistock, if he ever got the chance, for defending the ex-Kaiser. As Pa aimed his shot gun, guests flinched. In such an alcoholic condition he had the unnerving habit of changing his intended target. There was a blast. Glass shattered and curtains singed as a window took the force of his wrath. 'I'll have the lot of you,' he threatened, then dropped the shot gun and crashed into the ruins of crystal, silver and a large assortment of ripe cheeses.

I was removed from my small kindergarten in Lambourn and packed off to an educational establishment far away in Somerset. It was to be the first of many times that I was loaded into a large, shiny car and deposited in the care of odd characters who'd mistakenly decided their vocation lay in teaching children. Nanny wept and promised she'd still be at College House when the holidays came. I also wept. The fear of going to a strange place caused apprehension, but my tears were also for the Mama I so dearly loved. She seemed genuinely distressed at being parted from her child. Trying to explain that it was all for my own good, she kissed me before rushing sobbing into the house. Pa shook my hand and asked that I not blacken the family's good name. I was five years old.

The establishment was one of those awful schools that had prompted Charles Dickens to write with such passion in *Nicholas Nickleby*. Run by two elderly sisters who the pupils were instructed to call Aunt Maud and Aunt Edith, the new intake of juniors quickly discovered who was the villain and how she should best be avoided. Aunt Maud was a big woman. With her purple cheeks, fanged teeth and enlarged nostrils from which stubbly bristles flared out, and carrying a slipper, she padded around the school always on the lookout for a buttock to whack. For months I managed to remain reasonably unobtrusive, until she caught me staring at her bunions. Aunt Maud smiled and sized up my buttocks with malicious anticipation.

A little light relief came in the form of my first dramatic experience. Given my family's general contempt for law and order, I was inappropriately cast as a policeman in the school pantomime. The play went off well enough, but the dressing-room was hardly up to West End standards. The junior cast were marched on to a railway track, and ordered to strip and change into their theatrical costumes. Supervising the undressing was Aunt Maud's other half, Aunt Edith. A gentle mouse of a lady, forever blinking and twittering, her nerves must have been ruined by Aunt Maud. 'Now, come along children,' she'd stutter. 'Take off your clothes while I keep a look out for the trains.'

With the pantomime in full swing at a nearby hall, those not on stage swopped sweets and cigarette cards while awaiting their call. When it came, they walked backwards towards the hall, watching Aunt Edith who was still on the track and blinking into the distance for the sight of a train. Thoroughly enjoying my first acting part, I forgot about Aunt Edith until a bloodcurdling scream sliced its way through the hall. With Aunt Maud in the wings hissing fatal consequences if we left the stage, the cast soldiered on; but they did so with visions of Aunt Edith's squashed corpse stretched out across the track like a blob of raspberry jam. At the end of the evening, we ignored a second curtain call and stampeded back to the track with an enraged Aunt Maud in pursuit. Aunt Edith could be seen wandering up and down the rails in a state of hysteria. Apparently, something nasty had crawled up her leg.

Vacations did mean an occasional visit home, but most of that time was spent on further obligatory grand tours around the mansions of my numerous relatives. Best described as a 'tweedy' lot, some spoke as though a plum was stuck in their throats, while the rest sounded as though they'd swallowed the orchard. They also had traditional ideas about the making of a gentleman. The first words I'd been taught had been 'Please' and 'Thank you'. Apart from that I was not encouraged to speak. It was likewise all but flogged into me that a gentleman never showed emotion. This was almost impossible, as I desperately missed my parents and Nanny, added to which, after my first stage appearance, I'd acquired a taste for acting. How could I act without showing emotion?

As for the lower orders, it was explained to me that they were on the earth to serve, and that we had an obligation to look after them. Appreciation of this primitive social welfare was expressed during prayers in the servants' dining hall:

'God bless the squire and his relations
and may we always know our stations.'

I had already learnt to nod benignly when forelocks were
touched before 'Master Patrick'. Given such formality, it
seemed quite contradictory that intimacy with Nanny was
socially acceptable.

Back at school, my chums were going down like skittles
under the weight of Aunt Maud's slipper. With escape out of
the question all one could do was await the summons to her
study. Mine came. Within ten minutes of entering that torture
chamber I emerged in tears rubbing a very sore bottom. Down
in the school chapel, a clutch of chastised boys threw themselves on the mercy of The Almighty. 'Dear God,' we be-
seeched. 'Please take Aunt Maud and her slipper unto you.'
He replied with rare alacrity. Some weeks later, the old
dragon was driving back from Minehead during a thunder-
storm. As her car skidded across a wet road, lightning struck
a tree which then crashed down on the top of her automobile. Mercifully, she was killed outright, but the school's
pupils had difficulty showing genuine grief at her memorial
service.

Come that Christmas, Mama 'went missing' once more.
Remembering my relations' lectures on the vulgarity of emotional outbursts, I managed as best I could to forget the thrill
of cuddling up to Mama. Half-heartedly shrugging my shoulders, I made a beeline for the nursery. Nanny's response was
intoxicating. Serving up a tea of potted chicken sandwiches
and cream buns, that night she allowed me to share her bed
for the very first time. All but fermenting with excitement, I
was further intoxicated by the aroma of a beeswax polish that
had been rubbed into the linoleum covering the nursery floor.
Nanny extinguished the lights and began to undress. I peeped
at her over the embroidered edge of my sheets. Her ample
silhouette was illuminated against the flames of a fire crack-

ling in the grate. Although her back was turned, Nanny cautioned, 'Now, now, Master Patrick. No peeping!'

We cuddled up together in bed, and the kindly girl recited my favourite stories about Winnie the Pooh. Cushioned in Nanny's opulent curves, I was grateful for such affection and drifted for once into a happy sleep.

Mama and Evelyn were back in London again. They'd received an invitation from Mrs Meyrick to attend the opening night of 'The Silver Slipper', her new night club near Piccadilly Circus. Booked in at The Connaught, the pair of them got drunk in the bar and rolled up to the club hours late. Through her alcoholic haze it must have occurred to Evelyn that something was amiss when she spotted a traffic jam of Black Marias stuffed with assorted riff raff, heading for the police station at West End Central. Grabbing Mama, Evelyn did an about turn and raced back to the Connaught. The next morning's headlines said it all.

With vintage champagne 'on the house', half of Burke's peerage, the world of show business and a contingent representing the criminal fraternity had streamed into her club. The evening began on a rowdy note which quickly roared to a crescendo when the cabaret began. Some way into the third act, an audience of several hundred drunks catcalled, cheered or threw champagne bottles at anything that moved on stage. In the midst of this bedlam, in minced a well known member of the French aristocracy with his entourage of young boys. Although it was an open secret that the nobleman hunted wild boar on his estate wearing make-up and corsets, even the jaded audience at Mrs Meyrick's gasped when they saw the boys. Clad in breast plates, tight buckskin pants and thigh length, black patent boots, the boys' *pièces de résistance* were gleaming helmets surmounted by double-headed eagles. Any authority on military uniforms would have recognized a troop of subalterns from the First Cavalier Guard Regiment of Tsar Nicholas the First.

Confronted by this vision of pre-revolutionary Russia, the band quickened the tempo and struck up some wild Cossack numbers. Smashing uncorked champagne bottles, the subalterns pranced on to the glass dance floor, joined hands and skipped around before breaking into a slick Gopak routine. The audience went mad. So did the police. A whistle was blown and a regiment of beefy constables charged the subalterns. Eagled helmets flew and patent boots kicked before the subalterns were brought to their knees; but as police and poofs untangled themselves, a lone subaltern with a blushing constable held tightly in his grip could be seen waltzing along a side of the dance floor.

By now, my parents were barely on speaking terms. There was an occasional exchange of grunts about the decline and fall of the British aristocracy, the Kilkenny Cats miaowing in agreement. Lady Ossulton only confirmed their fears by opening a laundry. As the cats complained, 'Opening a laundry, indeed. One can only assume she'll be taking in washing next.'

Unknown to the family, Pa had drawn up secret plans to escape to India. He dropped the hint to his old boozing chum, Henry Young, during a meeting at York races, but Henry was too absorbed with a personal problem to take the matter seriously. He was the owner of a mare who'd never lost a race and whose best friend was a goat. While the mare's ability wasn't in dispute, it was evident that she was encouraged to run flat out whenever the goat was taken to the races. Although the odds were lowered, the bookies had still lost a fortune. Determined on revenge, an unscrupulous few made abortive attempts to kidnap the goat. Fully pre-occupied with his mare and goat, Henry paid scant attention to Pa's ramblings about the Raj.

Before Pa could escape, the Equal Franchise Act was passed. This gave the vote to all women of twenty-one and over. Recognizing a feminist victory, Mama talked Pa into buying her a gramophone as a celebration gift. As he knew nothing of politics, his compliance was probably a form of humouring her. One evening, what sounded like an elephant trying to keep time to tinny piano music could be heard in one of our reception rooms. A female voice shrieked encouragement while a man's irritation was expressed by an increasing number of oaths. Creeping down a staircase and across to the door of the reception room, I squinted through the keyhole. Partnered by Mama, and still wearing breeches and riding boots, Pa was dancing his own very individual version of the Fox-Trot. She kept him at it half the night.

Counting off the years to her wedding, poor Nanny didn't realise that her 'intended' was cheating on her. It wasn't a serious affair, and as Nanny was essentially a 'nice' girl, who could blame the chauffeur for revolting against celibacy? As I watched him wander off to some woodland with a rounded young blonde, my curiosity was aroused. Whistling to Stinker, the two of us followed at a safe distance. We lost the couple down in the woods and wandered about for a time before strange sounds directed us towards a bed of primroses in a small clearing. I'd long since realized that grown ups were peculiar, but why on earth should they want to roll about stark naked in the chill of early spring whilst making primitive grunting noises? With a woof of triumph, Stinker leapt forward. Wagging his tail, he pounced on the chauffeur's backside, which he proceeded to sniff. As the enraged man fought off the dog, he spotted me and roared, 'Get out of it, you little bastard, and take your bleeding dog before I murder the pair of you.' I'd only wanted to be his friend, but given such hostility, blackmail did cross my mind.

Mama was spending more of her time up at Rooksnest, where she complained to Evelyn, 'My husband knows more about horses' hocks than human beings.' As a form of consolation and a sign of her regard, Evelyn presented Mama with a newly published book called The Well of Loneliness, by Miss 'John' Radclyffe Hall. The book was an honest account of a lady's struggle to cope with her lesbian tendencies. Such candour was not well received, even in the nineteen twenties. The *Sunday Express* trumpeted, 'A healthy child would be better off with a phial of prussic acid than that book.'

Mama discovered she was pregnant again. Of course, it must have happened when she was drunk and a lecher had taken advantage, but this excuse did not impress an angry Evelyn. Her rage was further increased when Mama coyly refused to name the father – but it certainly wasn't mine.

Pa's temper had become so unpredictable that even Henry Young advised him to take medical advice. With his liver the size of a walnut, what could the physicians do but advise him against drinking. Angered by their unhelpful advice, he stormed out of Harley Street swearing he'd never see a doctor again. A veterinary surgeon friend supported Pa and warned him against the malpractice of the British Medical Profession. Over a few gins in their local, the vet told Pa, 'Ignore the buggers. Maybe the sauce has twisted your livers but life would be a darn sight worse without the daily dose.' Such was Pa's trust in the man that he went to him for his future medical check-ups.

With my parents not speaking to each other or me, my social circle was confined to Nanny, Stinker and a new addition to the staff at College House. This was Arthur, the head gardener. Paid one pound a week, Arthur began his working day hand-pumping water into a five-hundred-gallon tank for the household baths. During spare moments, he'd help me sail my toy speed-boat across the tank. An earthy soul, Arthur leered blatantly whenever he saw Mama wiggle her curvaceous figure. Mama was graciously appreciative of such attention and within weeks Arthur had become her favourite. One day, leaning out of a bedroom window wearing a low-fronted dress, Mama ordered Arthur to bring out the family's black and yellow Rolls-Royce. Not wishing to disappoint the lady for whom he lusted, Arthur obeyed, omitting to mention that he couldn't drive. Crashing through the gates of College House, both Arthur and the Rolls rumbled down through the streets of Lambourn before smashing into the premises of Mr Weeks the saddler. As he helped Arthur push the wreck back to College House, the wooden-legged saddler explained the advantages of driving lessons to Arthur. Arthur did acquire a licence, kept it for fifty years, but never learnt to drive.

We awoke one morning to discover that Pa had vanished. Through his connections with the Maharajah of Patiala and Lord Irwin, the British Viceroy, he'd finally made a bolt for India, where he was employed in an official capacity at Bombay racecourse. Quickly becoming part of the British Raj, he forgot the old mother country and also embarked upon a new drinking career. With Pa on the run in India and Evelyn in a huff since the announcement of the latest pregnancy, Mama was in trouble. In short, she'd run out of cash. Her trustees even shook their heads. All had been squandered years ago.

On the look out for a patron, Mama briefly considered taking up with an old acquaintance, a perfectly revolting Fascist named Colonel Barker. Looking more like a beached whale, the Colonel's breath was repellent, as was his habit of always leering, instead of smiling, at me. Even at that age, I could only groan and deplore Mama's taste. Before Mama could make up her mind as to whether the Colonel would be a sound investment, he was arrested for failing to appear at a bankruptcy examination. There'd been some gossip about the legitimacy of the Colonel's claim to a military title, and in the publicity surrounding the hearing, this was indeed proved to be bogus – as was his claim to masculinity. The Colonel was in fact one Lillias Arkell-Smith, who'd married a girl several years earlier before vanishing after the wedding breakfast. On hearing this, both 'The Colonel's' estranged wife and Mama fainted. A week later, my younger brother, James, was born.

Evelyn must have forgiven Mama, as she was invited back to Rooksnest to sign a peace treaty. I was wheeled out to be inspected by this formidable looking lady, who announced that she'd been made my guardian and suggested I'd look better wearing a dress. Terrified both by Evelyn and her views on suitable clothes for little boys, I was hauled off to be measured up by a dressmaker. In the event, it was decided a kilt would be more appropriate. From that moment on I was allowed into Rooksnest only when wearing a pleated skirt of Macnee tartan.

Mrs Meyrick left Holloway prison in a blaze of publicity. Everyone had quite forgotten how many terms of imprisonment she'd served, but these days she'd be met at the great doors of Holloway by her three daughters, two of whom had married into the aristocracy. Ten days later, Mrs Meyrick was re-arrested. This time the charge was one of bribing police officers. But, ever gracious, she announced that 'His Majesty's Constabulary have always been so kind to one.' When the Great Crash came in October 1929, Mrs Meyrick was one of the few people who acted sensibly. Leaving the world to fret, she returned to prison.

Alongside the chaos and ruin of the crash, my own worries seemed infinitely greater. I was informed by Mama that she and I were going to live with Evelyn on a permanent basis at Rooksnest, while my baby brother would have to be farmed out. Eyeing me warily, the terrifying Evelyn warned, 'Remember, it's kilts and no trousers.'

Dressed in 'that' kilt, a black velvet jacket, buckled shoes and knee-length tartan socks from which a dirk protruded, I clenched my fists against my sporran and shuffled along the magnificent drive which led to the south front of Rooksnest. My hair, which had been twisted back into an absurdly short pigtail, not only gave me a headache, but also the appearance of a Chinese boy dressed up as a Scotsman. This confusion of cultures may have satisfied the whims of Mama and Evelyn, but dressed as I was I'd have felt conspicuous at a fancy dress party, let alone in the country houses of rural Berkshire. I scowled at the stone lions mounted on plinths on opposing sides of the lawns where the drive ended. The lions had been scowling at each other for several hundred years, and my hostility went unnoticed by them; but not by Evelyn and Mama.

'The boy is sullen,' Evelyn stated, 'Boy' being underlined with resentment.

'Now, Patrick dear, do behave,' Mama twittered. 'Evelyn's so very fond of you.'

Perhaps, but I was left wondering what form this fondness took when Evelyn announced that 'Given time, we'll make a good woman of him.'

Even Mama blinked at such an ambitious project, while Evelyn's pet monkey remained perched on one of her shoulders making faces at me.

Clutching one of my arms, Evelyn marched me into the stately Elizabethan mansion while Mama trailed along behind us gossiping away to herself and gulping back occasional slugs of gin from a hip flask secreted between her breasts. I was then whirled into an about turn before being led to the great hall, where a long line of people, dressed in uniforms of black and white and standing to attention in respectful silence, stared at me. Here was the army of servants whose task it was to cater to our needs properly and promptly.

The housekeeper was polite, if reserved, and Cook, predictably fat and jolly. I thought the ladies' maids, parlour maids and housemaids exceedingly pretty. Their flaxen hair and flushed cheeks spoke of wholesome country living. I later discovered it was the footmen and not wholesome country living that brought such a flush to their faces. Given Evelyn's obvious distaste for anyone born wearing blue, it was surprising to discover that she did employ men.

The female staff bobbed and whispered 'Master Patrick'. When it came to cook's turn she got stuck in mid-bob, and had to be hauled to her feet by the maids. A quartet of footmen eyed me warily. Now convulsed with giggles, I gave them what must have resembled a twisted leer and tried to look friendly without appearing familiar. Having decided I'd need all available masculine support in this house of female lunatics, my hopes soared upon being introduced to Winter, the butler. He was an eerie looking man with rolling eyes and a blue nose shaped like a tulip bulb. Bearing an extraordinary resemblance to Robert Newton in his combined roles of Long John Silver and champion lush, Winter went through the motions of the expected grovelling routine, but in such a way as to suggest that inwardly he was blowing raspberries – especially at Evelyn. I liked Winter.

Evelyn possessed an exceptional mind and outstanding powers of perception, however, and she eyed the two of us suspiciously.

'I hope you're behaving yourself,' she snapped. Uncertain as to whom she was referring, I looked chastised while Winter gave a floppy salute. Still suspicious, Evelyn instructed me to follow her to the stables where I'd be introduced to the grooms and other outdoor staff. As she sailed towards the front door, Winter winked at me.

Those first weeks in my new 'home' were among the most

wretched in my life. My baby brother, James, was not allowed into the house. I discovered that he'd been farmed out to a wet nurse in Lambourn, where Mama tried to fit in a couple of visits each week. Although showing me great warmth, Mama could be a puzzling creature. She quite deliberately submerged her fine qualities of kindness and affection beneath a surface of supreme superficiality. She was also afraid of something, but of what I could not be certain. When Mama had informed me that we would be living at Rooksnest, I was the one who'd been afraid. Not only for my own future security, but also for Mama's. Filled with a dark sense of foreboding, I'd begged her not to go. My protests were hushed by assurances that such a move would be for the good of us all. Thus began an uncertainty that haunted me then, and still haunts me to this day.

In rare moments, Mama would hold me close to her in dark corners of that terrifying house. She said little, preferring to gaze upon me with great sadness. I felt she longed to speak, but probably thought I was far too young to understand what she wished to say, as I was to appreciate the circumstances that had brought us to Rooksnest. I said nothing, but my large, pleading eyes must have told her how I longed to return to College House, where I assumed the two of us could live happily with baby James and my father.

What of Evelyn, this strange and apparently sinister woman whose thrall we found ourselves in? Having lost her mother at a young age, she had inherited a wicked step-mother who beat her and dominated her father. Evelyn's salvation had been her governess. An intelligent and kindly lady, she educated her charge to a high standard. In turn, Evelyn later tried to do the same for me and several other children. At the age of twenty-one, Evelyn received a fabulous legacy. Now financially independent, her emotional life seemed fulfilled when she married. In the event, her husband treated her atrociously. Disappointed by a father and betrayed by a husband, Evelyn spent the rest of her life hating men.

Yet another union of 'new' money to old blood was forged when Evelyn took a wife called Augusta, known as Gussie. A grand-daughter of the Earl of Mar and Kelly, Gussie persuaded Evelyn to buy Rooksnest, where the two of them settled down to enjoy married life. Since Evelyn was not a faithful 'husband', Rooksnest saw a succession of secondary wives and concubines. But Gussie remained unruffled; while Evelyn enjoyed affairs, Gussie effectively ran the estate, secure in the knowledge that she was the number one wife. Then, Mama arrived. Realizing that she'd been 'divorced', Gussie continued to farm by day, chain-smoke by night and quietly bide her time.

Evelyn's numerous lady friends who alternately stayed and lived in the house were not all lesbian, but with few exceptions, they ignored me. I was made nervous by these 'tweedy apparitions' stomping about or chasing each other around the public rooms and up the staircases. But it was the atmosphere of the house itself that was most alarming. To me, the Tudor mansion had the smell of death. Come dusk, I felt overwhelmed, not only by the house, but also by an eerie countryside which seemed to echo with sounds of the unknown.

I was invariably packed off to bed shortly after tea and would lie awake for hours listening to the noise of carousing ladies as they drank and laughed away the night. One evening, having floated into a semi-sleep, I awoke screaming. When Mama came in, she was confronted by a shaking child who sobbed hysterically. 'Don't leave me,' I begged. Holding me closely, Mama kissed my head and tried to calm me. Evelyn then appeared, and, observing our intimacy as she entered the bedroom, looked resentful. She usually called Mama 'darling', but on this occasion used her Christian name.

'You've deserted me, Thea,' she said with just a hint of sulkiness in her voice.

'It's Patrick, darling. He thinks he's seen a ghost.'

'A lady,' I sobbed. 'She was grey and wore ruffles about her neck.'

For a moment, Evelyn eyed me with sympathy. Then, turning to Mama suggested, 'Why not re-join me downstairs?'

I had yet to learn that such seemingly pleasant suggestions were actually orders.

'In the circumstances, Evelyn, it would be sensible if I stayed with Patrick.'

Mama looked worried. For my sake, she'd taken a gamble, and she knew it. Grateful and surprised by such unexpected courage, I glanced at Evelyn to gauge her reaction. Her eyes sparkled with anger. Turning to leave, she paused briefly and in a voice choked with emotion, said, 'Then, I will bid you good night, Thea – darling.'

For the first time I realized that Evelyn was very fond of Mama and jealous of me, but I could not understand why.

I was now due to leave my boarding school in Somerset, and there were lengthy discussions as to where 'the child' should be sent to complete the next stage of his education. I was now referred to as 'the child' instead of 'the boy'. Since Evelyn was paying the school fees, I felt there was a fair chance she'd put me in a convent. In the event, I was sent to Summer Fields, arguably Britain's best prep school. Mama would be discouraged from visiting the school, but at least I'd be with boys.

Ticking off the days before being sent away, I noticed a full moon was imminent. Filled with apprehension, I volunteered to go to bed exceptionally early that evening. Even at the risk of suffocating, I intended spending the entire night closeted underneath the sheets and blankets. This potentially suicidal decision was motivated by the fear previous full moons at Rooksnest had provoked.

Come nightfall, I would hear a rustling sound in some undergrowth just outside my bedroom window. As the rustling ceased, violent snorts would puncture the air, to be replaced in turn by what sounded like the sharpening of knives. When this stopped, there would be a silence which was shortly broken as a pair of high-heeled shoes click-clacked their way across a nearby courtyard. While the heels continued to click and clack, there'd be a roar intermingled with feminine screams and the rush of what I assumed was a trumpeting cart horse. It all made fascinating, if frightening listening. I had mentioned this once to Mama, who shrugged off the matter as something of no importance.

That night, at about eleven o'clock, half choking I flung back the bed clothes and, now more curious than scared, tip-toed across to the bedroom window and opened it a little way. Some time later, I saw a man crawling into the undergrowth. This was followed by the usual rustle, snort and sharpening routine. After a while, I spotted Cook totter across the courtyard in a pair of dangerously high-heeled shoes. What I'd assumed to be a snorting cart horse was in fact a snorting Winter who, brandishing a couple of gleaming knives, now leapt from the undergrowth and chased Cook around the yard at a steady canter. That canter increased to a gallop as she fled across the estate with Winter hot on her petticoats. Being Hungarian, Cook was not blessed with Winston Churchill's command of the English language. 'Me collapsee, me collapsee,' she shrieked as Winter foamed and lunged. Given his gleaming knives and blatant animal lust, whatever it was Winter wanted, I've not doubt he squeezed it from those plump Magyar loins.

Wildly excited by this discovery, I couldn't wait to tell Mama. It wasn't until after lunch that the two of us could be alone together. Mama's breath was overpowering, and I could only assume that the meal had begun, continued and ended with gin soup. Blinking and concentrating with difficulty, Mama listened to my story. Surveying her cigarette from glazed eyes, she commented in that carefully enunciated tone so favoured by grand drunks, 'How perfectly D-I-S-G-U-S-T-I-N-G.'

The British upper classes have two particularly nasty habits. The first is beating their children and the second is sending them away to be brought up and beaten by other people. Consequently, generations of boys have entered the adult world thoroughly grounded in Latin and Classical Greek syntax, but riddled with sexual and social problems. In those days, each autumn, splendid motor cars would be polished up and stacked with initialled trunks while a uniformed chauffeur stood to attention by an open rear door of the automobile. Some moments later, a frightened looking boy would appear, drag himself towards the car, climb in and listen with a feeling of utter hopelessness as the chauffeur closed the door. Pressing his nose against a window, the boy would observe his waving and rapidly disappearing parents.

'Now, don't forget to write, dear.'

'And don't come back without making the First Eleven, you little bugger. I made it, my Father made it and his Father made it. Keep it in the family, what?'

'Good-bye, darling.'

I pressed my nose against a window of the car. This time, there was no one there to see me off.

On arriving at Summer Fields, I was slightly consoled by the sight of numerous small boys who looked just like me. Laced up in tweed suits which seemed one size too large, we all appeared to have been dumped like packages alongside our trunks. Each boy was allotted a number. As my name and number, 'D.P. Macnee – number 8' was called out, I felt not only like a criminal, but also totally rejected by my family yet again.

We boys sized each other up through red-rimmed eyes. Once initial suspicions had been allayed, tentative overtures of friendship began with the swopping of sweets, or the discovery that Nanny had an aunt who'd looked after someone else's father.

'Are you going to be alright, Master Patrick?' This sole voice of comfort belonged to Emlyn Owen, Evelyn's handsome Welsh chauffeur. I nodded. He'd joked and tried so hard to make me laugh all the way to Summer Fields, and I still remember this kindness with such gratitude. 'Then, I'll be off. But if there's anything you need, just write to me down at the cottage.'

I nodded again, wanting to speak, but knew I'd cry if I did.

That night, a dormitory of eight-year-olds wept and spewed into their pillows. I expect the thoughts of my contemporaries were much the same as mine. 'What have I done to be sent away?'

As the boys were 'broken in', they began to learn something of their school and its masters.

Founded in the mid-nineteenth century, Summer Fields had really taken off when it was discovered by the Macmillan family. With distinguished past pupils including Harold Macmillan, Field Marshall the Earl Wavell, Harold Caccia, later to become Head of The Diplomatic Service, and a clutch of Privy Counsellors, Bishops, Judges, Admirals and war heroes, the boys had a broad choice of good examples to emulate. My problem lay in trying to be good.

Believing that their parents had dumped them, the boys began to transfer their affections to each other. This affection developed over three stages, beginning with forlorn looks and wistful sighs as the object of one's adoration passed by. If the passion was reciprocated, excited boys plunged into stage two, where expressions of admiration would be whispered in first year Latin while prized possessions were exchanged. Stage three was far more daring and dangerous.

School dormitories have little privacy. During their first days at school, the boys went to comical lengths to avoid exposing private parts. Apart from the usual stripping off under sheets and behind curtains, the more imaginative removed their trousers in cupboards. One fearless soul even clambered out of a window, slid down a drainpipe, changed and climbed back in.

Come the first half-term, however, inhibitions were a thing of the past. Private parts became public parts, and there was a mania to compare notes on size, shape and shade. With several love affairs also on the boil, stage three began. After 'lights out', boys leapt out of bed, debagged each other and probed each other's buttocks. This part of the anatomy was most popular because it was recognized as 'cane bait', and therefore had a purpose. Although there was much tugging at 'that bit' in the front, it was generally regarded with suspicion. Apart from being a funnel through which gallons of lemonade could be siphoned off, no one could be certain of its having any additional functions — although there were peculiar suggestions from a boy who'd once caught Mummy and Daddy without their clothes on.

Passionately in love and deeply involved in my first affair, I was soon well into the advanced part of stage three. It was a perishing cold autumn day when my partner and I scuttled into some bushes near that part of Summer Fields known as Old Lodge. Extremes in temperature are no bar to physical love, especially at the age of eight. Pulling off our trousers and underpants, we flung them on top of the bushes and settled down to probe and giggle. Suddenly my partner gave a strangled gasp and paled to a colour of sick yellow. Forcing myself to turn around, I saw another strangely coloured face glaring at us over the bushes and holding our trousers up with both his hands. It was the Reverend C.A.E. Williams. That he should be a clergyman was bad enough, but he was also the Headmaster.

The Reverend was something of a maestro with the cane. A well built-man with thin, black brilliantined hair that was parted down the middle, his purple face was in mottled contrast to his white dog collar. One senior boy had even wagered his entire collection of gramophone records that the Reverend was the same colour all the way down, though no one ever found out.

As a sad queue of boys awaited their punishment outside the Head's study, they reminisced about previous canings. Alongside some veterans of nine, I felt a little inadequate, Aunt Maud's slipper forming my only previous experience. Some boys expressed concern about a boy called Macgrigor, a younger brother of the Earl of Inchcape. He had a fine mole on the centre of one of his buttocks. To date, the mole had survived a couple of canings, but, shaking their heads, the veterans took the view that a cane would eventually lift it off.

When my number was up, with whispers of 'Good luck' reverberating in my ears, I entered the study, and bit my lip as I closed the door behind me. Watching the Head swish the cane about in practice strokes, I thought for one happy moment that he was using it only to swat flies. Then I remembered it was autumn. Placing the cane on his desk, the reverend gentleman looked at me more in sorrow than in anger before beginning his sermon. I seem to remember something about my body being a tabernacle of The Lord which I'd defiled through my wickedness. About half an hour later he was still rambling on. I began to nod off, but woke up with a start when he threatened possible expulsion. Muttering expressions of repentance that were inspired by fear rather than shame, I looked pleadingly at the Head. He nodded, but still picked up the cane. Lashing into my backside, he droned on about the aims of the school, though I considered his remarks about it being a seat of wisdom somewhat confusing.

Leaving the study with my backside in flames, I was accosted by the veterans. As I'd somehow managed not to cry, there were congratulations all round. I'd earned what was to be the first of many campaign medals. Thinking back on this experience now, I'm reminded of the words of that great apostle of reason, Jean-Jacques Rousseau, who once remarked, 'Who would have believed that this childhood punishment would have determined my tastes, my desires, my passions for the rest of my life?'

That day I discovered the existence of the Black Book. As old as the school itself, the book was a register in which offences were recorded. One entry, and a boy had to watch it. Two, and he was marked. Three entries, and he was obviously set on a course of depravity. Four might well mean expulsion. Offences varied in character and degree of moral decline. There were the predictably boring crimes of unpunctuality and untidiness, but more interesting misconduct included 1. 'Disgusting greed,' 2. 'Misbehaviour with a razor blade,' and 3. 'Deliberately walking into a snowdrift in his ordinary clothes.'

Back at Rooksnest, Christmas was in full swing. Even the dreaded Evelyn was remarkably civil. Nodding with approval, she said she'd heard good reports of me at school. I could only assume that news of my caning hadn't filtered back to her. As a reward, she promised me my first fishing lessons with the British dry and wet fly champions the following year. That I hadn't the slightest desire to fish didn't matter. She was determined I'd spend hours immersed in icy water while casting my rod. Perhaps news of my caning had in fact filtered back, and this was the horrible torture she'd thought up. 'Oh, and another thing,' she said as an afterthought. 'From now on, you must always call me uncle.' I now began to seriously wonder whether Evelyn just might be a man wearing woman's clothes.

Shuttled about as I was in a Rolls-Royce between the enclosed worlds of Rooksnest and Summer Fields, I was completely unaware that half the globe was in the throes of economic depression. While my own world wasn't exactly a laugh a minute, as I helped decorate the house with Christmas bunting and looked forward to searching for sixpenny pieces in the plum pudding, how could I know that many boys of my age would awake on Christmas Day looking forward to nothing?

Evelyn's good humour continued. Among the elaborate

Christmas decorations at Rooksnest was a mock up Spanish galleon which some of the estate workers erected in the main hall of the house. It must have measured about twenty feet in length and was loaded with Christmas gifts for intimates, friends and servants, gifts which Evelyn would distribute that Christmas Eve dressed as a pirate of the Spanish Main.

Upon arriving at Rooksnest, I'd been distressed to discover that Mama was not there. As Evelyn and her chums were quite incapable of looking after a child, Nanny had been summoned to take charge until Mama's return. There'd been yet another row with her 'intended' over naming the day, so like me, Nanny wasn't exactly brimming with the yuletide spirit. But it was so good just to be together again that the two of us hugged each other and all but cried with joy. Mama eventually rolled back in a fearful state. The Duke of Leeds had convinced her that the end of the road was nigh for the aristocracy. Indeed, he'd just auctioned his Coronation robes to an impressario who had announced he'd be using them in his next theatrical venture.

Decked out in my kilt, I was allowed to join Evelyn and her harem for dinner. It was to be the first of many nerve racking experiences. My trousers had been taken away as soon as I'd returned from school and, resplendent in the kilt and its accessories, I was led into the dining room. Ten female faces surveyed me with surprise and hostility, the most resentful stare coming from Gussie, Evelyn's 'divorced' wife.

Evelyn then beckoned to me. As I stood by her chair at the head of the table, she handed me a Christmas present. Encouraging me to open the gift, Evelyn studied my face as I removed the wrapping paper. At first, I thought she'd given me a set of bagpipes with a feather stuck in its navel. It was actually a hat. A Glengarry Bonnet to be precise. Evelyn thought it would add a nice finishing touch to my costume as junior Highland chief. When this tartan oddity had been arranged on my head, there was an uneasy silence. No one seemed to know whether they should ignore me or cheer. Uncertain faces looked to Evelyn for guidance. She lifted her glass. There was much clinking as the coterie scrambled to follow suit.

Dinner was hell. I felt utterly humiliated, and Mama got drunk. My fear returned about her living at Rooksnest. I was convinced that one day she'd go too far and Evelyn would fling us into the gutter. I didn't really mind, but we had nowhere else to go.

After the King had been toasted, everyone settled down to light up. One drunk even offered me a cigar. Then suddenly the mood was shattered. 'Tallulah,' Mama shrieked. Conversation ceased and there was a second uneasy silence. As Mama was Evelyn's wife number one, fidelity was expected. Surely she hadn't been unfaithful with the famous actress during her recent jaunt to London? 'Tallulah,' she shrieked a second time, and started crying. What on earth was she trying to say? Evelyn coaxed an explanation out of her. Tallulah's boyfriend, 'that swine' Sir Francis Laking, had recently died of an overdose of yellow chartreuse. Although he'd apparently left Tallulah his entire collection of vintage cars, it transpired that he didn't own even a pogo stick. Evelyn nodded sympathetically. All men were swine and she'd toast to that. While they toasted, I fretted. Given her reckless drinking, Mama would make one outburst too many and finish her days in disgrace. I glanced at the faces around Evelyn. Clearly they were waiting for Mama to fall.

But, for the present, Mama was the bright flame in the harem. Decorative, witty, and ever anxious to please, she was adored by Evelyn. Christmas passed in a whirl of glitter and gaiety. Evelyn presented Mama with an M.G. Classic sports car. After the festive season, Evelyn and Mama went away for a few days. On their return, Mama took me for a long walk.

'And how is school?'

'All right, but I'd rather be with you.'

'Bless you, dear. Now, can you keep a secret?'

I nodded.

'One day we'll be very rich. Evelyn has left me the estate and its accompanying fortune.' After Tallulah Bankhead's unhappy experience, I did wonder whether the estate was actually Evelyn's to leave, but assumed Mama knew best.

'Aren't you pleased?'

'Suppose so.'

Mama sighed at her difficult child, and then promised to buy him a new bike. We could now afford such luxuries. But for how long, I wondered?

Before returning to Summer Fields, I was determined to discover whether Evelyn was really a man. As my experiences in the dormitory had taught me there was only one sure way to find out: I took to loitering outside Evelyn's bedroom, which was sandwiched between the rooms in which her monkey and pet parrots resided. Winter passed by a couple of times, rolled his eyes and warned me I'd be better get out of it unless I wanted a thick ear from Evelyn or one of her friends. Undaunted by his advice, I sneaked into Evelyn's room, and hid under her enormous Charles the First bed. It must have been around three o'clock in the morning when a light was switched on and I saw two brogue-clad feet enter the room. Peeping out a little way, I watched as Evelyn tossed her tweed jacket and skirt on to the floor. She stood for a moment resplendent in men's underclothes, brogues, long socks and a hat of the kind favoured by bookies. Unfortunately I had peeped out a little too far, and Evelyn spotted me. She all but torpedoed her cigarette into my face as it peered up at her. Sparks and bits of pungent old shag flew as she screamed 'You horrible child.'

I was sent back to school in disgrace. As dear Emlyn drove me towards Oxfordshire, I was more than ever determined that one day I'd find out whether this strange lady was really a man.

Although I was unhappy at school, I derived great pleasure from learning. English and history were fascinating. I was allergic to mathematics, though my trigonometry later helped me navigate a boat in the Royal Navy. But my first love was acting. Since my stage debut at the late Aunt Maud's Dickensian establishment, I'd been nurturing a secret ambition to get back on stage at the earliest opportunity. Summer Fields gave me my long awaited break.

Among my closest chums was Felix Hope-Nicholson. Like me, he had loathed being sent away to school. A boy of great sensitivity and vivid imagination, Felix was related to half of Debrett's, and those to whom he couldn't claim kinship, he seemed to know. Although I'd tried my hand at a couple of scripts, Felix wrote a complete play in my honour named *The Jellico Mouse*. But even greater theatrical glory lay ahead.

It was decided to perform Shakespeare's *Henry the Fifth* with me in the title role. Cast as the Dauphin was the young Christopher Lee, who excelled himself by speaking his words both in French and English. It was only later that the cast of eight-year-olds discovered that the play had been performed in its uncut version: a hard but effective way of training would-be thespians. To my extreme embarrassment, Mama rolled up for the performance. Of course I was thrilled to see her, but she cheered loudly whenever I made an entrance.

Christopher and I acted again in *Richard the Second*, in which I played Bolingbroke, Robin Sinclair played Richard and Christopher played Mowbray. Christopher's splendid chain mail armour was made from old wool plastered with an evil smelling silver paint. As we stood together in the wings, I noticed Christopher scratching himself in the most unusual places. Thinking he's been invaded by fleas, I kept my distance. In fact, the heat from Christopher's body coupled with the heat of the spotlights had melted the armour and it had glued itself to his skin. Towards the end of the show, every time he moved silver flakes floated on to the stage. He resembled a walking advertisement for dandruff. When the armour was eventually peeled off, we stared at Christopher with pity. His entire body was covered in a pattern that resembled a ship's rigging. It took weeks of scrubbing before he lost his nautical appearance.

I put the horrors of home from my mind and continued to enjoy academic life. Summer Fields was a highly progressive school where talents were not only encouraged but channelled in such a way as to be of use in adult life. While the emphasis was on Classics under the admirable tuition of Geoffrey Bolton, the boys were instructed in a broad academic curriculum and numerous sporting activities. Those who applied themselves were rewarded, but those who didn't learnt the hard way via a swish across the seat of their pants.

If the Head was a maestro with the cane, Geoffrey Bolton was a virtuoso; but never once did he go for me. Having dubbed me 'Smee', after a pirate in Treasure Island, not only did he show immense kindness, but went to extraordinary pains to ensure that I'd thoroughly mastered the more complicated Latin and Greek verbs. His efforts produced a precocious nine-year-old who delighted in writing classical verse and flinging chamber pots out of windows.

Shell-shocked in the Great War, G.B.'s red hair had turned white and was combed back to reveal a bloodless-looking face. A man of outstanding intellect, his quick temper could be easily roused. One day as we sweated our way through a translation of Tacitus' *The Annals of Imperial Rome*, we encountered an especially tricky paragraph about a consul with the boozey sounding name of Gaius Calpurnius Bibulus. Smiling pleasantly, G.B. asked 'And what can you tell me about Bibulus?'

'Wasn't he the landlord of The Net and Trident?' sniggered one bright spark.

G.B. looked puzzled and enquired 'And what is The Net and Trident?'

'A pub next door to the Coliseum.'

Contributing their respective instruments to this orchestra of floggers were Mr Evans, the assistant head, and handsome Mr Mullins. A South African by birth, he often broke into a Zulu war dance, and when not dancing he played rugger in and out of season. Being a hearty soul, Mullins wasn't a natural beater. He preferred to chase overweight boys up to the gym horse, knowing they'd invariably get stuck in mid-leap. As his 'victim' heaved around Mullins would sidle up waving a cane and smirking from ear to ear.

'We're in for a thrashing, aren't we boy?' he'd chuckle.

'Yes, Sir,' came a resigned reply.

'One, two, three – WHACK.' And with that, he'd smash his cane into the side of the horse.

While such a bizarre sense of humour could be unnerving, it was preferable to the antics of some other masters.

One of my favourite pastimes was the musical drills run by Sergeant Morley. The very model of a military man, his waxed moustachios bristled with discipline as he barked out orders to platoons of marching boys. When he'd decided we were drilled to a suitable standard, the Sergeant would sit at a piano and smash out a repertoire of Strauss and Souza marches while we strutted around the gym in perfect time. I don't know whether the Sergeant was going deaf, but as the terms passed, his smashing into the piano increased in violence. There came the memorable day when the entire platoon did an 'Eyes Right' just in time to notice a couple of piano hammers break loose from their wires, soar into the air and perform an Immelman roll before spinning down to the floor.

Apart from Felix Hope-Nicholson, my greatest chums were Henry Thorold, who went on to receive holy orders, Robin Sinclair, who later became Lord Thurso, and a musical genius called Lumley-Saville whom I secretly adored. With each of them contributing their particular talents and engaging characteristics to everyday school life, not only were they a credit to Summer Fields, they boosted my confidence with their loyalty and cheerful ways. Of all the boys in the school, the one with the most dominating presence and hypnotic personality was an aspiring politician named Julian Amery.

By the age of eleven, Julian had already decided he would one day occupy Number Ten Downing Street. A serious little boy whose hair was combed immaculately, Julian always displayed a perfectly arranged handkerchief in his breast pocket. Such was the pristine state of this cotton construction that the rest of us assumed he never blew his nose. There was one obstacle to Julian's ambition, however, which was that perched precariously on a politicial seesaw of indecision, his views veered from left to right from term to term. A one time supporter of Lloyd George, he used to march around the school clutching his autographed copy of the Welshman's book, *How We can Conquer Unemployment*. But when he finally took his seat in Parliament, it was as a Tory. Perhaps he took the view that if Winston − as he confidently called the great man − could cross the floor of the Commons several times, then so could he.

Unlike Churchill, Julian did not become Prime Minister, but he did marry the daughter of one and still enjoys a distinguished and influential career as a politician. Not having the remotest interest in politics at that time, I was impervious to Julian's oratory and views on American Isolationism, but I am indebted to him on one point: I'm sure that Julian Amery was the first person who steered my attention towards an Austrian politician who was making something of a racket on the European Continent. His name was Adolf Hitler. With the coming of summer, however, National Socialism and the Japanese occupation of Chinese provinces were mysteries on a distant planet as I settled down to enjoy some of the British Season's traditional celebrations.

Situated near Oxford, Summer Fields possessed an aura of quiet order and detachment that was possibly an overspill from university cloisters in which centuries of learning have passed undisturbed. To this was added such a reverence for tradition that the school became a flawless backcloth against which the upper classes could act our their rituals and play their games.

There's little to compare with a truly glorious English summer, when idle days are passed under a sky of cornflower blue and when meadows are rich with clover and alive with the drone of nimble bees. It was on days such as these that the boys of Summer Fields played that most English of games, cricket, swung tennis raquets across lawns of green velvet, and took swimming lessons in the River Cherwell. Supervised by the Reverend Williams, swimming was not without its dangers. Dressed in red trunks, a clutch of boys would fling themselves into the river with lemming-like enthusiasm, before thrashing about as the Reverend, from his position on the bank, yelled instructions on how to swim. But for those last out of the river there'd be a swish across the backside from the ubiquitous cane.

The highlight of summer was probably Sports Day, when over-excited boys cheered on their teams, ran with the speed of Derby winners and danced about clutching trophies and medals. Politely applauded by an audience of parents, the whole throng would then troop in for tea. With strawberries, cream, ices and meringues in unlimited supply, there were always a few green-faced boys making a quick exit for a quiet corner where a boy could do what a boy had to do. As I'd long given up hope of my family making an appearance, I joined in the celebrations with great enthusiasm. To have done otherwise would have increased my unhappiness, and I was determined to survive.

As my mail was infrequent, I was surprised to receive a letter just before the end of the summer term. The surprise turned to shock upon discovering that the writer was Pa. As always, he had little to say and came straight to the point: 'Big trouble on the way. Don't tell your Mother. Pa.' Greatly concerned for Pa, I thought it better to show the letter to Mama when I next returned to Rooksnest. Reading it through several times, she commented, 'I suppose I should pay a visit to India. He's obviously drinking heavily.' And away she went for a brief visit. After several weeks of parties, she tired of Bombay, looked in on Pa and then sailed home. 'I was right,' she informed me. 'It's now two bottles a day.'

Evelyn was very friendly during my next summer holidays. Pleased with my academic progress, she promised me my first holiday abroad. Mama and I were to accompany her to Switzerland. Unsure as to how I'd fit into the trio, I tried to wriggle out of the trip, stating a preference to stay with my cousin Josephine. This request was refused. I couldn't really complain, as Evelyn had also encouraged my growing interest in drama by presenting me with a marionette theatre. Also, I was informed that wearing a kilt on the Continent would not be obligatory. Switzerland was enchanting. At the last moment Nanny had been brought along to keep an eye on me when Mama and Evelyn wished to be alone. I was taken to swim in Lake Lucerne, fought with some Italian boys, and stuffed myself on Swiss chocolate. As I still had to call Evelyn 'Uncle', I just prayed that the Swiss were as insular as the British about learning a language other than their own.

One morning, I came down to breakfast to hear Evelyn and Mama sermonizing in a way that would have done credit to the Pope.

'What filth.'

'The fellow's depraved.'

'And with men!'

'Well, he is a homosexual, darling,' Evelyn pointed out to Mama.

'Good morning,' I said, during a self-righteous lull in the conversation.

Evelyn glared at me. 'One day you will grow up to be a

man,' she accused, adding, 'you nasty pigeon-toed little boy.'

I glanced at my feet and then at Mama as Evelyn stomped off.

'Evelyn's right, dear. We must do something about those feet.'

It transpired that Earl Beauchamp, the Lord Warden of the Cinque Ports, had suddenly made a bolt from one of his ports and fled the country. The official reason had been a breakdown in health, but thanks to his brother-in-law the Duke of Westminster, darker rumours prevailed. Mama glanced around conspiratorially and whispered, 'They say he does strange things with men, but I expect you're far too young to know about that sort of thing.'

'Oh, no,' I piped up enthusiastically. 'We have a master at school like that. In fact he quite enjoys touching us now and then.'

We arrived back in England to find that the economic situation was sliding towards catastrophe. Such was the gravity of the crisis that King George the Fifth terminated his holiday at Balmoral and returned to London for an emergency meeting with the Cabinet. As an example to the nation, the King took a pay cut, as did the Prince of Wales and other relations on the Civil List.

Isolated as they were in their fantasy world at Rooksnest, Evelyn and Mama appeared oblivious to the state of the nation. It was only when the Marchioness of Curzon went broke and Lady Mountbatten was forced to put her town house on the market that Evelyn was driven to go to London to consult with her financial advisers. I can only assume that her consultation must have proved satisfactory, since she returned with a sapphire and diamond brooch for Mama and a film projector complete with several reels of Charles Chaplin films for me.

My unusual background had made me a little nervous of ladies. I certainly hadn't begun to hate them, but given the unpredictable behaviour of Evelyn and her harem, my feelings towards the female sex were confused.

My first overture to a girl was a nervous one indeed. Her name was Susan, she was enchanting, and her father was also a trainer who lived in Lambourn. I suggested we watch one of my Chaplin movies.

'Chaplin?' she asked.

'Yes. The comic genius.'

'Oh, of course. Isn't he one of those film star people?' she sniffed.

'Actually, I wouldn't mind being a film star when I grow up.'

'Hmm. Daddy thinks such people are nothing more than vulgar tinkers.'

'Oh well, I suppose I could always become a jockey. At least it would please Pa.'

'That's entirely up to you, but personally speaking, I much prefer owners.'

For some time, Evelyn had been looking peculiar. She'd wander around Rooksnest with a vacant stare on her face and with her hands clasped as though in prayer. For a brief but very happy time I thought she was ill and might even die. I sought Mama's opinion.

'Is Evelyn going to die?'

'Why do you ask?'

'She doesn't look very well.'

'Have you been tampering with her Scotch?'

'No, Mama.'

'Then, it must be God.'

'God?'

'Yes. She's discovered the Good Lord.'

Not a lady who understood moderation, Evelyn treated her conversion to Roman Catholicism with the utmost seriousness. The old chapel in Rooksnest was cleaned out and spruced up before the Archbishop of the Wales and Cardiff diocese was invited over to sanctify the place and say Mass. As I'd been brought up to believe that Protestantism was the one true faith, I was fascinated by the idea of watching a bunch of Holy Rollers at prayer. The Archbishop turned out to be a cheery old bugger who arrived at Rooksnest in an enormous car from which he waved graciously rather in the manner of Queen Mary. Heaving himself out of the car, he blessed me on the spot and swept off towards the chapel. He appeared to be the one man Evelyn actually liked.

The Catholic Mass turned out to be both a fearful and fascinating experience. The Archbishop mumbled away to himself in Latin and every few minutes threw his hands into the air. Taking this as signal to genuflect, the congregation spent most of the service jumping up and down, glancing around to make sure that everyone else was following suit. After Mass, there was a reception. With the exception of the Archbishop, everyone drank too much. Taking me aside for a few minutes, an emotional Evelyn gave slurred instructions on how to reach Heaven. Believing that everyone destined for eternal paradise spent an average of one thousand years in Purgatory to atone for their sins, Evelyn explained how I could knock a few years off my sentence. There was, for instance, three hundred days remission to be had every time I kissed the Archbishop's ring. And so, leading me over to the Archbishop, Evelyn forced me into a genuflection and pushed my face into his right hand. 'The child wishes to atone,' she beamed as I slobbered over a ruby ring. 'All right,' she snapped. 'Don't overdo it.'

I was blessed for the second time that day and wandered off to contemplate the benefits of this ceremony. Having worked out that I could avoid Purgatory altogether if I kissed the ring about forty thousand times, I went back to the old boy to begin some repeat performances. He was standing alone and looked bored out of his mind.

'Know where the pond is?' he muttered.

'Yes, Your Grace.'

'Meet me down there in five minutes and for Christ's sake bring a bottle of Scotch.'

'Yes, Your Grace, but please could I kiss your ring?'

'Eh?'

'I'd like to kiss your ring as I want to go to Heaven.'

'All right, but don't forget the Scotch.'

I was blessed for a third time; my hopes of salvation were looking up.

Assisted by Winter, I managed to smuggle a bottle down to the pond. The Archbishop took a liberal swig and passed the bottle to Winter, who did likewise before passing the bottle to me. Not wishing to appear bad mannered, I had a drink and passed the bottle back to the Archbishop. As this game continued I managed to kiss his ring every few minutes. When the Archbishop finally staggered off, I noticed a flock of crows pass overhead. Winter, being a fund of country folklore, crossed himself, muttering, 'When the crows be high, the devil be nigh.' He then tottered off in the direction of Cook's room.

When the time came for the Archbishop's departure, he allowed me to finger his rosary and gave me a sly wink. Smiling up at him, I noticed that one of the crows had left its mark down the front of the Bishop's robes.

Although I always seemed to be in some kind of trouble, Evelyn continued to be materially generous. As she was still most jealous of any affection Mama displayed towards me, I thought it was her way of trying to buy me off. By now, I'd become so wary of adults and the stupid games they played that I was quickly mastering the art of practicality. If Evelyn wished to load me with baubles, I'd no objection to building up a private fortune. But as the recipient of my Mama's love, I was determined to take precedence over Evelyn.

As Stinker had departed to gnaw on that big bone in the sky, I was delighted with Evelyn's latest offering, a lovable Welsh cob that I christened Louis. Since Pa's lunatic attempt to make me the youngest jockey in the history of British horse racing, I was a little apprehensive of horses, just as I was of women. Matters weren't helped by the fact that girls seemed to perform more daring feats on horseback than boys. My sole consolation lay in fantasy. Intoxicated by the aroma of saddle soap and linseed oil, I would dream of luring those plaited, giggling creatures into a tack room where I could rip off their breeches and give them a sound thrashing.

The only girl for whom I had any respect was my cousin, Josephine. She was one of the very few people I knew who possessed that rare combination of common sense and humour. So that I might stay with Josephine more frequently, come the school holidays I took to lathering Evelyn into such a state of exasperation that she all but horsewhipped me across to Silchester where my cousin lived with her parents.

I arrived to find Aunt Peggy in a vile temper. She'd driven out in a trap using horses whose tails weren't docked. This oversight resulted in a lot of natural equine waste being flicked back in her face. Very sensibly, Uncle Joe fled into the garden to hide in a camouflage he'd built. There, he spent many hours undisturbed shooting jays with a shot gun he'd poked through a side of his hideaway.

When Evelyn recovered from her state of exasperation, I was allowed back to Rooksnest for the rest of the holidays. Apart from seeing Mama again, such a prospect didn't particularly thrill me, and my indifference veered towards nervousness when Evelyn summoned me to her study. At school, such an order invariably meant a caning; given the lunatic conditions prevailing at Rooksnest, why should this bidding be any different? As I had yet to learn that Evelyn was opposed to corporal punishment, I went well anaesthetized against my expected walloping. A chum of mine had sworn on all he held sacred, which with hindsight wasn't much, that the regular application of saddle soap on the buttocks was the one sure way to cheat the cane. The theory supporting his claim sounded spurious, but anything was worth a try.

Stinking of saddle soap, I entered the study. Ignoring me,

Evelyn bustled about for a while, and then instead of producing a cane, gave me a book and commanded me to read from it aloud. It was a volume of Robert Browning's poetry.

'Which poem would you like me to read, Uncle?'

'Oh, I think "Childe Roland".'

I groaned to myself, for there were thirty-four verses. Around verse four, I was instructed to sit down, but did so only with great reluctance. Come verse twelve, I was writhing on the chair, my backside submerged in a mud of pale coloured toffee as the coats of saddle soap began to melt.

'Oh, do stop wriggling,' said Evelyn.

'Sorry, Uncle.'

At verse twenty-two, I glowered at Evelyn over the top of the book. She was apparently far away in a world of her own, however, her eyes closed, her hands gently conducting the flow of verse. Now seated in a quagmire of saddle soap, my bottom itched unbearably. Reading the words 'Toads in a poisoned tank, or cats in a red-hot iron cage,' how Browning's words reminded me of the seraglio at Rooksnest.

My reading must have pleased Evelyn, as she and Mama took me up to London to see Noel Coward's latest musical, *Cavalcade*. The show had so delighted the King and Queen that they'd invited Mr Coward to visit them in the royal box. He spent so long with their Majesties that word got around he'd been knighted on the spot. It would be another forty years before he received his knighthood, and another fifty before I saw *Cavalcade* again. But then, with the thrill of the West End still in my mind, my thoughts were turning with increased determination towards a theatrical career. I didn't dare tell Evelyn and Mama. Along with painting, acting was still regarded as a profession to which gentlemen did not aspire. But I knew that my paternal great-grandfather had, against considerable odds, succeeded as a painter, and I was determined to follow his example and in my case succeed as an actor.

Christmas passed pleasantly until Mama received a telegram. For days afterwards, Mama hit the bottle, and finally
took to her bed. As no one would tell me anything I cornered
Winter. Within minutes he cracked and told all. Pa had been
asked to leave India.

— 3 —

Pa returned quietly to Lambourn, where he wasn't seen in public for weeks. During that time, Mama tried, without success, to enter College House so that she might discover the cause of his fall from grace on the Indian turf. The obstacle to Mama's entry was a self-appointed sentinel, my Aunt Tibby. Fifteen years Pa's senior, this formidable spinster was the youngest of The Kilkenny Cats and guarded her baby brother with a maternal love. There is no doubt that Aunt Tibby was outraged by Mama's informal life-style, and resentful of her beauty. Still wearing the bustles and beaver-trimmed hats of her Victorian teens, my Aunt's frizzy white hair, bright yellow teeth and huge nose did nothing to enhance what physical attributes she did possess. As she watched besotted admirers of both sexes pursue her lovely young sister-in-law, the septuagenarian virgin must have wondered where she'd gone wrong.

While Mama continued to besiege College House, Aunt Tibby stood her ground, Pa retired to his bedroom with a crate of gin, and Lambourn was rife with rumours. It appeared the situation would remain at stalemate until Evelyn entered the fray. Ordering Mama to drive her down to College House, Evelyn marched up to Pa's front door carrying a glass of Scotch in one hand and a West Highland Terrier in the other, a cigarette clenched between her teeth.

The cigarette bobbed up and down as Evelyn demanded to be let in. An upstairs window opened, and out peeped Aunt Tibby, whose hostile face began to twitch when she saw who it was. Everyone was frightened of Evelyn. Calling Mama to follow her, Evelyn swept into College House and insisted on seeing Pa immediately. After he'd been hauled out of bed and tidied into a reasonable state of respectability, Pa was taken to his study, where Evelyn sat in the chair behind his desk with Mama seated on one side. Evelyn ordered Aunt Tibby to leave, close the door and not to listen at keyholes while the Lambourn Inquisition enquired into the case of Major Daniel Macnee.

It was all over very quickly. As they left the study, Evelyn looked saintly, Mama goggle-eyed and Pa mortified, albeit in such a way as to suggest he was playing along for his own good. Referring to him as her brother in Christ, Evelyn not only forgave Pa for what he'd done in India but promised to help him resume his career as a trainer in Lambourn. Keeping her word, she had her horses sent to College House at once.

'Well, darling,' Mama told me years later, 'it all began at the races.'

Apparently there had been a meeting of some minor social significance where the British Raj turned out in full to ignore the horses and look at each other. Pa, a little the worse for drink, had brandished a starting pistol and delivered a speech from a balcony. There were cheers as he praised the virtues of Queen Victoria, before breaking into a rendition of 'Rule Britannia'. But the cheers quickly dissolved into roars of fury as Pa undid his flies and sprayed the assembled Raj with a shower of golden rain. The Raj swayed back. It then surged forward towards the balcony howling for revenge. Again it was forced to sway back as Pa fired a pistol that he'd 'borrowed' from the starter.

'Away, you bastards,' he raged.

There was another roar of fury.

'It's the finest malt, you fools.'

This information provoked yet another roar.

'Single grain.'

The quality of the Scotch consumed by Pa failed to impress the Raj. When he was finally overpowered, Pa was asked to leave India.

Pa's return had placed Mama in something of a domestic No Man's Land. Her actual marital home being Rooksnest, she was committed to keeping up appearances with her husband at College House, as well as maintaining a further obligation to the owner of Stork House, which was a mile down the road from Pa's establishment. This house took its name from an elegant statue of a stork standing on the rear lawn. The owner of the house, Captain Oswald Marmaduke Dalby Bell, who had trained winners of the Thousand Guineas, the Derby and the Oaks, had also sired my baby brother.

Determined to remain on the best of terms with Evelyn, Pa and 'Ozzie', as everyone called the Captain, Mama drew up a plan of action whose success was either the result of her skill in maintaining relationships, or an unusual tolerance on the part of her admirers. Driving her M.G. Classic sports car, every day come sunset, for many years Mama followed an identical routine. Tooting a fanfare on the M.G.'s custom built klaxon, she roared out of Rooksnest and raced the car down Hungerford Hill quite oblivious of the fact that there were others who used the road. Whinnying stallions reared up, dumped their riders and cantered off across meadows as the M.G. shot past and accelerated into Lambourn before screaming to a halt outside College House.

'My darling,' she'd announce to her startled husband and half of Lambourn, gliding into College House with the splendour of an imperial sunrise. Now mindful of Evelyn's role as Mama's guardian angel, a terrified Aunt Tibby would lock herself in cupboards for the duration of such visits. For the next half an hour there would be a tattoo of 'Darling, darling, darling,' interrupted only when Mama tippled a glass of sherry in one gulp. Five glasses down, Mama would extend a gracious hand, which Pa dutifully kissed before ushering his pseudo-royal guest back to her car. Mama would then drive to Stork House.

The domestic arrangements at Stork House were a little more complicated. Although Ozzie Bell had sired my baby brother, he had a wife, Renee, who still shared his home. The daughter of Major-General Sir Edward Northey, a former Governor of Kenya, there was a time when the gorgeous Renee might have been Lambourn's answer to Elizabeth Taylor. Divorced from Sir George Beaumont, she married Ozzie before finally settling down with her third husband, Wyndham Tor. Aware of her husband's dalliance with Mama, Renee behaved with rare dignity and courage. Not only was Mama a welcome visitor, but her son by Ozzie spent much of his childhood at Stork House where Renee brought him up with her children by Sir George.

After another round of 'darlings' and sherries, Mama would pat her son on the head before tearing back to Rooksnest just in time to fulfil her role as Evelyn's wife at the dinner table.

Dinner at Rooksnest was always served at eight o'clock. A meticulous observer of time, Evelyn expected identical standards from others. Late-comers could expect instant expulsion from the dining room, though with luck, there might be an egg of caviar cadged off Cook. One autumn night, having done the 'sherry and darling' routine, Mama headed back to Rooksnest with her foot slammed hard on the throttle. A shroud of fog had descended upon the countryside, and, missing a turning, Mama's concentration was distracted and along with the automobile she careered into a ditch. It must have been nearing half past nine when my dazed Mama staggered into the dining room. Once more, the knives were out as secondary wives and concubines gloated over what they assumed would be the downfall of Evelyn's favourite. They were in for another disappointment. Mama was saved by her bruises, her tears and Evelyn's regard. A posse of estate workers were aroused from their beds and dispatched to search for the car while Evelyn feted Mama as her honoured guest. But this did little to allay my fears about Mama's precarious position.

Come the school holidays, I was pressed into joining the household staff. As I joined the ranks of footmen who served dinner in dark green coats adorned with silver buttons, they surveyed my kilt with curiosity and presumably regarded me as a substitute head waitress.

Still doubtful of Evelyn, I imagined that the other ladies were genitally female, although sexually some had obviously elected to become men. Such decisions did cause certain anomalies in the otherwise rigid etiquette observed during dinner. After the serving of a savoury, Evelyn, the host would stand up and bow to the lady of the highest rank who, in this instance, was Mama. In turn, Mama rose to her feet and, followed by those ladies who'd decided to retain their sex, would retire to take coffee in the drawing-room, leaving the 'gentlemen' to enjoy their port and cigars.

I'm not sure whether anyone has successfully defined normality, but by my twelfth year, I'd long since regarded the socially conventional as abnormal and vice versa. All the same, the madhouse I had to call home was having a most unhealthy effect; so much so that I began stripping off and staring at myself on a daily basis just to ensure I was still a boy.

Humiliated by the rank of 'head waitress', I complained angrily to Mama. On the one hand, I'd been taught not to fraternize with the servants, while on the other, I'd been ordered to work with them. This was hardly a consistent upbringing, was it? Such simple logic went quite above her.

'Oh, I shouldn't worry, dear,' she soothed. 'I've always so envied the servants. The stuff they pick up.'

'Stuff?'

'Gossip. I tell you, they know more than me. Oh, and perhaps you could pass on any snippets that might amuse, though spare me Daisy Warwick. Along with the late King's other old girl-friends, these days she's somewhat passé.'

Mama did have a point. Indeed, many of the servants were downright nosy. Consequently, Evelyn acquired something of a locking mania, and there were nights when I retired to find my bedroom door bolted. The staff's curiosity also led to an elaborate postal ceremony. Every afternoon, Emlyn Owen was summoned to Evelyn's study. There she would hand him a locked black leather pouch bulging with sealed mail. Emlyn would then drive to Lambourn Post Office, where the post-master personally received the pouch and unlocked and emptied it, before handing it back to Emlyn. The same procedure was practised in reverse with the incoming mail.

Alcohol so often destroyed this bid for privacy, however. By the time Evelyn changed for dinner each evening, she was invariably well on the way to being drunk. Frequently she would leave her day clothes lying on the floor of her dressing room, their pockets crammed with opened envelopes containing that day's mail. During dinner, a rush of maids would scale the stairs with the speed of Jesse Owens, read the letters, and stampede back to the Servants' Hall bringing the latest news. As the maids gossiped away their evenings, I realized that Mama had been quite right in one of her observations. In what I hoped would be a temporary role as head waitress, I too, was quickly picking up 'the stuff'.

Having fiddled the elections, Adolf Hitler was entrenched in the Reichstag while his Fascist side-kick south of the Brenner Pass was ruling a send-up version of the Roman Empire. The two dictators seemed close to running Europe as a double act until Stalin glared out from the Kremlin. Unable to ignore these continental dictators, sections of the British public formed themselves into opposing factions whose battlefields scarred the gutters of the British Isles.

The street brawls of the Communists and Fascists did little to inconvenience the average person unless they were inadvertently caught up in them. One such soul was Lord Berners whose misfortune I heard of from Winter, the butler. Something of a music lover, Lord Berners had a piano built into the rear of his Rolls-Royce. I'm told it was a remarkable sight to behold this gifted musician tickling the ivories as his chauffeur drove him through London.

Then came the day of a political rally. As the Fascists goose-stepped their way up one end of the street, the Communists marched up from the other end, while jammed in the middle and without any means of escape was the piano-playing peer in the back of his car. Quite ignoring the stationary car and determined on a punch-up, the opposing sides continued to converge upon each other. As they closed in, the by now terrified peer ordered his chauffeur to wind down the car's windows and with considerable presence of mind, swung into a repertoire which, every few bars, alternated between the *Horst Wessel* and *The Internationale*.

Still ignoring the car, the Fascists and Communists rushed each other, squashing the automobile up against some railings. Extricating themselves from the tentacles of piano wires, Lord Berners and his chauffeur squeezed out of a window and over the railings to safety. They were lucky. In the ensuing fray people had their clothes torn off and someone was even pushed down a drain. Upon hearing this, Mama was thrilled and I was now ordered to pass on all useful snippets of gossip.

As my school-days at Summer Fields were drawing to a close, my parents assumed their son's education was completed and argued passionately about his future. For years, Pa had been badgering me to be a jockey. To his disappointment, I'd grown into a tall boy, so he was forced to consider an alternative career. He casually suggested I should work for Henry Young in his brewery. The speculative look in his eyes told me what he was up to. He was dreaming about a life with unlimited supplies of free alcohol. Mama glared at her husband. A life in the diplomatic corps was more befitting to 'the young gentleman'.

I ended their dispute by courteously pointing out that as a twelve-year-old crammed with Classics and with several years of learning still ahead, I was currently fit for little in the way of employment, and that anyway the choice of my next school would probably be Evelyn's, as she paid my fees. In fact, Evelyn had already decided my fate. The child would be sent to Eton. I felt utterly wretched, as I'd set my heart on going to Radley. From what I'd heard along the prep and public school grapevine, Radley was a more relaxed establishment with kindly masters, and matrons just like Nanny, whereas Eton was akin to a gladiatorial training school. Exacting tutors and sadistic fag masters would demand almost impossibly high standards, and anyone failing to achieve a permanent Grade A trembled away his days under the shadow, prior to the painful reality, of the cane. Explaining my reasons to her, I begged Evelyn not to send me to Eton.

'You know I disapprove of violence,' she lectured. 'Hitting a child only proves one is physically stronger than they are. I will not accept that Eton is that kind of establishment.' Unaware that Evelyn had been beaten by her step-mother, I wailed, 'Eton's awful. Please send me to Radley.'

'No. I intend that you should follow in the footsteps of Sir Robert Walpole, William Pitt the Elder, the Great Duke of Wellington and the Earl of Derby.'

'Weren't they all Prime Ministers?' I asked suspiciously.

Evelyn nodded, adding, 'And they served their country well.'

'But I don't want to be Prime Minister.'

Whatever her ambitions for me, Evelyn was sufficiently shrewd not to commit herself. 'You will still go to Eton,' she insisted.

I was still determined on Radley. When Emlyn drove me back to Summer Fields for the last time, I sat in the back of the Rolls plotting how Eton might be avoided. Of course! The answer lay in The Common Entrance Examination.

Each year, Geoffrey Bolton coached a flock of boys sitting their Common Entrance Examination for Eton. Thanks to the dedication of this great teacher and other masters at Summer Fields, my academic standards were high and there seemed no reason why I shouldn't pass – unless I made blatant display of cheating. It didn't occur to me that such idiotic conduct would also slam the doors of Radley and every public school of repute in the British Isles. On the day of the exam, Geoffrey Bolton calmed his over-excited charges, while at the same time skilfully weaving in a final caution on correct Latin usage. Without Evelyn's money and my teachers' devotion I'd never have been in such a privileged position, but with the thoughtlessness of a child, I proceeded to behave disgracefully.

The examination papers were easy, but between answering questions, I made a great show of staring at the papers of those nearest me. As I continued to do all I could to draw attention to myself, it became slowly apparent that no one, least of all the supervisor, was taking the slightest notice of me. As to why this should have been, I never discovered, but when the examination results were announced it was obvious that my scheming had boomeranged. While staring at my neighbour's papers, I had disagreed with some of the answers and replied to the questions using my own knowledge. I obtained high marks, and could only respond with a forced grin as a delighted Geoffrey Bolton congratulated me upon passing my Common Entrance Examination to Eton.

Trying to forget Eton, I did what I could to enjoy the summer holidays. With the roles of Brutus and Bolingbroke now added to my Shakespearian repertoire, I felt well on the way to becoming the next John Gielgud. Such expectations rose further when I was told that Rudyard Kipling was visiting Rooksnest to watch a short film being made there. Entitled *His Apologies*, it was the tale of a Highland Terrier. Evelyn lent the director one of her forty-five dogs, Winter was roped in as a 'heavy', and I, Daniel Patrick Macnee, was to be the star playing opposite my cousin Josephine.

Two days prior to shooting, I went down with measles. All I could do was watch, enraged, from quarantine as Josephine pranced before the cameras with her new leading man – my brother! He'd been allowed to enter Rooksnest for the first time. My scowls deepened as they then sat down to an enormous tea with the unofficial Poet Laureate, before receiving their fees of eleven shillings and six pence. Though I didn't know it at the time, this was to be the first of many setbacks in my career as an actor.

Eton College has always been something of a lunatic asylum, an aristocratic reform school and a nuisance to several British governments. Having arrived at this conclusion within a week of starting my first half term, I felt optimistic about the future, since it appeared I might fit in.

Nevertheless, I arrived at Eton in a state of near mutiny. This was the latest of numerous occasions when evil adults had placed me in the custody of people I regarded as equally evil adults. Determined to revenge myself against Evelyn and Eton, I remembered the story of a revolt at Rugby. A boy named Willoughby Cotton had used gunpowder to blow up the headmaster's study. Cotton later became something of a military disaster in the Afghan campaigns, and the Rugby exploit was his greatest success with the use of explosives. I'd emulate Cotton and blow Rooksnest, Eton and their adult populations to fragments.

M'Tutor, a Mr Sladden, conveniently taught science. I've no idea how Evelyn ever got my name put down for Eton, but the usual procedure is for parents to approach a housemaster before their son's seventh year. One master who I know of touted actively for pupils in the stewards' enclosure at Henley Royal Regatta. An absent-minded man, he scribbled accepted names on his shirt cuffs.

Eton was run like the Hilton Hotel chain. The trade name, Eton, was held by the Upper Master (the Headmster) who nominally watched over twenty-five houses. When a housemaster retired, his house became vacant, then was sold, complete with furniture and boys, on something of a franchise basis to a new housemaster. While the house would be named after the new housemaster, the twenty-five houses were collectively known as Eton College. Housemasters collected school fees, passed the teaching portion to the Upper Master, and kept the rest to run their house and save up for their old age. With a niggardly retirement pension of only one hundred pounds on offer, a master's future sometimes took precedence over the boys' standard of living. I soon discovered that housemasters also ran lucrative rackets selling playing fields, hiring out boats and taking in washing.

Mr Sladden and I greeted each other politely, but beneath his pleasantries I sensed caution and unease. Had my bad name preceded me, I wondered? His enormous Adam's Apple appeared larger than his tiny head and these two lopsided domes wobbled precariously above a winged collar.

'Macnee, isn't it?' he squawked.

'Yes, Sir.'

'Hmm.'

'I hear you were knocked about rather badly in the Great War,' I piped up tactlessly. 'Have you recovered?'

The little head jerked up and down while the Adam's Apple distended and subsided in a rapid rhythm. I was reminded of a mangy old turkey scratching about its yard. 'You will be a good boy, won't you?' This would be the longest conversation we were to have until five years later when the lid blew off my pornography and tote scandal.

Being a tall boy for my age, I was immediately put into a tailcoat instead of the standard 'Bum Freezer' usually worn by younger boys. Coupled with long pin-striped trousers, waistcoat, paper collar (changed daily, by most), a silk topper and my haughty demeanour, the tailcoat surely lampooned me as an epitome of the little English gentleman. Crossing Barnes Pool Bridge, which links Eton and Windsor, I had no reason to doubt my superiority over the lower orders until I was spotted by a gaggle of toughs loitering alongside a bank of the River Thames. My cheeks reddened as a barrage of catcalls was hurled at me, but amid this offensive was a strange remark about 'bleedin' undertakers'. Apparently there are those who genuinely believe that the Eton dress was specifically designed for George the Third's funeral in 1820.

Although I was only twelve, I already felt most sophisticated and grown up. Eton did not entirely discourage this attitude. Each boy was addressed by his surname, allotted a private room and taught to develop independence and adopt lofty attitudes early in life. A monument to tradition and language, Eton was a great school, but it was also a school quite ruthless in seeking retribution from those who failed to fit in. Respect for authority was paramount and adherence to custom obligatory. There appeared to be one very obvious way of surviving, however. With most of the masters wearing strait jackets underneath their gowns, a boy simply emulated them and with luck, did survive. Given my domestic background, behaving like a lunatic came quite naturally and I soon found my own niche into which I settled until my seventeenth year.

Among the boys who became my closest friends in Sladden's House were Peter Barnes, who was later appointed an assistant Director of Public Prosecutions, and Arthur Innes who was killed in the Battle of Britain. On our first night at the school, the fagging system, that most sacrosanct institution, was explained. For a couple of years a lower boy literally became the servant of an upper boy. Duties included cooking meals, running baths and warming lavatory seats. Scorched sausages, flooded bathrooms and chilled superior bottoms resulted in canings. With years of lashings behind me, I'd become something of an old campaigner, but I still wanted to heave upon hearing the swish of that vicious rod before it tore into my buttocks.

I was assigned to fag for Tom Egerton. A very handsome

boy with soft blond hair and a languid manner, Tom regarded me with considerable lack of interest.

'So you're Macnee,' he all but yawned.

'Yes,' I faltered.

Tom pondered on this a little before staring at me in a way that suggested recognition.

'Macnee, Macnee,' he murmured. 'There's a trainer called "Shrimp" Macnee. Any relation of yours?'

'Actually, he's my father.'

'My God. That's marvellous. He's one of the best trainers around. Tell me, what does he reckon on the four o'clock at Epsom next week?'

'I've no idea.'

'Then find out.'

I somehow managed to reach a telephone and got through to Pa at Lambourn. At first, his reaction was one of surprise, then pleasure when it appeared his son might be showing an interest in the turf. Laden with 'dead certs', I returned to Tom, who put me an irresistible deal. In return for a steady stream of winners, whatever my errors I'd be spared a beating. Not only did this arrangement prove immensely successful, but it taught me my first major lesson in the art of becoming streetwise.

Before going to bed on that first night at Eton, there still remained one very private but most important task to be completed. I wrote a letter, and it began as follows: Dear Uncle, I do hope you will not mind my writing to you but there is a question that I must ask. Why have you taken Mama away from my Daddy? Evelyn never replied to the letter, but from that time what had been an unsettled truce based on necessity developed into a cold war.

A week or so later, I found myself cooking sausages for Tom's tea on the end of a toasting fork over a fire in my room. Life had become quite pleasant. My academic studies were up to standard, beatings could be avoided, there was money to be made in selling Pa's racing tips, though God help me if Mr Sladden discovered — and someone had given me a packet of cigarettes. The sausages browned well, the kettle sang away, and I was thoroughly enjoying tobacco. Eton wasn't too bad after all, so perhaps I should blow up Rooksnest only. Such idle thoughts were suddenly disturbed, however, by a quite violent shout. It was Tom, and he was hungry. Throwing my cigarette aside, I piled the sausages, buttered toast and the tea on a tray in one revolting heap and, all but colliding with similarly laden fags, ran to Tom's room. Having left Tom chomping contentedly, I then met Peter Barnes, who wanted to chat. But Peter broke off mid-sentence and sniffed. 'Can you smell something burning, Patrick?'

'No.'

'I can.' He sniffed again, then added gleefully, 'I think someone's on fire.'

Peter raced off in the direction of what he assumed must be a heretic sizzling at the stake while I ambled back to my room. I then realized this was the direction in which he had raced. I broke into a gallop, the kind of which Pa would have been proud. 'My room,' I yelled. 'It's burning down.'

Mr Sladden hopped and jumped about as he surveyed the damaged room. Apart from a smouldering bed and charred wall, there was little to worry about.

'Calamitous, calamitous,' he wailed. 'The entire house could have been destroyed.'

A week previously, such a possibility would have greatly pleased me. Now I was more concerned about my singed hair and missing eyebrows, which Mr Sladden quite failed to notice. But at least the incriminating cigarettes had been destroyed by the fire.

My routine at Eton was invariable. Hauled out of bed at dawn, I'd grab a mug of cocoa, fight for a dry biscuit and take early school in the dark. At breakfast, I retched over a slimey, oatmeal blancmange which passed for porridge, then yawned through chapel and froze in an outdoor assembly before struggling with Virgilian texts. Exhausted and very hungry, Arthur Innes and I often treated ourselves to a splendid tea in Rowlands, the Eton sock shop, or tuck shop.

'What do you think of Sladden?' Arthur asked.

'Brilliant on science, useless on catering.'

'That porridge was particularly nasty.'

'But for Rowlands, we'd starve.'

'There's a boy in the school who does.'

This wasn't strictly true, but on account of his stammer a fellow pupil certainly had difficulty explaining his nutritional needs to those who fed us. The boy's affliction was no common stammer. He simply couldn't speak. Chatter ceased and everyone stared whenever this slight boy with dark good looks entered Rowlands.

'Yes, dear,' the assistant would ask.

The boy would say nothing.

'If it's a strawberry mess you're after, they're not in season, luv.'

The boy would open his mouth. The entire clientele of Rowlands would lean forward to listen. Without managing so much as a hiccup, the boy would close his mouth and flee.

'Who is that boy?' I asked.

'A Peruvian called Bearskin,' a boy named Burdett-Coutts suggested.

'No, idiot,' Arthur corrected. 'His name is Bentine. Michael Bentine.'

Michael's arrival had caused a tidal wave of excitement. Jaded by centuries of aristocratic pupillage, Eton craved the unusual, which Michael has always been. The son of an outstanding aviation pioneer, the stammering boy was passed from master to master for examination, analysis and opinion. Probably attracted by a shared unhappiness, Michael and I quickly became friends. Still unable to speak, he communicated by paper and sent me the following note: 'The beaks are only interested because I'm a Peruvian and the idiots don't even know where South America is.'

The stammer had to be corrected. The man most determined to see a cure effected was Michael's housemaster, William Hope-Jones. This master's height neared seven feet, he sported twirling black moustachios, travelled on a 1910 Post Office bicycle and shrouded himself in Victorian knickerbockers and a greatcoat once worn by Gladstone. A kindly man who shared a passion for chess and mathematics with Michael's father, he placed Michael in the care of a speech therapist who began, as he said, 'To break the boy's silence.'

One day Michael and I joined a large gathering of masters and boys in School Hall for a film show. Among those present was Captain Knight, a noted ornithologist, who happened to have a giant golden eagle perched on his shoulder. I never discovered his connection with Eton, but it wasn't unusual to find eccentric squatters scattered throughout the school buildings. Well used to this partnership, the audience acknowledged them and other friends while waiting for the camera to roll. But for Michael and me, the bird was blocking our view. 'Er, excuse me,' I ventured. Captain Knight had dozed off, but his eagle flapped its wings, screeched and thrust a vicious beak at me. The precociously bright Michael handed me a note that read: 'Be silent. Eagles are not trained in the science of reason.'

Lights were extinguished, the film began and everyone, including the eagle, settled down to enjoy themselves. I was furious. Unable to see a thing and spoiling for a brawl with the bird, my anger turned to alarm when it began a twitching and hopping routine on the Captain's shoulder. Michael passed me another note that read, 'It looks like Mr Sladden covered in feathers.'

My giggling was curbed by a screech from Mr Sladden. 'Macnee – behave.' By now the eagle was decidedly fidgety. Even the Captain stirred to rebuke his dearest friend.

Obviously bored to its beak, the eagle emitted another screech, took off and flew around School Hall. The place was in turmoil. No one could find the lights, the ensuing stampede fell over itself and sprawled on the floor in a jumble, while the flapping gowns of terrified masters made them indistinguishable from the eagle, who soared and plummetted through Hall, flattening what remained of the seated audience. I didn't mind. With the bird now watching from 'The Gods', I could see the film. Struggling to his feet, Captain Knight mounted the shoulders of Conybeare, the Lower Master, and attempted fruitlessly to lure the bird down with a repertoire of squawks and twitters. He was ignored. Sliding off Conybeare, the Captain perched himself on a chair, repeated his repertoire, this time adding an accompaniment of twirling arms and facial spasms. The eagle glided back to earth, order was restored and the film continued, though once more my view was blocked.

Not wishing to receive a dreaded white ticket for idling, I submerged myself in work. This dedication also distracted me from the moods of intense despair which were now becoming an affliction.

Having talked my way out of rugby and the Field Game – Eton's version of football – I took up beagling. Writing another letter to Evelyn, I asked to be measured for a beagling outfit of tweed jackets, breeches, stocks and peaked caps trimmed with velvet. Given my previous correspondence, she was remarkably agreeable. Perhaps it was a sense of guilt. I didn't know or care. Suitably kitted, I started beagling and pursued my version of that sport with boundless enthusiasm. Removed from the beady eyes of authority, I let the hounds run wild while I sat upon a hill reading everything from Pliny to comics.

My talents, such as they were, lay in creation, and I was advised to join the Drawing Schools. A vast complex of buildings on the river bank, the Drawing Schools were run by

Robin Darwin, later Sir Robin Darwin and President of The Royal College of Art. Resembling a scruffy Sir Francis Bacon, this remarkable individualist taught the skills of pottery and woodwork, encouraged dramatic interests and constructed a marionette theatre whose wooden puppets the boys were inspired to craft. When I joined, the Drawing Schools lay under a pall. A couple of their masters had just tumbled off The Matterhorn, so I began this phase of creative development in a funereal atmosphere. With Dennis Pullen-Thompson and the Michaels Benthall and Warre among my contemporaries, I was fortunate to be involved artistically with boys whose exceptional literary, dramatic and graphic talents would mould a period of British theatrical history.

There was one boy called Heinrich with whom I did not want to be involved. This son of a European aristocrat had taken a liking to me and made his feelings known backstage at the school's marionette theatre where my friends and I had constructed scenery and wooden puppets, and done voice-overs, for such productions as Max Beerbohm's *Happy Hypocrite* and Elmer Rice's *Adding Machine*. Then Robin Darwin decided to stage what he hoped would be a first-rate production of Laurence Housman's *Victoria Regina*, with my unbroken treble voice behind a puppet of that most remarkable of ladies. Wearing a lightweight shirt and a pair of grey shorts I stood behind the backcloth with my script in one hand and used my other hand to dangle the Queen onto the marionette theatre's stage. I was startled by Heinrich.

'Why not visit me in my room?' he suggested.

Given the Prince Consort's recent death, sex was the last thing on my mind. Rebuffed, Heinrich turned nasty. Twirling his puppet into a spin, he threatened, 'Visit me in my room or you'll find something greasy in your bed.'

'Do not desecrate the Prince Consort's corpse,' roared Robin Darwin at this particularly poisonous thirteen-year-old who was working Prince Albert.

Heinrich became more daring. During our final rehearsal one of his hands slithered up my shorts.

'Stop it,' I complained, nearly dropping my script onto the marionette theatre's stage.

'Then visit my room.'

'Alright,' I grumbled, but didn't.

A lump of rancid butter was found in my bed and Heinrich promised further revenge on the first night of *Victoria Regina*. With the curtain hardly up, again his hand slithered into my shorts.

'Take your hand off my bottom,' I hissed.

Scanning his script, our puzzled prompter whispered, 'I say, that's not in the dialogue.'

I was now shaking nervously and instead of seating Queen Victoria on a chaise longue, inadvertently launched her into a cartwheel. Robin Darwin frowned from his front-row seat in the audience while a couple of fathers behind him guffawed. My buttocks were then tweaked by Heinrich, I dropped my script onto the stage, and twirled the Queen into a daring spectacle of high kicks. The guffaws increased. Suddenly losing my balance, I all but tumbled onto the stage myself. Heinrich yanked me back, the Queen broke into a hornpipe, and the show was stopped until my script could be retrieved. As I reddened, the guffaws increased further, and someone even shouted, 'Encore', but from the look on his face, Robin Darwin had obviously marked me as trouble.

Christmas was greeted with general jubilation. Peter Barnes invited me to stay with him and his parents at their happy Bayswater home.

'It'll be such fun,' he said. 'My parents are great theatre buffs, so you'll all get on famously.'

'But I'll be expected down in the country,' I replied. 'How about Easter?'

'Marvellous. Come then.'

'Perhaps you'd care to visit Rooksnest,' I suggested.

No sooner had I spoken than I regretted inviting him to that nest of termagants, and I did not repeat the invitation.

Rooksnest had the warmth of an ice palace. Evelyn avoided me, and from the nervous expression etched upon Mama's countenance, it was evident that my reproachful letter had been passed around the harem. With her great rival, Gussie, temporarily back in favour, Mama drifted in and out of an alcoholic haze. Ignored, I decided to try my luck with Pa at College House. Bicycling down Hungerford Hill, I skidded into a ditch as a classic M.G. Sports Car chased past. It was Mama beginning her social round. Watching the car zig-zag its way along the road, it was evident why she hadn't recognized me.

Mrs Rose came out of College House and hugged me. A cook who combined substance with artistry, this skilled countrywoman always served my favourite dishes. Pa wandered about snorting in a manner not dissimilar to his horses.

'Here,' he mumbled, proffering a couple of half-crowns.

'Oh, thank you.'

'No, boy. That's not for you. Pick up my laxative. You've time before dinner.'

Pa's laxative was still two bottles of gin a day.

The New Year, 1935, opened with a screaming row. Evelyn accused Pa of drunkenness, a charge he denied on his rare occasions of sobriety. Evelyn was scarcely qualified to sermonize against the evils of liquor, but in fairness, her complaint was not without justification. Measured in crates, Pa's intake was awesome. Concerned primarily for the well-being of her horses, Evelyn dithered over leaving them in the care of a fellow inebriate. But still regarding Pa as her brother in Christ she left the horses where they were.

Nanny was in tears. After a thirteen-year wait, her chauffeur fiancé had become, as she so coyly phrased it, 'frisky'. Was I, she begged to know, at last old enough to look after myself? With Rooksnest, floggings and Eton on my curriculum vitae, I felt sufficiently experienced to spar with Adolf Hitler. Reassured, Nanny married. It was apparent that her husband's dislike of me had not diminished. A witness to his infidelity, I'd always be a potential blackmailer. Near to adolescence, I felt sufficiently mature to tip him a man-to-man wink. Staring coldly, the chauffeur seemingly misinterpreted my familiarity as a hint to pay up.

It was good to return to Eton. I'd survived my first term, made friends and was even having fun.

At that time, twelve-foot knitted scarfs were *de rigueur* for the fashion-conscious Etonian. As a parting gift, Nanny knitted me one, and I joined the ranks of muffled boys who tripped through the school and over the ends of their own tassles.

In a rare moment of misjudgement, Robin Darwin advised me to audition for the school choir. The real judge of my musical ability would be Henry 'Daddy' Ley, the Director of Music, who doubled as talent scout after Sunday Chapel. That Sunday's sermon was given by a batty retired master, whose numbed side gave him an uncanny resemblance to Victor Hugo's heroic occupant of Notre Dame. An emotional man, the master unleashed his passion in the pulpit. For his subject, the good man chose Christ's confrontation with the money men in the temple. A largely Gentile congregation, we had no wish to be embroiled in what was essentially a Jewish financial dispute until the master thundered, 'He drove out those who sold and bought, and overthrew the tables of the bankers.' The offspring of eminent financiers took umbrage at this and stared coldly as he continued, 'And he overthrew the chairs of pigeon sellers.' Since I had recently acquired a racing pigeon, everyone turned to stare at me. As they stared, the master shifted his numbed side into 'Walking' position and limped out of Chapel, leaving his congregation in mid-sermon.

The masters hushed chattering boys and peered anxiously

towards the exit through which the master had departed. Claude Aurelius Elliot, the Headmaster, marched up to the pulpit, intent on standing in for him, but before he could say a word, a quivering voice intoned, 'My house shall be known for a house of prayer.' We all turned to see the master limping back in. 'And you have made my house into a den of thieves,' he continued.

Was he so very wrong? I wondered, feeling my pockets crammed with betting slips, unpaid bills and photographs of nude sunbathers whose sale was supplementing my income.

When the sermon was finally over I duly reported to Henry Ley. 'Daddy' Ley's organ was a magnificent instrument sporting a particularly splendid fantail of rear-view mirrors. Smiling into the mirrors, 'Daddy' Ley whispered, 'I can spot the great buzzard.' I assumed he was referring to Captain Knight's golden eagle.

'So you're intent upon an operatic career, Macnee?'

'Not at all.'

'Then why did Robin Darwin send you here?'

'He thinks I might have possibilities.'

'Another boy castrato,' he groaned. 'Let's try "Rock of Ages".'

'Daddy' Ley had a mania for re-vamping old tunes. Given a simple waltz time of three/four, he'd attempt transpositions into a tricky six/eight rhythm whose success is usually the triumph of a Tchaikovsky. 'A six, an eight, a six, eight, six,' he warbled. 'Rock of ages cleft for me, Let me hide myself in thee.' I was reminded of a New Orleans jazz band with half the players entering on a late cue.

'I see you're at it again,' a voice boomed. It was Bill Hope-Jones, a fierce traditionalist who disliked musicians meddling with their minims.

'Oh God,' wailed 'Daddy' Ley. 'It's the great buzzard.'

Hope-Jones was followed by a chorus of boys from his house, and supported by them he began to bellow 'Rock of

Ages' with the volume and musical technique of Gigli backed by the entire company of La Scala.

'You bloody fool, William,' raged 'Daddy' Ley, resuming his organ thumping in what had seemingly degenerated into a previously unheard of thirteen/eleven beat.

'Keep it going, Macnee,' he cheered me on.

'But Sir . . .'

'Let the water and the blood,' he urged.

'From thy riven side which flowed,' roared the Hope-Jones ensemble.

Clambering off his organ seat, 'Daddy' Ley regarded me with pity. 'Forget your operatic aspirations,' he advised , 'You can't even sing.'

'But I never wanted . . .'

My protestations were stalled. 'Send me a Caruso,' he demanded.

Returning to more familiar pastures, one day I opened an account with a new bookie named William Hill. Having backed a stream of winners, I was collecting my winnings when a skeletal gentleman with a broken nose and cauliflower ears sidled up.

'You,' he rasped.

'Good afternoon, Sir.'

'Git out the back. The Guv wants yer.'

His minions might be thugs, but William Hill was a gentleman. With great courtesy, he explained that given my Father's reputation, my patronage was no longer acceptable.

'But I do so enjoy doing business with you, Mr Hill.'

'Yes son, but I can't afford you.'

'Go on, git out of it, you saucy little bugger,' said his minion, 'else Oi'll give you a nose like mine.'

I wasn't too dispirited. Back at school, I began guiding gullible visitors around Eton for a fee, and founded my own tote.

'It is your duty to die with your men and with the name of

the King upon your lips.' This fearful admonishment had been Mama's theme in a lecture upon the meaning of life. Hoping to fulfil at least one duty with distinction I joined the Officers' Training Corps, where I was moulded into cannon-fodder and taught to lead the lower orders into glorious death and destruction. Wearing a uniform of sand and brown khaki, I was sent down to Tidworth Camp for military exercises against Charterhouse. None of us could have possibly guessed that within a decade the ranting maniac ensconsed in the Berlin Chancellery would be responsible for sending so many beloved friends to their deaths.

Communicating through scribbled notes and sign language, the mute Michael Bentine had 'talked' his way into OTC, where his creative talents, though useful, occasionally back-fired. What should have been a solemn parade for inspection was sabotaged when the troops' puttees unwound and settled in a tangled skein around their ankles. Burrowing into a knapsack crammed with curiosities ranging from blueprints to bath salts, Michael retrieved a bottle, ordered a line-up and glued the platoon's puttees into a neat criss-cross. Well into that long night he was still unpicking the trussed calves of some very fractious young soldiers.

Very soon the King's name was on the nation's lips when in the New Year of 1936 George the Fifth passed away. Michael Bentine and I stayed up for nights in front of my radio listening to the latest bulletins on the King's health, and in the early morning of 21 January, 1936 came the news that death had come peacefully to the King at 11.55 p.m. Barely fourteen, I was nevertheless affected by the apparent brevity of life, that most precious of gifts. Eton and Windsor were submerged into a shroud of gloom. Fellow-pupils included the two Lascelles boys and the sons of numerous crowned and uncrowned heads of Europe. This, coupled with a royal affiliation that was centuries old, meant that Eton played a unique part in the forthcoming great occasion of state.

Traditionally, Eton boys stood within the precincts of Windsor Castle, providing a guard of honour outside St George's Chapel for departed monarchs. Michael, myself and other friends were included in that guard. Drawn by sailors of the Royal Navy, the gun-carriage bearing the coffin was followed by the new King Edward the Eighth and his brothers, the royal Dukes of York, Gloucester and Kent. Behind them walked five of the late monarch's cousins: Carol of Rumania, Christian of Denmark, Boris of Bulgaria, Haakon of Norway and Leopold of the Belgians. Other dignatories included Prince Starhemberg, Umberto, Prince of Piedmont and three remarkable soldiers: Finland's Field-Marshal Baron Mannerheim, Russia's Marshal Mikhail Tukhachevsky, and a face I recognized as that of Marshal Pétain of France.

Out went the order, 'Present arms.' Amid the surrounding guards the coffin was difficult to see. There lay a good man who had ruled wisely for twenty-five years, a quarter of a century during which his Romanov cousins had been murdered, his Hohenzollern cousins deposed, the map of Europe re-drawn, and the war to end all wars had killed a generation of fine men who should have lived to serve and lead their countries. Michael and I glanced at each other. Perhaps it was the solemnity of the occasion or perhaps it was the realization that we were witnessing the passing of an age, but like me, Michael was fighting back tears.

— 4 —

The death of the King inflamed Evelyn's religious mania. She ordered masses for the repose of his soul, made spectacular signs of the cross and continually jiggled her rosary beads. I just spluttered in the surfeit of incense which had settled on the chapel like a pea soup fog. With Evelyn distracted by matters celestial, Mama and Gussie tussled for supremacy in the harem. Gussie's viperish tongue and overwhelming determination made downfall eventually inevitable for my charming if weak Mama. Convinced that her ruin was now just a matter of time, I resolved to conclude my education swiftly and with distinction, while attempting to effect a reunion between my parents. I still so longed for them to be together, and of course we'd need shelter when Mama was disgraced.

Having one day dropped a vague hint that she should return to her husband, I awaited Mama's reaction. She lit up a cigarette, inhaled the smoke and seemed to cluck in the manner of a broody hen. Dropping a stronger hint, this time I was rewarded with a soliloquy on her devotion to Evelyn and punished with an acerbic reminder that Rooksnest would be ours but only if I behaved. To Pa, I suggested that his estranged wife would not be averse to his attentions. But I watched with a sense of defeat as the little man paled and bit into his lower lip. Pa glanced at his watch. 'Come along,' he bellowed just a shade too loudly. 'We'll be late for the races.' I would not understand Pa's humiliation and hurt at the hands of a woman until my own manhood. But of one fact I was certain: Pa was deeply in love with his wife.

On the way to the races in Pa's red Chrysler, he noticed that I was reading an unfamiliar paper.

'What's that you've got, huh?'

'*The Stage*.'

Pa braked abruptly. 'The *what*?'

'It's *the* theatrical newspaper. I now take it regularly just like Gielgud and Leslie,' I boasted.

'Leslie?'

'Howard, of course.'

Pa replied by confiscating *The Stage*, suggesting I subscribe to *The Sporting Life* – 'Just like Gordon Richards' – and reconsider a career in Henry Young's brewery.

As always, the races were exciting and highly lucrative. And I watched admiringly as Edward Underdown, one of Pa's jockeys, described as the most handsome man in England, rode a winner. With a winner and a bottle of gin behind him, Pa mellowed and invited me to dine at College House. Over dinner, the going was heavy. Predictably, Pa's conversation developed into a symphony of spits, snuffles and snorts. Ted Peart, the head lad, entered, saluted and announced it was time for the Major to inspect the horses. Watching Pa reel off to the stables I realized sadly that we had absolutely nothing in common and could never converse with like minds. Remembering my Great-Grandfather, Sir Daniel Macnee, who'd run away to pursue his chosen profession, I resolved that the more restraints were put on me, the more determined I would become to be an actor.

Back at Eton, come summer, I pleaded a weak testicle in the hope of dodging cricket. Michael Warre stared at my crotch, said he didn't believe me, and called in a second opinion. The second opinion, a boy of bullish proportions and a rapine nature, conducted a more intimate examination.

'Cricket is not obligatory,' he assured me.

'Oh really?'

'Really. There's a choice of cricket and rowing and I think you are medically unfit for the first.'

'See,' I jeered at Michael Warre.

'So you can double with me in the second.'

The 'Bull' reminded me of Heinrich. Sensing potential danger I began protesting.

'I can't row either. Weak back, you know.'

'A pull at the oars should build you into a strapping boy.'

Surprisingly, the 'Bull' behaved with the utmost propriety. A keen and knowledgeable oarsman, he taught the rudiments of rowing, encouraged me to skull on my own and furthered my love of the water. Soon I was rowing confidently along the River Thames. Those idle hours on the river sheltered me from the growing menace of a war that would kill and maim so many beloved friends. Leaving the politicians to humour a bellicose Adolf Hitler, I dreamed away idyllic days, intoxicated by the bouquet of an English summer.

Such rapture was intruded upon by the reality of life on Queen's Eyot, the island in the river to which I invariably rowed. A buttercup yellow sun gleamed down upon half naked boys who snoozed, swam, chatted, swopped 'sock' or caught up on work. Ever short of money, I touted for bets on forthcoming races, sold my racing pigeon and bought a share in a greyhound which was run secretly at the nearby Slough track.

The environment of Rowlands was most congenial to my personal development as a sleazy aristocrat, however. There, I'd idle away time with other Etonian hell-rakes discussing gambling, wine and sex, in that order. There was much talk about seducing girls, but with none available we were still virgins – contrary to our boasts. With sisters out of bounds and mothers well plucked, that left the servants, whom no one quite knew how to approach on such a matter. There was further talk of ladies in London who obliged for a remuneration, but we were frightened by stories of what might be contracted from these bighearted girls.

Returning to Rooksnest for the vacation, I decided to trace the last known whereabouts of my brother James. Now aged ten, he'd been lodged with yet another family, and after our initial embrace he cried bitterly. Not knowing what to do with the boy, his well-meaning if confused guardians had squeezed him into a pram where, trussed up with string, he spent his holidays staring out at puzzled livestock.

It was during that same vacation that I truly fell in love for the first time with a girl. Called Joan Greville-Williams, she was a delicious looking marshmallow of pink and white and the daughter of an owner. I longed to kiss her, but such was my diffidence that all she received were adoring stares. Joan proved to be a sweet girl, and with my faith in ladies restored a little, I approached Pa for a 'man to man' chat.

'She's the most beautiful girl on earth,' I sighed.

'What d'you say her name was?'

'Joan Greville-Williams.'

'Her Father's got some damned good horses. Do what you can to get the blighters stabled with me. Oh, and for Christ's sake don't get her into trouble.'

One evening that autumn, the boys at Eton left their beds to hear King Edward the Eighth's Abdication Speech. As we sipped our cocoa and listened, I'm not sure whether many of us really appreciated the gravity of the occasion; but the departure of monarchs has always given me a sense of personal loss. It was like losing a parent. Come Christmas, school choirs across the country sang 'Hark the Herald Angels sing, Mrs Simpson's pinched our King.' Though the by now eloquent Michael Bentine confided, 'I feel sorry for George the Sixth. You see, I so understand the embarrassment of a stammer.'

In a rare letter, Mama enthused over numerous visits to the London theatre. She and Evelyn had become first night stalwarts. With my fifteenth birthday just weeks away, my request to accompany them was granted and the three of us booked in at The Connaught. As expenses were courtesy of Evelyn, I wasn't going to risk any adverse comment upon her public consumption of gin. But nevertheless the drunken antics of her and Mama quickly became a source of embarrassment. Within a day the two of them had been asked politely to leave a restaurant, nearly walked under a bus, and cheered Joachim von Ribbentrop, the newly appointed German Ambassador.

Our much anticipated visit to the theatre was more humiliating than my 'crowning' with a Glengarry bonnet at Rooksnest some seven years previously. My elders rolled in for a matinée performance inebriated, noisy and to my fury, very late. Trying to pretend I didn't know these people I cringed in a corner of our box as the two of them played musical chairs. Hissing from adjacent boxes brought a modicum of order, but still furious and deeply ashamed, I left during the interval and wasn't even missed. I roamed the streets of London, discovering the famous bookshops in the Charing Cross Road. Flush with Evelyn's money, I bought a number of books, before chancing upon a tiny bookshop whose back-street entrance was almost invisible. The owner, a man of fifty whose shapely eyebrows and luxuriant lips clashed with his tweed jacket and spats, was a blatant flirt. Shaking my head at an offer to join his sunbathing club, I was nevertheless fascinated by his sales pitch on 'adult' magazines.

Back at The Connaught, I pored over exotic titles such as *Hollywood Nights*, and a sprinkling of nude male photographs. I later sold the photographs on the open market at Eton, but *Hollywood Nights* I hid in the guttering above my bedroom window at Rooksnest. What the mansion's housekeeper was doing in the gutter was never quite apparent, but she informed Evelyn of a 'filthy' discovery. Mercifully, she also told Emlyn Owen. Out of pity, and perhaps curiosity, this lusty Welshman bagged *Hollywood Nights* and without the damning evidence the housekeeper's alleged find was put down to drunkenness.

Added to my academic curriculum I now had commercial interests which, apart from selling dirty pictures, included running a *Book* and part ownership in a greyhound which was raced regularly at Slough track. Race meetings were fascinating. After the formality of home and school, the Slough track provided a relaxed atmosphere where I could mix freely with bookies, gypsies and drunks. On those rare occasions when I observed the presence of housemasters, a quick exit was vital, else I'd face expulsion.

Further dramatic experience came when the school produced *Richard the Second*. It received mixed notices, as the saying goes. Michael Warre was praised for 'managing to give the impression of age and showing promising talent in John of Gaunt's dying speech.' As for me: 'Greater care in the pronunciation of consonants would have relieved the strain of hearing. Macnee alone was blameless in this respect, and for this reason he several times revived the play when it was flagging.' All very heady stuff, except I cannot for the life of me remember which part I played.

After the performance a venerable old gentleman and an exceedingly pretty young woman introduced themselves.

'The name is Peter Henry. I'm your maternal Grandsire, and this is Daphne, my wife.'

'I didn't realize you were still alive,' I blurted out. Giving Daphne an appreciative glance, I said, 'How do you do, Grandmama.' This amused Grandpapa greatly. Daphne was the old boy's newly acquired third wife.

During a later stay with this devoted couple I found them to be remarkably forthright. A medical practitioner, Grandpapa Henry enjoyed his gin and hinted that his medical skills had been acquired while treating cattle in West Africa. Daphne's tender years and stunning looks had apparently aroused jealousy on the part of her husband's older female relations, who were further peeved that she was the main beneficiary of his will. The more malicious even suggested he'd picked her up in Piccadilly. During my week with the Henrys at their elegant home on the borders of Richmond Park, I forged a more intimate bond of affection with Grandpapa than I ever would with my own Father. Such relationships are not uncommon between the very old and the very young. But while I was grateful for Grandpapa's understanding, I still so longed to make Pa my best friend.

'Please come again, my boy,' Grandpapa Henry urged.

'I'd love to.'

'And would you be averse to some advice from an old man?'

'Of course not.'

'Flirt all you want with Daphne, but don't join the Labour Party.'

Once again I was sent away. Although my command of French was reasonable, Evelyn decided I'd master the language of diplomacy with fluency only by living among the natives. Destined to stay with the de la Morandière family at their graceful St Brieux home in Britanny, I sulked as Emlyn Owen drove me to the port of Southampton. I was determined to annoy someone, and it didn't matter whom. I stood alongside the rails of the ship's deck and waved to the crowds gathered at the dockside. Then, with a grand flourish, I tossed my passport into the air and watched with glee as it dive-bombed into the sea. Attempts at salvage proved useless, not to say dangerous, and I giggled as harrassed officials squeezed water from their trouser legs and handed me a temporary replacement.

Madame de la Morandière was also accommodating two girls of my age. The first, a Swede, had the build of a Valkyrie and a veil of flaxen hair. The second, a native of my own country, was blessed with mousy hair, a rice pudding of a face and a lumpy bottom. Forgetting Joan Greville-Williams, I fell in love with the Swede. She spurned my timorous overtures, however, preferring a dally with packs of Gallic admirers. Unwanted compensation came when the Rice Pudding offered to show me her bottom.

On a balmy summer's eve, Madame invited me to walk

alongside her in the grounds of the Morandiere home. With her husband snoring in the family vault, perhaps Madame was lonely, I thought. She led me to a mound of rocks. Buried beneath them, she explained, was the family silver and a collection of seventeenth-century weaponry. Madame exclaimed, in the manner of a modern Joan of Arc, 'We shall guillotine the Republican traitors.'

Unknown to me, there was at that time, an enormous Royalist revival in western France. Rallies and plots abounded. The French authorities took the view that given sufficient licence, this particular spurt of Gallic enthusiasm would soon fizzle out. But Madame's boyfriend, an elderly baron, informed me that he personally would lead an advance upon Paris. He spent hours shooting clay pigeons to practise for the hour of retribution. The Baron was also a friend of Paul Eugene Louis Deschanel, a former President of the French Republic who years previously had tumbled off his presidential train, later to be found roaming France in half his pyjamas. Which half was never specified. The tumble must have had an effect, for Deschanel took to sitting in a pond near his chateau and refused to budge.

I'd been banished to France to improve my command of the language. Thanks to some original French lessons I returned to England almost fluent. Nearly every evening I'd spend hours with the Baron, who taught me to play poker and drink Armagnac. He also fascinated and intrigued me with his stories of the Great War. Praying to God that the answer would be negative, I asked the Baron whether he truly believed a second European war was inevitable. Putting down his cards, the Frenchman sipped his Armagnac and pondered my question. There were tears in his eyes. I suppose he was thinking of the last German advance into his beloved France. Then, lifting his shoulders into a characteristic Gallic shrug, he replied fatalistically, 'But of course there will be war.'

I returned to Rooksnest. Now into my last year at Eton, I

was still the topic of innumerable rows between Evelyn, Mama and Pa as to what my future should be. That they exhausted themselves in these quarrels was of no concern to me. I was going to become an actor.

It was in my last year that Michael Bentine announced he was returning home. 'The male progeniture is short of the drachmas,' he explained, in what was quickly becoming a colourful and most individual verbal style. Michael's house-master, Bill Hope-Jones, offered to waive his fees, but not wishing to impose upon his old friend's generosity, Michael's father gratefully declined. Although we wrote for a time, I wouldn't see Michael for another twenty-three years.

During my last year at Eton, I was obliged to spend a lot of time immersed in academic work. Although the theatrical profession did not ask for a double first from those about to enter its ranks, in a world of unemployment I recognized the necessity of sound educational qualifications. I also longed to be a credit to my parents, and perhaps to earn their approbation, and indeed that of Evelyn.

She had instilled in me, and in several other children educated at her expense, the sense that privilege must be earned. And loath as I was to accept that Evelyn possessed virtue, I had to admit that my desire for success and what sense of obligation I did possess was a consequence of my upbringing at the hands of a woman I hated.

A master named Prescott Hedley announced his forthcoming production of *Macbeth*. 'Dear God,' I prayed on my way to casting. 'If you really love me, don't let him make me one of the witches.' The Good Lord was magnanimous. I was cast as Macduff, while the versatile Michael Warre played a witch, a porter and a murderer. It was a joy to act with so many old friends. John Balfour, with whom I'd done hours of play-reading, would be Lennox, Peter Barnes would be Fleance, and an abashed Simon Phipps, who was later to become Bishop of Lincoln, would be Lady Macbeth.

Claude Aurelius Elliott, the Headmaster, regarded the theatre as a hotbed of sexual immorality and had reputedly remarked, 'I don't mind plays so long as they're performed badly.' Ignoring this puritanical and philistine attitude, we began rehearing.

A sweet lady called Mrs Allsopp laboured for days on the design and sewing of the costumes, but even this innocent ran foul of Claude Elliott who nearly banned the production. The point at issue was Simon Phipps' bust. Elliott was determined that Simon should play the part flat-chested. Shapely Lady Macbeths only encouraged immoral thoughts. Unable to alter her costumes without Elliott's permission, the exasperated Mrs Allsopp eventually persuaded this ascetic to accept a modest 32A cup. In the event, however, she cleverly constructed a stunning thirty-eight-inch bust from formidable pieces of metal she had once used to protect herself while fencing. To Claude Elliott's fury, Simon Phipps was practically wolf-whistled off the stage by hundreds of sex-starved Etonians. The play was well received. For the first and only time during my five years at Eton, Mama visited me, and as she'd done when watching me in *Henry V* at Summer Fields, cheered loudly when I made my stage entrance. After the play, she was not only sober but now sympathetic to my theatrical ambitions.

'You were quite good, darling.'

'Thank you, Mama.'

'It's what you really want, isn't it?'

I nodded.

'Oh God. I'll have the devil's own job trying to persuade Evelyn and your Father.'

'Do they have any say in the matter?'

Mama sighed. 'Of course. Unless you enter diplomacy or brewing they'll offer no financial support.'

'Then who'll pay for me to go to drama school?'

'Oh, I suppose there's someone out there your loving Mama can flirt into coughing up.'

The play's reviews in *The Eton College Chronicle* were encouraging. 'Phipps was a fine Lady Macbeth whose make-up added to her purposefully evil character,' I read out. If 'that' bust had been noticed, comment had been censored. 'Macnee played Macduff admirably and his voice sounded very well. He acted the scene at the English court so movingly as to make fully dramatic what is too often a mere détour from the principal business, but alone of the main actors his hands appeared uncomfortable.' A grinning John Balfour suggested I should have grabbed Lady Macbeth.

In the middle of my matriculation examinations I received a letter from Evelyn. Complaining about the excessive bills I was running up, she told me to curb my spending. I panicked. This was the first time that my profligacy had even been commented upon. I was used to unlimited expenses, and my academic concentration was distracted temporarily as I wondered how I'd survive. A friend with legal ambitions explained that I might have a case against my guardian. As a minor, I was entitled to be supplied with what the English law defines as 'necessities'. There'd even been an instance, he went on, where a deprived boy had taken an action against his father for refusing to pay for his sixteen handmade waistcoats. Greatly cheered, I asked about the verdict. 'Ah, well I'm not sure about that,' was the uncertain reply, 'but you could try.'

The examinations went well and confident of matriculating, I focused my attention on the tote. With my silk topper perched at a rakish angle and my shirt sleeves rolled up, I lit a cigarette and studied the form. Royal Ascot was a week away, and for me there'd be a lucrative four days' work.

Royal Ascot turned out to be a disaster. My face must have resembled that of a New York stockbroker when Wall Street crashed as furious punters hammered the door of my room demanding their winnings. I had funds available for a partial pay out, but as the hammering increased, it became imperative that anything I possessed which had a market value went at once. This would include a number of salacious magazines I had recently taken possession of. Unknown to me, however, possession had already passed on once again. One of the maids had found them and turned nark. In due course a message came that Mr Sladden wished to see me. The interview was painful for both housemaster and pupil. 'What are these?' Mr Sladden screeched.

Playing nervously with my collar, I mustered a semblance of dignity and muttered, 'In the parlance of vulgar tradesmen, Sir, they are what is referred to as erotic material.'

'Oh God. Claude Elliott will have to see these.'

'I say, that's not allowed. You have to buy them before you can look at the pictures.'

I was asked to leave. It was not only the magazines, for the school was rife with rumours regarding the collapse of the Macnee tote. Switching from bookie to auctioneer, I sold off my personal effects, including virgin condoms, a chest expander and my share in the greyhound. I don't know whether Claude Aurelius Elliott ever got to see those magazines, but during a painful interview he remarked that my personality and character did not bode very well. He then gave me a small parcel containing a volume of Gray's poems. Once a much bullied pupil at Eton, this sensitive poet's verse has, over the years, afforded me delight and consolation. It is signed personally by Claude Elliott, and is now a well-thumbed volume. It brings back memories of so much that was dear, but also much that was fearsome.

The most poignant part of leaving were the farewells. Friends such as Peter Barnes, the Michaels Benthall and Warre, and Simon Phipps I would meet later on, either professionally or socially, but there were those I'd never see again. Upon reflection, it was not so much their deaths, but more the way in which they died, that has subsequently caused me such grief. I do not remember what Arthur Innes said when we shook hands, but I do remember the smiling face of a handsome, talented and loyal friend who was sent to his death by a German pilot in the Battle of Britain.

Too frightened to return to Rooksnest, I arranged to meet Mama.

'What a wretched business,' she sighed. 'Aunt Peggy tells me you've been sending strange letters to your cousin Josephine.'

I coloured.

'Well?'

'Um . . .'

'Don't try to explain. I can guess. You're at that silly stage boys go through. If only you'd been a girl. We could have found a place for you at Rooksnest.' She sighed. 'Still, at least you matriculated. So what are you going to do?'

'Michael Warre's invited me down to Dorset. His family are staging a production of *The Taming of The Shrew*.'

'Do you have any money?'

'No.'

Mama handed over a wad of notes. Then she looked at me thoughtfully and said, 'You have both your Father and me in you, dear. A lethal combination that can only bring great success or complete ruin.'

— 5 —

I was determined to romp through the summer of 1939 – and I did. There just remained the immediate problem of where to go. I could not join Michael Warre immediately, so invited myself to stay with friends where I set about enjoying myself with the enthusiasm and optimism of youth. My generation did not then appreciate how brief 'The very May-morn of our life' would be. Chasing off to the Isle of Wight, I spent a few weeks sailing and swimming as the self-invited guest of the Greville-Williams, whose splendid yacht was moored at Cowes. My passion for their second daughter, Joan, was re-kindled when she appeared on deck in a beach robe which she proceeded to slither out of with the seductive skill of a stripper. I gawped, as the robe slipped over the curves of a superlative shape which was accentuated by a swimsuit that clung and clung.

I slavered as Joan plunged into the sea, and ignoring inner warnings of social disgrace, determined to chase after her and do what sex-crazed youth had to do. I belly-flopped into the sea and hacked my way after the teenage Venus as she gracefully cut her way through waves of aquamarine. This enthusiasm merely prompted her to remark, 'Golly, Patrick. You're such a dashing swimmer.'

I spent hours examining myself before a cheval-glass. Given my height, slim physique and what I'd convinced myself were saturnine good looks, why hadn't Joan fallen in love with me? This question was answered by one of the many handsome young men who crowded Cowes that summer, who explained kindly that the beautiful Joan's wealthy Papa would never consider a son-in-law without a future, while she could not contemplate a husband with blackheads. I was now more than ever determined to convince the Greville-Williamses that I was the heir apparent to Leslie Howard.

A few nights later I arrived at a glittering ball. I had painted a plaster cast of calamine lotion over my facial spots, over-brilliantined my hair, and newly learned a Shakespearian speech. After a couple of perfunctory waltzes with dowagers, I joined the queue waiting to dance with Joan. The ballroom sparkled with laughter, careless chatter and the music of Strauss. I longed to say that I loved her but, overcome by diffidence, kept mumbling about Leslie Howard. It was only when the dance was over that I realized she had said nothing, so I took a gulp of lemonade, which seemed to imbue me with new-found confidence. Marching up to Joan's Father, I gave him a soliloquy on Leslie Howard which was interspersed with quotes from my Shakespearian speech and assurances about my dazzling theatrical future. Nodding kindly, Joan's Father heard me out and wished me well, but he appeared mesmerized by my calamine lotion. Having remarked that there was indeed a vague resemblance between me and Leslie Howard, he then excused himself. I later learned that he was convinced I must be a 'nancy-boy'.

I fled to Dorset and quickly settled down with Michael Warre and his family in their gracious Elizabethan pile. Rehearsals for *The Taming of The Shrew* had been in progress for a couple of days. Cast at Hortensio, I would play suitor to the Shrew's baby sister. Maria Britnieva, whose superb looks and sweet nature later inspired Lord St Aubyn to make her his wife, was cast as Katharina, whilst Michael Warre played Petruchio and his sister played the piano. We rehearsed in a great rambling barn which the Warres had converted into a theatre. For the first time in my life I participated in sublime domestic happiness. Michael's family appeared united by love, care and laughter. While possessing so many material advantages, I felt deprived of emotional security, and cursed the Gods for extracting such a price from those they seemingly favoured.

Such harmony was marred only by the news that Winston Churchill had put away his paint brushes and canvasses, remarking, 'I shall not be painting in peacetime for some years.' Trying to forget the ever creeping horror of war, I began to look forward to our first performance. It was while we were on our way to church one Sunday that a neighbour of the Warres told us of the advent of the inevitable. After the neighbour had informed us of the Prime Minister's impending announcement, Michael's Mother began to cry. We drove on to the church in silence. I seem to remember many weeping ladies in the congregation. Apart from that, I recall little. Sitting in a place where the faithful had worshipped their God for nearly one thousand years, I harangued that same God for letting his planet slip towards the brink of destruction.

Over lunch, Michael's Father informed his guests that given the forthcoming hostilities, *The Taming of The Shrew* would be cancelled. Our hard work, dedication and enthusiasm had been in vain, and I experienced a second setback to my theatrical ambitions. There was no alternative but to accept this decision, but it meant an immediate return to Rooksnest, where an angry Evelyn would demand an explanation over my expulsion from Eton.

Borrowing a bicycle, I made my way to Lee Lane. Having dismounted from the bike, I laid it on the side of a bank and wandered across to stare at a grey stone that stands at the junction of Lee Lane and the Dorchester Road. It had been erected to commemorate the escape from England of Charles the Second after the Battle of Worcester, some three hundred years before. I read the stone's inscription, which had been taken from Fuller's *Worthies*: 'When 'midst your fiercest foes on every side, For your escape God did a Lane provide.' I could only despair. Even God was my enemy, for had he not sent me Evelyn, Hitler, and old age? Upon that September day what little youth I'd known had been snatched away and was gone for all time.

Evelyn had all but turned Rooksnest into a military barracks, convinced she could smash the Germans single-handed. Sandbags had been ordered, gas marks issued, and rationing already introduced. Those members of the harem who couldn't shoot were given lessons in the use of military hardware, while vegetable allotments were cultivated for the war effort. With the Fuehrer to contend with now, Evelyn had obviously forgotten my expulsion. Indeed, we even found a mite of common ground in our mutual loathing of Hitler.

Having seen a revival of *The Importance of Being Earnest*, Mama now appeared even more determined than me that I should tread the boards. She had been so smitten by John Gielgud's performance in the play that she decided her son should follow in his footsteps. Since Evelyn had effectively cut me off, I was dispatched to care for the pigs on her estate. Beginning my working life as a swineherd, I waited impatiently for Mama to find a wealthy patron who'd put me through drama school.

Shortly afterwards, Mama brought my attention to a newspaper headline. Wishing to contribute to the war effort, David Niven, 'The Famous Hollywood Film Star', had returned to England. Impressed as I was by the actor's patriotism and eminence, I could only wonder at the irony inherent in our respective situations, for David Niven was renouncing the very position I craved to achieve.

Mama suggested that I should make myself known to David Niven. I stared at her with amazement, an amazement that became disbelief when she announced for the first time that he and I were cousins. She was vague as to the exact nature of our blood relationship, but such was the fervour with which she made this statement that I willingly believed her. Like all true believers I was subsequently plagued with doubts. Submitting Mama to rigorous questioning, I unearthed the existence of a previously unheard of 'Uncle Max'. Mama assured me that this mysterious gentleman was the link between David and me.

Given a probable Luftwaffe attack upon the capital, some of Evelyn's London friends sought refuge in the concrete of the Dorchester Hotel. Other friends, Mama informed me, would be staying at Rooksnest. When a car load of tweedy ladies eventually rolled up, I threatened once more to run away. Then, both fascinated and amused, I watched as a shambling figure staggered into the hall of Rooksnest before passing out on a sofa. It was Augustus John. A dishevelled looking gentleman with uncombed hair and rolling eyes, this bohemian painter was once summed up most perceptively by that brilliant soldier and noted martinet, Field Marshal Viscount Montgomery of Alamein: 'The fellow drinks, he doesn't wash, and I suspect there are women in the background.'

While the ladies sipped gin and destroyed reputations, I was despatched to take care of Augustus John. When he came around, I enquired whether he'd care for tea. Such a suggestion was not well received. Uncertain as to what I should offer, I sat next to him upon the sofa with a growing sense of unease until he lunged forward, grabbed my throat and growled 'Brandy'. Having settled him on the sofa with a couple of bottles, I was hastening to leave when he ordered me back and asked whether I was artistic. I explained that a great-grandfather had been President of The Scottish Royal Academy, and that for myself I hoped I was sufficiently artistic to succeed as an actor. Upon my mentioning the theatre, Augustus John took a liberal swig of brandy and lunged forward yet again. Then he smiled and hissed, 'Women, boy. Big women with generous hearts. The theatre's full of them. Good luck to you, but don't catch the pox.'

Upon the outbreak of war, all stable lads of fighting age had been called up. With a shortage of labour in Lambourn, Pa contacted Gussie and asked if I could be spared for part-time work at his stables. Gussie seemed amenable but pointed out that Pa, and not the Rooksnest estate, would be responsible for my wages during working hours at College House. This demand was not unreasonable, but in the event Pa 'forgot' to stump up a solitary farthing.

Pa said he'd heard I was a Socialist and glared when I smiled in agreement. Ordering me to keep my politics to myself, he reminded me of a recent stable lads' strike in Lambourn. This unprecedented event had shaken racing's higher echelons and Pa didn't want further agitation emanating from his stables.

Although I was employed only as a fill-in, Pa set about training me as he would an apprentice jockey. Perhaps it was his way of seeing a lifelong dream fulfilled, but whatever his motives, I discovered quickly how harsh a life with horses could be. Dragging myself from a hard bed at five-thirty on frosty mornings, still half asleep, I'd shuffle my way down to the stable yard. There, I'd crack ice on a rusty pump before returning to my tiny room with a bucket of water for washing. Having doused myself with the freezing water, I'd make my way to the stables, muck out two loose boxes and be ready for the first ride at approximately six-fifteen. By then the ink black sky of night would have softened to a deep navy blue that was streaked with the first hues of a livid pink dawn. A string of lively horses carrying us yawning lads clopped their way through Lambourn and up to the Downs, a razor-sharp wind carving into our pinched cheeks.

During those mornings on the Downs, it was Pa who taught me how to judge pace, come into line, sit properly and ride a finish. Having failed to form a bond with this funny little man, I believed his face glowed with pride when one day he watched me gallop to where he stood in his Buick shouting instructions.

'Well, what do you think?' I asked.

'You're on a nervous colt, but there are possibilities.

Handled properly, he could have quite a future,' he snorted, showing more interest in the colt than in his son.

Upon returning to Rooksnest, Mama informed me that come Christmas, funds would be available for drama school. The relief was immense, for it appeared that my fallow period was drawing to a close. She further explained that the name of my patron could never be divulged; suffice to say that he owned four magnificent homes and was related to royalty, albeit on the wrong side of the blanket. Given Mama's many and influential connections, I accepted the wealth and antecedents of this mysterious patron without comment.

I was taken to see Margaret Rawlings. She'd already caught my attention in the spring of 1937 when, dressed in a bathing suit, she had starred in a production of *Black Limelight*. With that bathing suit flitting through my mind, auditioning before this formidable actress was no easy matter; but she appeared sufficiently impressed to write a letter of introduction for me to give to Sir Kenneth Barnes, then principal of the Royal Academy of Dramatic Art.

I telephoned this exciting news to my old school friend, Derek Beecham. His response was disappointing. He explained that RADA was most conservative in outlook and far too large for a student to receive individual tuition. The Webber-Douglas School of Drama, where a cousin of Derek's was studying, was a more relaxed establishment, and had something of a family atmosphere. Derek had unintentionally hit my rawest nerve, as I'd always longed for a family. So, forgetting the advice of an established actress, I listened to the views of Derek's cousin and decided to audition for the Webber-D.

For my audition I settled on the part of King Henry the Fifth. The staff watched in wonder as I capered around the estate rehearsing my speech, waving a rapier borrowed from a collection of seventeenth-century weaponry and armour hanging in one of the state rooms.

During my rehearsals Mama returned to College House, hoping to discover the truth of certain rumours concerning her husband. Within days she was back at Rooksnest spluttering with outrage at the behaviour of the man she'd married. Apparently she had walked in to discover her husband crawling down the stairs. Turning towards the open door of Pa's study, Mama had been treated to the rear view of a very large cleaning lady on all fours with her skirts hoisted high as she scrubbed the floor. But that was not the least of it. A few days later, having piled up several wooden boxes in the barn, Pa climbed to the top and peered through a slit in the wall. From there he could enjoy an uninterrupted view of a naked lady washing in a downstairs bathroom. His excitement must have been frantic, for the boxes wobbled and over he tumbled. The real tragedy, however, lay in the fact that this object of his admiration had been Mama.

The Webber-Douglas School of Drama, located in Clareville Street, South Kensington, was housed in a couple of adjoining Victorian villas which contained a miniature theatre called The Chanticleer. There, I joined a large group of other hopefuls. Aware that the intake was limited, I glanced around to assess the competition and was left pleased though puzzled. Apart from myself and three other boys, the place was packed with girls, most of whom wore skimpy vests, leotards and practice tights. Forgetting Henry the Fifth, I settled down to study vital statistics. Then a voice hissed, 'Macnee, Daniel Patrick? It's your turn.'

I wandered on to a small stage dreaming of bosoms and buttocks. Seated in front of the stage were a row of people who included Johnstone Douglas, a one-time warbler of opera, and the Irish actress Ellen O'Malley, who was so old that she'd performed in the first nights of many Shaw plays. Though revelling in fantasy, I did notice the kindly, encouraging and keen expressions upon the faces of my adjudicators. They were willing me to succeed, so boldly announcing the extract from my chosen play, I burst forth. When I reached the line, 'Creeping winds drawing the huge bottoms through furrow'd sea,' Johnstone Douglas raised a hand to halt my words. A man possessed of inordinate courtesy and a mellifluous voice, he gently pointed out that I was reciting the Chorus instead of Henry the Fifth. My fantasies had got the better of me. Now, my reverie broken, I blushed and mumbled, 'Oh God.'

'That was conceivably uttered by The Bishop of Ely,' said Douglas, referring to another character in the play. 'Now, why not relax and start again?'

Having stumbled through the correct speech, I sat in a sweat scratching my spots. Shortly afterwards a bespectacled and stringy secretary announced that the adjudicators wished to see me. I left the Webber-D. in a trance: not only had I been accepted but I'd been awarded a scholarship. Standing in a bus queue, I nudged a complete stranger to announce, 'I'm an actor, you know.' 'Well, another few months and you'll be a soldier,' came the sane reply. The thought of a third setback in my fledgling career was too cruel to contemplate, but there was truth in the stranger's words. It was only then that I realized why there were so few men at the audition.

Before long, Evelyn was informed that the Army would be taking over the grounds of Rooksnest come the New Year. At once, she spent hours closetted away with Gussie planning as to how the two of them should run the British military. Though I couldn't wait to leave the house I'd always hated, my last Christmas at Rooksnest was an emotional occasion. I felt sadness that the old house was testament to so much misery, regret that my parents had parted, and fear for what would become of Mama.

Back at Webber-Douglas, for the first time in my life I attended school with enthusiasm. The teachers were bohemian, the lessons fascinating, and there was that wonderful preponderance of girls. Geoffrey Hibbert, Christopher Willard, David Baker and myself comprised the male intake in a class of girls who left me dithering and drooling. Given this disparity of the sexes, Geoffrey, Christopher, David and I acted every male role in the Bard's repertoire, while the girls competed with, and clawed at each other to play Cleo and Cordelia.

My singing lessons were a disaster, however. As the music mistress hammered into a top G sharp, I burped at a steady Middle C. Exhausted by her efforts, the lady locked the piano lid, applied rouge to her wan cheeks and advised me not to audition for musicals. The fencing classes were much more thrilling, as were the dancing lessons, which were conducted together with the leotard-clad girls.

I told myself that I mustn't touch, but such temptation was irresistible. Leaping towards a girl in front, I noticed a glare from the dancing mistress, so leapt backwards in retreat. At the end of that morning's class, I was told to stay behind.

'Are you a virgin?' the dancing mistress demanded to know.

'Er, well . . .' I faltered.

'That means, yes,' she cut in.

I coloured, scratched my face and was told not to pick spots as they festered.

'And you were going to molest that girl?'

'Um . . .'

The lady nodded sagely, said she'd had trouble with my type before, and warned there'd be no cabrioles (goat leaps) in her dancing classes. Recalling some French I'd learnt from the old Baron, I remembered his enthusiasm for cabrioles. It was the only way to take a woman, the old boy had advised.

Other classes included voice production, modern dancing, mime and the speaking of verse. Ellen O'Malley was a sympathetic but quite absent-minded teacher of drama who had a habit of crying 'Push out your diaphragm' at the slightest provocation.

Home was a single room at Roland Gardens in Kensington.

Christopher Willard shared the room and introduced me to another drama student who resided on an upper floor. This student came from Hull, where his family owned a jewellery shop. I noted the name of Ian Carmichael and decided where to go should I need a cheap deal on an engagement ring.

It was around this time that I was introduced to Barbara Douglas, a fellow-student at the Webber-D. A tall blonde with perfect features, a divinely willowy figure and better legs than Betty Grable's, her haughty demeanour had previously deterred me from making an approach. I would later discover that this apparent aloofness was a front used by an essentially shy girl who placed great value upon her privacy. I discovered she was already 'spoken for', however, and that my rival in love was none other than Geoffrey Hibbert. Having been told that Barbara lived in a hotel on the Cromwell Road, I took to hanging around the hotel until, pestered by prostitutes, I was forced to seek refuge in its foyer.

After what seemed an interminable wait, the beautiful Barbara made her entrance. Dressed in a well-cut camel coat which accentuated her golden hair and seductive brown eyes, she walked past without noticing me as she tugged at the leash on her fierce-looking German Shepherd dog. I rushed up, reminded her who I was and was about to suggest dinner when an older lady interjected and demanded to know what I wanted. It was Barbara's mother, and she shared the same hotel suite as her daughter. I mumbled some incoherent explanation, and scratched my acne. Barbara asked her mother if I could join them for tea, and her eyes twinkled with merriment as we sipped from cups and chewed cardboard sandwiches with curled edges.

In an attempt to impress Barbara's mother, I boasted of my family connections. The earls, knights and race horses seemed to please her. I also mentioned the name of David Niven but was somewhat thrown when she suggested we all meet him for dinner. I hadn't dared approach Niven yet. At any rate, I sneaked in a request to walk out with Barbara.

The old girl considered the matter. Explaining that her daughter already had a young man, she nevertheless permitted a first tentative step in my courtship. I would be allowed to walk Barbara's dog – who disliked me on sight – alone. For weeks afterwards I propped up lampposts whilst that bloody dog sniffed at the bottom of my trouser legs and legions of tarts propositioned me. I confided my passion for Barbara to Christopher Willard who, in turn, told me of his unrequited love. Perhaps I could persuade a beautiful redhead to reconsider him? he suggested. I did what I could but brought back bad news.

'What?' a horrified Christopher exclaimed. 'You mean to say she prefers women to men?'

I nodded.

'But I don't understand it. Do you?'

I understood.

Convinced I'd never make Barbara my own, I found refuge in nicotine and neat Scotch, and took to hitting the town. A fellow-roisterer was Michael Warre who introduced me to a nineteen-year-old from his drama school. A good-looking boy with a formidable reputation, his name was Peter Ustinov. As the three of us sat at a table in Lyon's Corner House, Peter Ustinov said little, preferring to scribble on lined sheets of paper. I was told he'd been a child prodigy, spoke several languages fluently, wrote, and played every musical instrument from the banjo-zither to the pipes of Pan. He was scribbling a play called *House of Regrets* which, in my humble opinion, is one of the best he's done.

June was a depressing month. After the humiliation of Dunkirk, Churchill told the world we'd never surrender, then repeated this celebrated speech for American radio. He afterwards confided to Ed Murrow that the British would crack German heads with beer bottles, adding: 'It's about all we've got left.'

I became bored. Bored with London and the inevitable restrictions that are imposed by all educational establishments, including even liberal-minded drama schools. I knew that a lifetime could be spent learning stagecraft, but I longed to run off and acquire the basic skills of that craft with a repertory company.

I noticed an advertisement in *The Stage*. Squeezed between notices requiring resident pantomime dancers and artists for special weeks in Manchester and Leeds, it read: 'Wanted for Rep. Theatre nr. London. Char. Actor and Actress about 40; Juvenile Man, and two young Actors; good wardrobe essential. – Photo. full pars., lowest terms (s.a.e.). Box 4763, c.o. *The Stage*.' I auditioned and was offered employment as a young actor with a repertory company in Letchworth Garden City.

I was torn briefly between ambition and duty when, on 7 September, Hermann Goering ordered his Luftwaffe to bomb London. A blast of bombs battered the capital, which took on the appearance of an enormous bonfire. Crouching in a doorway near South Kensington tube station, I considered postponing my theatrical career in favour of joining the RAF. With no family to advise me, I asked Johnstone Douglas for an opinion. He said that call-up would eventually be unavoidable and advised that until the papers came, I should learn all I could about my craft.

I departed for Letchworth just as the Webber-D. was hit by a fire bomb. During the journey I reflected on my past. I'd survived prep school, Eton, Rooksnest and the disastrous marriage of my ill-matched parents. But would I survive the war?

— 6 —

I departed for Letchworth with two pieces of luggage and one lady's handbag. The first piece of luggage contained my everyday clothes and the second held my theatrical wardrobe. This included some bullfighting gear, a smoking jacket, plus fours, my childhood kilt, oilskins, a riding habit and the obligatory lounge suit. In the handbag was my range of theatrical make up. I'd also acquired a fez, a Salvation-Army bonnet and a nightcap.

The repertory company in Letchworth Garden City was run by a most personable theatrical named Forbes Russell. The welcome he gave me as the junior member of the company was both kindly and encouraging. Forbes Russell promised to teach me all he knew and advised me to look at, listen to and learn from the many accomplished thespians in his employ. He also had a warning for me. Enunciating with the clarity of a trumpet, Forbes Russell pointed out that Letchworth Garden City was a 'dry' town. Still, should I need either barley or grape, there was a distant hostelry named 'The Fox'. Forbes Russell then sank into a reverie, murmuring 'The Fox, The Fox.'

Those first days in repertory didn't offer much in the way of acting, but I raised curtains, helped paint scenery, understudied the assistant stage manager and bicycled through the lanes of Hertfordshire, whose trees had coloured to a leafy harvest of burnt orange and old gold.

My fellow-actors included Brenda de Banzie and Geoffrey Gunn. Brenda, an acerbic and unpredictable lady, would later give a brilliant performance as Laurence Olivier's drab wife in the first performance of John Osborne's play *The Entertainer*. I first met Geoffrey when he was perched upon a piano stool.

Indeed, as the months passed, this piano stool appeared to be his sole place of habitation. It was one of those stools which, if spun, would soar to the height of skyscrapers or sink to an ocean's bottom. A vague twilight creature who'd yet to make a decision regarding his gender, Geoffrey spent his days twirling and whirling on the stool while giving me lessons in the art of comedy. Never once was he heard to complain of vertigo.

By now I was determined to lose my virginity to anyone making a serious offer. I received one, from a very forward and very big blonde, whom I'd picked up at The Fox. I promised to call her and stumbled into the theatre where I told all to a spinning Geoffrey Gunn. Swivelling his stool to a standstill, Geoffrey warned me against involvement with this woman. She possessed a thug of a husband, he explained, who was away in the Merchant Navy, and using the local Scottish Dancing Club as a front, she was running a gin-smuggling racket within the dry town of Letchworth Garden City.

Naturally I telephoned her. Conversation was initially confined to Scottish Dancing, though my expectations rose when she asked me whether I could dance a jig named 'Kiss Under The Stairs'. Assuming that this was the lady's code for a rollicking romp between the sheets, I said I could dance anything she cared to name, and she promptly invited me to an evening at the Dancing Club. I got out my childhood kilt. How I'd grown! In fit and length, it resembled a tartan loin-cloth, but it would do. I siphoned off a velvet jacket, ruffles, sporran, tartan stockings, garter flashes and dancing pumps from the repertory company's wardrobe, and bicycled off to the big blonde's house on the other side of town. She eyed me in what I thought was a salacious manner, remarked that I was a well-developed boy for my age, and yanked me in.

The club's membership comprised a large number of ample-bosomed ladies with snaggle-teeth, and about four gentlemen who must have been well into their eighties. My arrival was greeted with a gust of self-conscious giggles by the ladies and complete indifference by the quartet of Methuselahs. Heaving herself on to a small wooden podium, the big blonde clapped her hands for silence before ordering everyone to select partners for 'Jimmy's Fancy'. Before I could protest ignorance of 'Jimmy's Fancy', I was all but flattened by a cavalry charge. Hitching up their long white dresses and yards of tartan sashes, the ladies cantered towards me, each one intent upon claiming the youngest man in the room for herself. The big blonde dragged me out and partnered me up with a Methuselah. That way, she explained, rebellion in the ranks would be avoided.

My partner and I sized each other up. He stated that under no circumstances would he be dancing the lassie's part. I thought it prudent not to argue as the gentleman was wearing a pair of heavy surgical boots. The strains of a fine strathspey creaked forth as everyone except me wheeled into 'Jimmy's Fancy'. It wasn't long before I managed to step firmly on my partner's foot. He was carried off the floor in agony. In a moment of exasperation, the big blonde broke up her class and ordered everyone into the kitchen, where exotic-smelling cigarettes were passed around and a golden malt consumed. Then each of the dancers plonked hitherto concealed bottles of spirits upon the large kitchen table. The big blonde appeared well pleased, paid everyone off and gave instructions as to where they were to collect their next quota of alcohol. Amid a hullabaloo of 'Good night' and 'God bless you', the Scottish Dancing Club packed up its pumps and departed. At last I was alone with the big blonde.

Having apologized for my lamentable performance upon the dance floor, I resolved to give an unforgettable performance in bed. I referred meaningfully to a 'Kiss Under the Stairs'. Giving me a tired smile, the big blonde dodged the issue by asking whether I'd like to earn myself a few bob on the side by joining the Letchworth smugglers. She was clearly more attracted by my bicycle than by me, since its mobility made me a valuable addition to her little team.

Given my paltry wage of one pound ten shillings a week and an increasingly erratic allowance from Mama, I threw in my lot with the big blonde. She instructed me to cycle to Luton every Sunday afternoon, and handed me an address from where I could pick up my cargo of gin. For this I'd be paid half a crown a journey.

Upon arriving in Letchworth I'd been lodged with a couple of esoteric publishers. A husband and wife team, this cultured pair published such tomes as *Into the Snows with Captain Scott* and *A Journey through the Nooks of Ancient Bukhara*. Given their discouraging sales figures, they were forced to take in paying guests. One day the couple shyly invited me to join them for afternoon tea. After much fidgeting and polite coughing, the conversation turned to my marital prospects. Given my parents' fiasco, I'd little enthusiasm for the state of holy wedlock. Perhaps I already had a young lady? came the discreet enquiry. I shook my head sadly and remembered Barbara. Within days they introduced me to another of their guests. She was an enchanting ballerina of elfin proportions with a penchant for bicycling ten miles a day without stopping. But still dreaming of hearing from Barbara Douglas, I could not give my love to this sweet girl who, to my delight, seemed quite happy to be a good friend.

Soon after this little idyll the Luton gin run was busted and, with the police sniffing up our tails, I was switched to the Bedford run. At the mention of the police I began to sweat. I had assumed I'd done nothing more than contravene a puritanical ruling of the Letchworth elders, and the realization that I was probably a marked bootlegger played havoc with my nerves. But I decided to risk it, and by now demanded five shillings a journey. When I confided this turn of events to Geoffrey Gunn, he went spinning through the ceiling. I could jeopardize my career, he wailed, and begged me to make do with my meagre wages and concentrate on the theatre.

The company had just begun to rehearse five plays by Gilbert Nathan. I featured in three, playing a young man, an air force officer and King Richard the First respectively. There was even the possibility of a West End transfer. Geoffrey repeated his warning, but to no avail. The money apart, the gamble of a final run was temptation beyond endurance. I accomplished it successfully, though disgraced myself by dropping two bottles onto the floor of the publisher's hallway. I could only stare with dismay at the splintered glass, and pungent liquid that trickled from a pair of soaked underpants in which I'd hidden the bottles. My commission was cut, and the big blonde received my notice with bad grace. I wasn't sorry to be out of the racket since it had continued to wreck my nerves and my rep. company now had a definite West End booking.

Gilbert Nathan's five plays opened at The Comedy Theatre on 2 May, 1941. The company settled down quickly, and my eyes settled even more quickly upon a raven-haired spitfire who might have inspired Bizet's original dream of Carmen. Between performances and bombs, I managed to date the spitfire. With anything more advanced than a brief kiss quite out of the question, I tried to persuade her to go further by pointing out that given the prevailing conditions I could well be dead within the week. She retorted that her mother had warned her daughters against 'my sort', but finally allowed me to visit her room.

Half an hour into play, I'd scored two brief kisses and undone a single blouse button. Yet again I recalled the French Baron's advice on cabrioles and tried a leap. It was only when I'd ripped off the blouse that the spitfire called me a filthy animal. If I was looking for that kind of woman, she said, I'd be better going down to Shepherd's Market. I'd never heard of the place, and in my innocence I asked a police officer the way. Since he warned me against being a public nuisance, I confined further enquiries to little old ladies. After innumerable difficulties and confusions, I found myself wandering down Curzon Street. Sniffing a mug punter, the girls of the market jostled and shoved to get at me. A fight broke out between a couple of girls who each believed the other had 'pinched her patch'. When the general tumult had died down, everyone crowded around and waited expectantly. I was touched by their concern that I might be lonely and selecting a pert little redhead I followed her back to her room.

I watched entranced as the girl climbed a set of creaking stairs. Beneath a short and very tight skirt, her bottom swayed from side to side with the precision of a pendulum. Quite mesmerized, I continued to watch until she glanced back and suggested I move myself. Taking the steps three at a time, I bounded up those stairs and into her room.

Sex was surely the most agreeable discovery I'd made since food. My ecstasy turned to embarrassment, however, when the girl asked for recompense. I said that I hadn't got enough money. She sighed, explained she wasn't running a bleeding charity, and asked what I could leave as surety. I gave her my watch, and agreed to return the following day with five shillings.

This enjoyable new activity was cut short by the plop of an envelope through my letter box. A summons arrived ordering me to report to a call-up board. Recalling Johnstone Douglas's advice, I decided to ask for a six-month deferment, and after a terrifying confrontation with the members of the board, I was granted it. I then promptly put as much distance as possible between them and me and journeyed to Bradford to join Harry Hanson's Players.

At that time, the first of what would be a long line of agents was a gentleman named Gordon Harboard. Gordon did his best to be agent, agony aunt, legal advisor and general factotum all rolled into one. But he was very blunt and when packing me off to Bradford he remarked, 'Your handsome mug has been ruined by the omission of a kisser.'

Harry Hanson cast me in a production called *Broken*

Blossoms. Our personal relationship wasn't effusive and, diverted as I was by thoughts of sex and war, it's unlikely that I contributed much in the way of dramatic concentration.

I resided at some third-rate theatrical digs, sharing a room with a seasoned old trouper who'd enjoyed something of a reputation in the heyday of the British music hall. Long out of work and behind with his rent, the old boy had taken to the bottle. Although stating a preference for vintage champagne, it quickly transpired that he'd drink anything from methylated spirits to French perfume. I fixed his rent problem with a whip-round at the theatre, but there was nothing I could do about the meths. Once I even caught him wandering around the house drunk and quite naked. As I hauled him back to his room I was invited to admire his 'fine cluster'.

Via Letchworth and about five other addresses a letter eventually arrived from Barbara Douglas. It offered no encouragement whatsoever, but the tone was friendly and I replied by return of post. As I read and re-read the letter, I convinced myself that Barbara must be secretly in love with me, and resolved to wait for her.

Such are the cruel ironies of life, however, that no sooner had I heard from Barbara than I was pursued by a blonde dancer who'd just moved into my digs. Shortly afterwards, this lovely girl was killed in a bombing raid. I had to forget her. I was not being callous; to mourn in war is not conducive to the survival of the living. This was a harsh lesson which my generation had to learn upon the outbreak of hostilities.

Soon afterwards, Harry Hanson summoned me to his office, told me I was more West End than repertory material, and fired me. On reflection, that was one of the most stylish ways I've been sacked. I went down to Bognor Regis to spend a few happy days with Grand-Papa Henry, whose seaside home adjoined Lady Diana Cooper's farm. One of the twentieth-century's great beauties, this remarkable daughter of the eighth Duke of Rutland concocted exotic cheeses from the milk of her goats. Samples were sent to Grand-Papa which we all enjoyed with excellent wine and conversation. Such privilege and escapism could not last, and soon I returned to London, broke and looking for work. At Victoria Station I ran into my raven-haired spitfire. Since our last unfortunate meeting she'd married a brilliant interior decorator who enjoyed royal patronage. Ever impulsive, this sweet girl took me home and asked her husband if room could be found for me; that night I snuggled down into a comfortable bed.

London had become a pot-pourri of international refugees. It was quite fascinating to observe British reactions and attitudes towards these fugitives. The French were viewed as notoriously unpredictable gourmets and womanizers; the Dutch and Scandinavians fitted in, being regarded as cousins who lived on the wrong side of the English Channel; the Czechs were adored on account of their humour, but public opinion was mixed on the Poles. As they'd gone to war over Poland, the British treated these brave people with a degree of superiority. Then rumour went around that a Poish officer had, in a fit of passion, ravished a girl – in fact had bitten off one of her nipples. Within days Polish stock had soared and no Pole, especially the officers, was safe from a now predatory British female population. Meanwhile, our Australian cousins boozed, womanized and carried on the many noble traditions whose cultural roots may be found in the Aussie outback.

With so many now called up it seemed quite extraordinary that employment was difficult to find. My allowance still filtered through and, thanks to the generosity of my hosts, I just avoided starvation. My break came in July 1941 when I was offered the part of Laurie in a stage production of *Little Women*. My joy was intensified upon discovering that the role of Jo had gone to Barbara Douglas. During rehearsals I barely knew what I was about. William Holles, the producer, took me aside one day. 'Look dear,' he grumbled. 'We know you're in love, but no rogering the girl in rehearsals.'

Such a lascivious remark appalled me. Although Barbara had come to an understanding with Geoffrey Hibbert, I had every intention of marrying her myself. Geoffrey was on top form when he saw off Barbara and the rest of the cast at the beginning of the tour. Having recently enjoyed celluloid success with Deborah Kerr, making her first film, *Love on the Dole*, he exuded self-confidence. Kissing Barbara, Geoffrey asked, 'Look after her for me, Pat.'

I obliged.

The tour was a progression of mischief, mirth and madness. As the company zigzagged from Bradford to Birmingham and Nottingham to Norwich it played to capacity houses, received respectable notices and enjoyed the hospitality of some of the most understanding and generous theatrical landladies in the business.

We stormed into London and gave our first performance of *Little Women* on 22 December, 1941. I was delighted for Barbara. The notices marked her as 'an actress to be watched'. I was described as handsome, particularly when standing sideways, and 'possessing an ability to show dog-like devotion', praise that resulted in an invitation to become a general understudy with H.M. Tennent, the leading production company in London.

As the Luftwaffe continued to pelt us with bombs, we lived in an eerie world of sirens, searchlight batteries, fires, ambulances and the ubiquitous drone of bombers' engines. The house of an old friend was hit. Grateful to be alive, he raised no objection to a missing leg and what would be a permanent dent in his head. In order to escape the nightmare of Goering's strafing, come the play's final curtain Barbara and I would change and head for one of the many underground clubs which proliferated in London at that time. Our favourite was The Music Box, which was always packed with couples dancing and smooching, and downing Scotch in copious quantities. But always there was the rumble of falling bombs, and our laughter masked the realization that perhaps, come morning, our broken and bleeding bodies would be dragged from a tip of rubble.

Then came that gruesome night when the Café de Paris was bombed. I can't be sure how many were killed, but the mangled corpses of too many men and women lay in the street barely hidden by white sheets covering them. The fear I felt can only be understood if experienced, but it was not to be the last time I'd see the bloodied and shattered limbs of people, so many of whom represented my generation.

I was then cast as Jan Marek, an idealistic young communist, in *Once There Was Music* at the Q Theatre. Playing the part of Heinrich Hunlein, my Nazi arch-enemy, was a grand old actor of impressive stature named Ernest Thesiger. Our final encounter ended in loud disarray when Ernest tried to shoot me as I scrambled out of a window. Ernest had a memorable face. Such was the angle of his nostrils that whenever he surveyed you, which was often, it was as athough you were being transfixed by his olfactory organ instead of his eyes. Ernest was a great mate of Queen Mary, and they shared the same passion: *petitpoint*. As Queen and actor stitched away the hours, conversation veered towards those members of the profession who were, and who were not, the more notorious kind of queen.

'And what of Mr . . .?' the royal widow enquired while embroidering the golden thrum of a daisy.

'Sound. Ma'am'.

'And young Mr . . .?'

'Happily married, they say.'

'Most reassuring.'

After a pause, the royal widow continued: 'And do tell me, Mr Thesiger. What about Mr . . .?'

Slipping his needle through the cloth, Ernest slowly withdrew the thread to an inordinate height before informing Her Majesty, 'As a coot, Ma'am.'

Toward's the end of the play's run a letter arrived from Mama explaining that my mysterious patron would no longer be providing me with an allowance. Although this appeared unfair at the time, in retrospect I realize he could hardly be blamed. Although I endured periods of rest, I was now a professional man. I spent a month selling theatre programmes to pay the rent, surviving on paste sandwiches and old buns.

An offer came to work on the film *Pygmalion*. I was only an extra, but at last the chance had arrived to act alongside my idol, the great Leslie Howard. Quite the most romantic gentleman I've ever seen, he was a golden creature. I'd often watch him stroll through the gardens of Denham Film Studios, his pipe lounging between his teeth, and I flushed when remembering my efforts to pass myself off as a Leslie Howard type during those carefree days on the Isle of Wight.

Confusing fact with fiction I recalled his portrayal of Ashley Wilkes in *Gone With The Wind* and thought he was cuckoo to reject the advances of Scarlett O'Hara, alias the delicious Vivien Leigh. Given my passion for this beauty, I assumed divine intervention had interceded when an offer arrived to work on Shaw's *The Doctor's Dilemma* at the Haymarket Theatre. Playing the part of Mrs Dubedat was Vivien Leigh.

H.M. Tennent asked me to understudy about three other understudies for the role of Louis Dubedat in *The Doctor's Dilemma*. I arrived at the Haymarket with my head in the heavens. Any realistic chance of playing opposite the beautiful Vivien was slim, but such are the dreams of youth that I was certain I would take the West End by storm and that Vivien Leigh would fall hopelessly in love with me.

She was perfectly exquisite to look upon. Her bone structure had surely been sculptured by a latter-day Michelangelo. Her emerald eyes were at once mischievous and seductive. Her arched eyebrows, retroussé nose and sultry lips were haughty but her smile was warm and natural. She radiated impetuosity, sensuality, energy and wit. Night after fascinating night, along with many other actors, I would crowd into the wings to watch this kitten claw and entangle her fellow-actors as though they were a skein of wool with which she was amusing herself. Vivien Leigh was one of the most compelling and beautiful ladies I have ever seen.

Daunted I might have been, but I was still sufficiently conceited to attempt a flirtation. I believed such a chance had arrived when, along with another understudy, Peter Jones, I was invited to take tea with Miss Leigh, John Gielgud, Hugh 'Binkie' Beaumont and other luminaries in the theatre's Green Room. But such was the throng surrounding the actress that Peter and I were squashed up against the walls of the room, where we spent a miserable hour munching the solitary sandwich we'd managed to snatch.

There were fewer guests at a second tea party. Blinded by conceit and confidence, I sipped tea from a Spode cup, and fixed my eyes upon Vivien Leigh. For a moment she seemed to be alone. Lifting my right leg, I thrust it forward intent upon taking my first gigantic step towards her. Just as my leg was poised in mid air, the door of the Green Room opened and in strode Laurence Olivier, resplendent in the uniform of the Fleet Air Arm. A respectful silence descended, and Olivier was received with much deference. With my leg still thrust forward I could only stand there enraged.

It was fortunate that the management had the foresight to employ so many understudies, for shortly after the first night the leading man was fired. His understudy was also fired, since he hadn't bothered to learn his lines, and his place was taken by a second understudy who was then beaten up by a gang of thugs in the Haymarket. I was the third understudy, and I thought that at last my chance had come to act with the beautiful Vivien.

At the same time my agent called to say I'd been given a part in a forthcoming film, *Tuesday's Child*. This, coupled with my West End break, naturally convinced me that I was poised for stardom in both the theatre and the cinema. Alas! The thrill of this dual triumph was marred. A gloomy letter arrived from Mama whose handwriting suggested a degree of intoxication. 'Stop being a "Little Woman" ', she'd scrawled, 'and fight for your country.' I think it was Pliny who remarked, *In Vino Veritas!*

Then on the day I was due to play my first West End lead, my call-up papers arrived. I was heartbroken, knowing that a second opportunity to star opposite the lovely Vivien would be unlikely. I realized there could be no more deferments, but felt my theatrical career was over. My film part went to Stewart Granger. I told myself that I'd never act again, and was probably destined to be blown up in a battle cruiser. I longed to say good-bye to Vivien Leigh but felt too miserable to even venture into the West End. This foul mood endured until my attention was caught by a *New York Times* article which had been reprinted in the *Times* in London. It read, 'Hitler has spoken and Lord Halifax has answered. There is no more to be said. Or is there? Is the tongue of Chaucer, of Shakespeare, of the King James translation of the scriptures, of Keats, of Shelley, to be hereafter, in the British Isles, the dialect of an enslaved race?'

I now realized that unless we did win the war, I'd be employed as a slave labourer, or obliged to sing Feste's song whilst an SS oompah band thumped out the *Horst Wessel*. Furthermore, I'd never play Shylock, the Jew of Malta, Jesus Christ or any gent with Hebrew antecedents. I went to war quite determined to fight for King, Country and Empire.

I've yet to see a film in which the sun shines on farewells. True to celluloid, it was an overcast day in October, 1942, when Barbara and I stood in a sooty railway station blubbing our eyes out. There were roughly five thousand other couples doing much the same thing. Promises to write were sworn, eyes wiped with soaked handkerchiefs, and lovers' keepsakes exchanged. Hanging half-way out of the carriage window, I waved as the train slid away. Soon, Barbara was quite lost in the throng of women left behind. I'd no idea where the train was heading, but with a mingled sense of excitement, curiosity and fear, I began my war as ordinary seaman Macnee.

The troop train wasn't up to the standards of comfort I'd come to expect, and the company comprised some very rough boys who swore and sang in accents I could barely comprehend. After listening awhile, I realized that the boys with whom I would train over the next few weeks came from Glasgow, Liverpool, the Humberside and other depressed areas of Great Britain. I must have been the only ex-public school boy there. I decided to keep quiet, or if I had to speak, to moderate what was a fairly pronounced Oxford accent.

Fortunately I smoked and wasn't averse to a drop of the hard stuff. Swigging from a communal bottle and puffing a Woodbine, I took a first nervous step to what I prayed was becoming one of the lads. As the train sped on, taking me further and further away from my beloved West End, my comrades broke into song. Then someone said we were going to Wales, a remark that gave rise to many Welsh jokes. I felt tired, and nauseous. When eventually we found ourselves at our destination, we extinguished cigarettes, emptied whisky bottles, and tossed them all from windows along with various packets of condoms.

A razor-sharp wind grazed our cheeks and wrapped our trousers around our legs, we were piled into lorries, and taken to a compound encircled with barbed wire. I doubt whether barbed wire had been part of his plan when Billy Butlin opened this holiday camp at Pwllheli, on the Welsh coast. I despaired. A few days earlier I'd been enjoying a carefree life in London's theatreland, smothered in grease paint and surrounded by gorgeous girls. But as I lay in bed on that first night of my six-week induction course, I derived comfort and even confidence from my memories of Eton.

Contrary to popular opinion, it is a hard school and except

for the fact that I was now working alongside the impover-
ished instead of the privileged, the first stages of naval training
were much the same as my first days at Eton. I realized how
essential it would be to remain unobtrusive during my term at
Pwllheli. As the sole Old Etonian among a crowd of mainly
working-class boys, I'd have to act my way out of public
school and the theatre and remember not to call anyone
'darling'. I began to regret not having joined the Guards
instead of the Navy. Such a view was reinforced upon
remembering I was one of those people who's chronically
seasick.

The first morning we tumbled out of bed at 6 a.m. reveille.
There was icy water to wash in and an inedible breakfast to
force down. Within the hour, a gaggle of us were square
bashing. From that very first morning, I had difficulty in
remaining unobtrusive. Remembering the drill I'd learnt at
OTC, I strutted the parade ground with pride, but when I
tripped over an untied shoelace, I incurred the wrath of the
petty officer, a bulldog of a man. Forgetting the rules of
military etiquette, I raised my hat and wished him 'Good
Morning'. Eyeing me suspiciously, he inquired what my line
of work had been. When I mumbled that I'd been an actor, the
entire squad craned their heads to stare at me.

I was more avoided than ignored. Though none of my
comrades was unkind, they regarded me with unspoken
suspicion and wariness. Given the disparity of our upbring-
ings, I shouldn't have been surprised by their attitude, but
during those first couple of weeks on the Welsh coast I felt
more alone than I'd ever felt in my life. My one lifeline to any
feeling of belonging and being wanted came with the letters
Barbara was writing regularly. I proposed to her by letter, she
accepted, and eagerly I ticked off the passing of another day
before 'Lights Out'.

Apart from the bulldog, the only other person to pay me
any attention was a quiet boy of about nineteen. He confided

in me his desire to be an ornithologist once the war was over. I advised him not to confide such an ambition to anyone else. A week or two into the six-week induction course, he approached me on the verge of tears. He'd spent hours trying to get up a shine on a pair of his shoes, but without success. As kindly as possible, I explained that polish should not be used on suede shoes. There'd been something of an uproar back in the nineteen-thirties when the then Prince of Wales had worn suede boots with his khaki uniform while inspecting troops; if HRH couldn't get away with such footwear, then neither could my comrade, especially with bulldog on the prowl.

The going on land had been punishing, and I groaned with dismay when it was announced that we'd be going to sea. The would-be ornithologist advised me that his mother always took one raw egg beaten in a glass of milk as an antidote against seasickness. I took to loitering around the cookhouse where, in exchange for a couple of Woodbines, I cadged an egg and a cup of milk off a rating. I swear the milk was off, and I nearly threw up. Puffing a Woodbine, the rating watched my contortions impassively. When the show was over, this black-marketeer swore on his mother's bones that the milk was fresh and slammed the cookhouse window in my face.

We were all taken down to Porthmadog, where our training ship HMS *Glendower* was based. I'd begun to feel very peculiar, and with great daring asked the bulldog whether I might be excused from the dinghy exercises that were to take place. He warned that I'd be disciplined for any more lip. It was with the gravest misgivings that I went out to sea. The waters were very rough that morning. As the dinghy bounced across the waves of the Traeth Bach inlet, my stomach began to churn. I threw up, my comrades backing off as a spray of curdled milk hit the bottom of the dinghy. After a second spray I noticed that the raw egg had come out scrambled. Mumbling an apology, I was astonished when a ginger-haired

Glaswegian patted my back and led a chorus of murmured sympathy.

I lay on my bed that night curled up in agony. I felt as though my innards had been yanked out through my ears. Huddled together in a corner of the room, my comrades smoked illicit cigarettes and talked among themselves. I thought they were planning to beat me up. After 'Lights Out', the ginger-haired Glaswegian sneaked over to my bed and, coming bluntly to the point, asked whether all actors were really queer, adding that Clark Gable didn't count as he was considered 'one of the boys'. Deciding that outright denial would not be believed, I asked whether anyone had a torch. Light was provided and while someone stood on guard by the door, I showed my comrades a photograph of the girl who would become my wife. The appreciative remarks made about Barbara dispelled any doubts they may have had about my sexual proclivities. The Glaswegian asked whether I felt sufficiently well to tell everyone about my life. My guts were still churning over but, determined to seize an opportunity that might never arise again, I regaled them with tales of my childhood without explaining the set-up at Rooksnest! Then, in return some of them told me about their own lives, growing up during the Depression. By now I was grateful for my sickness, for without it such a camaraderie might never have developed.

For the rest of the induction course that camaraderie was further strengthened by the exchange of Woodbines and the shared belief that the authorities were trying to break down our personalities. Drawing on what I'd learned in OTC, I did what I could to help my comrades with map-reading, weaponry and military etiquette. But my true moment of greatness came when I was asked whether I'd met Vivien Leigh. My answer was received with awe. Then a second question was asked. I had to say that although I'd longed to, I had not.

At the end of those six weeks, I felt as though I'd been

flattened by a hurricane. It was a battered Able Seaman Macnee who headed for London to march down that most precipitous of parade grounds, the aisle. A hotch-potch of relations and chums crowded into St Peter's Church in Cranleigh Gardens for my marriage to Barbara in November, 1942. My baby brother James was summoned from Stowe School to be my best man. He'd quite grown up since our last meeting, and appeared to enjoy the occasion more than me. For myself, I felt quite terrified. I glanced around and spotted Mama. As she waved, I noticed an old buzzard on the top of her head. It was actually a hat. I nodded to Barbara's mother, who just stared back. Such displeasure was understandable. Geoffrey Hibbert had been a much better 'catch' than Patrick Macnee.

The ceremony went off without incident, with Barbara looking stunning in an outfit of pale pink, but the reception was something of a shambles. Encouraged by Mama, several guests got drunk. Barbara and I quickly left to enjoy a brief honeymoon at a hotel in Half Moon Street. Our time together was all too short. Having settled Barbara in a basement flat at 22 Cranleigh Gardens, I paid advance rent to the Italian landlord, and prepared for war.

I returned to sea convinced that my life expectancy during active service would be no more than a month. I had survived many horrors in my twenty years, and could not believe that my luck would continue. I was posted north of the border to further my naval training upon a paddle steamer with the disconcerting name of HMS *Whippingham*. Barbara wrote suggesting I think about becoming an officer. Her thoughts appeared to coincide with those of my superiors, and Able Seaman Macnee was put down as Commission Warranted Candidate. Having heard the most evil rumours concerning selection boards, I faced my interview with trepidation. It was said that lunatic admirals delighted in playing practical jokes upon aspiring officers. A favourite wheeze, so the whisper went, was to knock a glass off a desk in order to gauge a candidate's reflexes. Enlisting the help of a shipmate, I whiled away my few leisure hours upon *Whippingham* playing net-ball with a tumbler.

The board comprised one admiral and two captains. Seated behind a huge table of a solid-looking oak, to me they all looked pissed. I'd hardly taken a seat when a captain, representing the Navy's educational branch, extended himself across the table and hissed, 'Where were you at school?' Eton seemed to please them, as did my training with OTC.

Then, giving me a perfunctory sniff, the admiral asked whether I'd ever contracted venereal disease. Before I could stutter a negative reply, the admiral poured himself a glass of water, though it could have been neat gin, and launched into a sermon upon the evils of syphilis. Glaring at me, the old sea dog warned that the wrath of the Almighty had been inflicted upon a society who believed promiscuity was acceptable.

Conversation was steered sharply from port to starboard when one of the captains drawled at me, 'Is it warmer in Murmansk than Pwllheli?'

I blinked. Had they assumed that I'd sailed with the Arctic convoys? I attempted to correct his impression, but my protests were silenced by a hubbub. The Admiral called the first Captain a bloody fool, while the second Captain suggested that the cold of Murmansk would be dry, whereas that of Pwllheli would assuredly be damp. The Admiral accepted this view, and then roared that I'd been admitted, though to what and where was not specified. A week later, kitted out in the uniform of a Sub-Lieutenant, I reported to HMS *Alfred*, an officers' training school near Brighton.

I entered the ranks of the officer class with conflicting emotions. This small advancement made me proud for Barbara's sake, but in more pensive moments I couldn't help but wonder whether I was the right sort of person to lead other men into battle. But HMS *Alfred* was fun.

Commuting between King Alfred, Lancing College and a commandeered prep school, we submerged ourselves in a curriculum of engine maintenance, flags, gunnery, keys, morse code, navigation, radar, signalling, mine laying and the use of torpedoes.

During our torpedo course, we were billeted in Rodean School. Unfortunately, the girls had been evacuated, but their absence was compensated for by some stunning Wrens who catered for nearly all our needs. Above our beds in the girls' dormitories of Rodean were notices that read, 'If you want a mistress in the night, ring twice.' But none of the Wrens ever answered my calls.

At the end of the course I left King Alfred as Sub-Lieutenant Macnee. Proudly sporting the wavy stripes of the RNVR, I was sent for further training to the naval bases at Devonport and The Royal Naval College at Greenwich, which might best be described as an officers' finishing school. At that time, the

Navy was devoting a considerable amount of time to building up officer strength for combined operations. Given the diversity of backgrounds from which the recruits were drawn, it was felt that the finer points of etiquette should be clarified for those gentlemen who'd never had the good fortune to enjoy an eight-course dinner or savour a fine Bordeaux.

To dine in the Painted Hall of the Royal Naval College is to dine in Paradise. Seated at a table, I stared quite spellbound at the ceiling in the hall's lower section. Painted by Sir James Thornhill, this ceiling depicts The Glorious Revolution of 1688. Using the mythological deities of Classical Rome, the artist salutes peace, and freedom and denounces despotism. Staring at this majestic and awe-inspiring celebration of good over evil, I could only pray that I'd live to admire a like monument commemorating an allied victory in the present war.

One evening dinner was served at an earlier hour, since the hall had to be cleared and the tables re-set for a banquet Winston Churchill was throwing for the chiefs of the American Naval Staff. With spare time on their hands, my friend Cameron Gough and his chum John Fisher, a grandson of Admiral Jackie Fisher, went down to the college basement to spend the rest of the evening playing skittles. Since it was the occasion of John's twenty-first birthday, the two friends imbibed unwisely and were startled when a Paymaster Captain, a great friend of Admiral Fisher, entered and informed the two men that the Prime Minister wished to see them in The Gun Room. Perhaps it was the influence of alcohol, or maybe he just had style, but like a latter day Sir Francis Drake, John drawled, 'I'll just finish my game of skittles.'

On arriving in the gun room, the two drunks quickly sobered up. Assembled before them were Winston Churchill and his American naval guests, John G. Winant, the American Ambassador to The Court of St James, Sir Dudley Pound, the Admiral of the Fleet, Mr A.V. Alexander, The First Lord of the Admiralty, and distinguished chiefs of the British Naval Staff. With their breath reeking of gin, 'Cam' and John believed their naval careers were finished. Instead, Churchill offered birthday congratulations to John Fisher; then, brandishing one of his famous 'Romeo y Julieta' cigars, he launched into an off-the-cuff speech, stating that the loss of young life was an inevitable price paid in hostilities, but the present war must be fought to ensure that future generations survived to enjoy a world free from the shadow of tyranny. When 'Cam' told me what had taken place, I felt inspired, and prayed I'd fight bravely for my country.

I was now a qualified officer, and I had to decide upon the branch of the Navy to which I wished to be seconded. During a brief spell of leave in which Barbara helped me brush up my trigonometry, I confided my feelings to her. I was fascinated by submarines, but found their claustrophobic atmosphere daunting, and I would have felt lonely aboard a gargantuan destroyer. Fortunately there was a compromise and I decided to join the British Light Coastal Forces, part of which was a fleet of Motor Torpedo Boats dedicated to the defence of the English Channel.

When I arrived in Dartmouth in 1943 to join the First MTB Flotilla, it was at the height of the German attacks upon our shipping. Our main line of operation was along the French coastline from Cherbourg and around the Channel Islands to St Malo. At that time, policy dictated that all naval bases on the south coast should be named after stinging insects. Thus Dover was known as HMS *Wasp*, Weymouth as HMS *Bee* and Dartmouth as HMS *Cicala*. I had previously undergone training on MTB's in the lochs around Fort William, but nevertheless I arrived in Dartmouth in a state of some apprehension; this would be the base from which I'd depart on my first serious foray against the enemy. The boat I would navigate through enemy waters was an MTB numbered 415. Rather like a Spitfire or Hurricane, the boat's hitting power was heavy for its size, for it was intended to attack German shipping. It was seventy-one feet six inches in length, with a beam of nineteen feet three inches and it was powered by American Packard V-12 supercharged engines. The MTB had a maximum speed of between 38–40 knots, and carried machine guns, torpedoes, depth charges and mines.

Though I was a lowly sub-lieutenant, I now found myself acting as navigator and sailed with a midshipman who acted as first lieutenant. The coxswain was usually a petty officer or leading seaman and there would also be a petty officer motor mechanic. In addition there were about ten members of crew whose task it was to man the guns and torpedoes and act as telegraphist or engine room artificers. Most of these jobs were interchangeable when the boat went into action.

On the night of my first mission, I felt exhilarated and reckless. Possibly influenced by the attitudes of my colleagues, I took the view that if the horror of death was inevitable, then so be it. Most missions in light craft took place at night, so as to avoid aerial strafing. Come dusk, dressed in thick jerseys, monkey jackets and fleece-lined boots, the Flotilla Commander, captains and lieutenants gathered in a briefing-room to discuss the outlines of that night's plan, which was given by a senior officer, usually a Flotilla Commander. By the time I reached my boat, however, I had quite blanked on the briefing and could only remind myself that aircraft, shore batteries, mines and, of course, the ubiquitous U-Boats and E-Boats must be avoided. An eerie silence hung over the harbour where our flotilla was moored, a silence that was suddenly shattered as orders were shouted, duty hands sprang into action and wireless operators clattered into their cramped quarters. But it was only when the First Lieutenant shouted for the guns to be uncovered that I truly realized that I was finally on my way to meet the enemy.

Taking my place in front of a tiny table at one end of the ward room, I tried to concentrate on what would be expected of me that night as the ship's navigation officer. I'd have to calculate tidal flow, file a mass of data including the number of engine revolutions per knot and the deviation of the magnetic compass which changed with each new torpedo. Charts were also marked up with corrections, and allowances made for wind drifts. My mind wandered and in a moment of panic I told myself that I wouldn't be up to the job. A terrifying roar interrupted my thoughts; this was followed by a second and a third. As my boat's engines exploded into a deafening throb, noxious fumes wafted through the lower deck. The racket was quite deafening. A rating glanced at me, I grinned back, and then, inhaling a whiff of oil, I vomited over the floor.

'First trip is it, Sir?' inquired the rating.

As the engines continued to rumble and roar the boat moved out into the water, spray drenching the decks. Scintillas of light flickered from the flotilla's leader, then the irregular roar of engines subsided to a more uniform din and the unit sped out towards hostile waters. As the shoreline of my country faded rapidly behind me, I began to feel such apprehension.

We left harbour in line ahead, but once beyond the boom we formed into a 'V', with the flotilla leader at the head and the other boats lining up two to port and two to starboard, rather like a gaggle of ducks. We had been given information that a British convoy was heading through the Channel. Aware that this would be a tempting target for German E-Boats, we followed instructions to go out beyond the convoy and act as a screen between the enemy coast and the convoy itself. Once in position, we cut the engines and stayed hove to for several hours watching and listening for the anticipated E-Boat attack. But no E-Boats appeared; this was to be the first of many nights when we waited and watched for an enemy that never came in that vast silent darkness of the English Channel.

We made a sweep along the Channel Islands, hoping to bump a likely target. As there was nothing to be seen, we turned back for Dartmouth. I felt intense relief when the order came to switch auxiliary motors for the entry into harbour. This was done to avoid waking the many old ladies then living in the town! As the roar of the supercharged Packard engines died away, I smiled in the knowledge that I had survived my first operation.

A couple of weeks later, Winston Churchill sent the following message to all light coastal forces.

30 May, 1943   10 Downing Street
                                              Whitehall

'I have noted with admiration the work of the light coastal forces in the North Sea, in the Channel and more recently in the Mediterranean. Both in offence and defence the fighting zeal and professional skill of officers and men have maintained the great tradition built up by many generations of British seamen. As our strategy becomes more strongly offensive, the task allotted to the coastal forces will increase in importance, and the area of their operations will widen. I wish to express my heartfelt congratulations to you all on what you have done in the past, and complete confidence that you will maintain the same high standards until complete victory has been gained over all our enemies.

                                              WINSTON CHURCHILL

Come winter, our nightly forays into the English Channel obviously increased in duration so as to exploit the extended cover of darkness. After up to twelve hours at sea, our hearts were light when we returned to the welcoming shores of England. We'd invariably alight from our boats tired and quite drenched through, but after the luxury of a hot bath and a wholesome breakfast served by smiling Wrens, our weariness seemed to recede, and we settled down to the necessary administrative work with renewed vigour.

After the hectic schedule of a busy morning, we would grab a quick drink before drifting off to sleep between sheets that crackled with starch. Greatly refreshed, we'd rise around 5 p.m. so as to be on the boats by seven o'clock. If that night's operation was cancelled for any reason, then off we'd go to the Imperial Hotel in Torquay for some relaxation.

The Head Waiter at the Imperial was named Joseph, and he affected French and Serbo-Croation origins. In fact he was a raucous cockney who ignored the rationing rules and served us enormous meals that were always rounded off with liqueurs and cigars we hadn't ordered. During one such evening I glanced around the table. 'Bussie' Carr, my commanding officer, Eric Archer, who would later succeed him, 'Cam', who would later succeed Eric, 'Topline' Broadhurst, 'Pop' Beck, Jamie Shadbolt, 'Stoo' Large, and so many other good friends were puffing cigars, downing the liqueurs and roaring with the sort of laughter that comes from wondering whether we would live to enjoy another such night.

Not all MTB operations began with instructions from a Flotilla Commander in a briefing-room. Sometimes the urgency of a situation meant that we were 'scrambled'. One such occasion came when information was received from Ultra, the Allied Special Intelligence decrypting service, that the German battle-cruiser *Scharnhorst* would be making a sortie against one of our convoys. On this occasion it wasn't the stench of oil that brought such a horrible feeling of nausea creeping up my throat, it was the formidable reputation of this particular battle-cruiser. I whispered to myself 'Oh God. Not the *Scharnhorst*.'

Scharnhorst and her sister ship *Gneisenau* had, through a spectacular series of naval victories and the brilliant use of Goebbels's propaganda machine, filled the Allies with some apprehension. Full load, *Scharnhorst* displaced 38,900 tons.

Besides its nine 28 cm and innumerable other guns, it carried torpedoes and four aircraft. *Scharnhorst* and *Gneisenau* had recently sunk the British armed merchant cruiser *Rawalpindi* and the aircraft carrier *Glorious* along with her escorting destroyers *Ardent* and *Acasta*. In total they had sunk, wrecked or captured over 116,000 tons of allied shipping and had at one time all but closed our convoy routes. Their reputation for invincibility was partially dented when the *Gneisenau* was retired due to damage, but the *Scharnhorst* continued to haunt the Channel and North Sea, and I could only compare our Vickers machine-guns and Oerlikon cannons with German firepower and assume that I'd been sent on a suicide mission.

We set out at high speed. I navigated by dead reckoning, until eventually we cut and lay in wait surrounded by the dark, cold, silence and wetness of the North Sea. During such waits, mens' feelings would alternate between fear and utter boredom. As we watched for the *Scharnhorst* that night, I said my prayers and thought about sex.

After we wallowed in the ocean for several hours, I was ordered to relieve the officer on the bridge. Up there, even my fleece-lined boots seemed scant protection against the bitter cold. Then, about midnight, I finally spotted movement. It was Able Seaman Parkin, carrying a large tray. 'Not a night for being out, is it, Sir?' he remarked jovially. I examined the tray to see what he'd brought up. There was a plate heaped with dripping sandwiches, and a huge mug of cocoa. Naval cocoa contained the original cocoa butter, whose greasy foam floated on the surface before hardening into a thick skin. My guts protested, my stomach heaved and I spewed into a bucket. 'Never mind, Sir,' sympathized Able Seaman Parkin. 'The Admiral Lord Nelson had a dicky tum.' By the time we headed back to the British shoreline, I was all but grovelling before The Almighty. In his mercy, He had persuaded Kapitan zur See Friedrich Huffmeier, the *Scharnhorst*'s captain, to stay in port that night.

It was only many years later that I learnt about the pantomime that had taken place on the *Scharnhorst*. Captain 'Poldi' Huffmeier might kindly be described as accident prone. While under his command, the *Scharnhorst* ran aground, one of her aircraft was shot off a catapult in error, avoided a mine just in the nick of time, and got a buoy wire wound around the ship's starboard screw. Had I known of this on that night, I would have gone to sea whistling Rule Brittania.

After the failure of Airborne Operation Market Garden to capture Arnhem and so liberate The Netherlands, our invasion had to be postponed. With so many escape routes blocked and betrayed, the First MTB Flotilla was ordered to the Dutch coast where it would pick up members of the Dutch Resistance.

On that particular night I went to sea with a feeling of exhilaration. It was a marvellous sight to see the boats creaming along at thirty knots. An order went out for an exercise in station keeping, or close formation sailing.

Using enormous skill, our coxswain managed to bring our boat so close to another that the two craft couldn't have been more than one foot apart. I remembered 'Cam' telling me of a similar experience when for a full half minute he'd managed to stand astride two boats as they sped along. Caught up in the excitement of the occasion, I decided to try this for myself. Steadying my balance between the two bouncing boats, I somehow managed to stand astride both craft and, waving my arms above my head, trumpeted a roar of triumph. Regrettably, this victory flourish had a somewhat unsettling effect upon my balance, and I began to fall. Fortunately a Petty Officer grabbed me, and we landed in a heap on the deck. When we stood up he shook his head wearily and with great courtesy reminded me of my responsibilities up on the bridge.

We headed towards the Dutch coast, and a gleaming moon came up. Apart from the roar of our engines, the Channel was quiet. As we approached the Frisian Islands we cut our main engines, glided towards the Dutch coast on the auxiliaries, and about a mile from the shore hove to. Only a faint blue navigation light gave the slightest indication of our position. I do not recall the precise hour at which we were due to liaise with the Dutch, but I do remember thinking that our wait was terrifyingly long. Although maintaining an outward appearance of calm, the entire crew of the MTB felt growing concern as we peered towards the direction of the Dutch shore. Given the seemingly impenetrable defences of the German 'Atlantic Wall', none of us could be blamed for assuming that the Dutch would fail to reach us. The beaches of northern Europe had been transformed from pre-war playgrounds into entanglements of barbed wire and treacherous minefields.

Then splashing could be heard. It sounded like a swish of oars. Someone whispered, 'It's them.' For a few agonizing moments we stared into the darkness, wondering whether it was indeed the resistance men, or whether perhaps it was a trap, and we were about to be attacked. It was the brave Dutchmen, and as they boarded our MTB I could only marvel at their courage in fighting so bravely for the Netherlands.

I don't know who it was who remarked that 'The whole of southern England looks as though it has become an armed camp', but this was most certainly the case by the spring of 1944. Every available park and open space in this part of the country had been turned into an ammunition dump, a vehicle park, or both. Many villages along the south coast were evacuated in their entirety and the inhabitants housed elsewhere, particularly in those areas where rehearsals for the invasion were taking place. The roads were crammed with lorries and tank transports, and soldiers of every nationality and colour were represented in this, the largest invasion force ever assembled.

My flotilla left Dartmouth for Portsmouth (HMS *Hornet*) to make preparations for D-Day. I was now the 1st Lieutenant on MTB 434. Navigating our little boat up through the

Solent, I remarked to my CO, Eric Archer, upon the great armada of ships that had been assembled for the forthcoming invasion of Europe. In Portsmouth my task was 'to prepare the ship in every respect ready for sea and to meet the enemy'. With the war so obviously nearing its conclusion I went about my duties with a sense of well-being. But now and then I wondered how many more would perish before final victory.

Later that week, I began to feel unwell. Terrible pains seized my chest as I coughed, sweated and felt like fainting. The doctors diagnosed bronchitis, and to my fury ordered me to a hospital in Chichester. While I lay in bed not in the best of tempers, a substitute navigator went out in my place. I'd got to know my crew so well, and given the marvellous camaraderie that existed, it seemed so unfair that I had to remain behind suffering what would be my only illness of the war.

The following day, a sombre-looking officer entered the hospital ward and, having questioned Sister, was directed to my bed. He was evidently in considerable distress. Coming straight to the point, he informed me that MTB 434 had been sunk the previous night. I must have looked perfectly idiotic as I lay there open-mouthed. Such was my state of shock that I couldn't move and such was the confusion of my emotions that I didn't know whether to cry or sigh with relief.

He proceeded to tell me what had happened. Our flotilla had assembled off Cap D'Antifer for an attack on a German convoy sailing out of Le Havre. Apparently there'd been some confusion on the radar screen since the echoes from ships had been picked up along with some back echoes from cliffs on the shore. As the MTB slowed down to make an attack, one of the German escort ships picked it out and scored a direct hit. The boat went up in an explosion of flame. Of the fourteen or so men on board, one was killed and four were wounded. After a short time in the water, the survivors were picked up by MTB 431. Two DSM's were won that night, the first by Able-Seaman Falk and the second by Petty Officer Jack Pacey, who had tried in vain to rescue Stoker Ernie Heywood from the blazing engine room. I felt a deep sense of shame at not having been there, a shame I still feel to this day.

The war came to an end, and my thoughts began to return to the theatre. During a brief visit to London I managed to snatch a meal in the Savoy Grill. Everyone was smiling, and there was an overwhelming sense of relief. But before all of us lay the daunting task of re-building our broken lives in a devastated world. I could only thank God that I had survived.

— 8 —

The war might have ended, but I was still a naval officer, and getting myself demobilized was not a simple matter. Nevertheless, I was determined to use my leave to look for work in the theatre. I made contact again with Kitty Black, a white South African who had been John Gielgud's secretary before joining H.M. Tennent and later becoming a leading agent of plays. We'd met briefly at Felixstowe during one of my wartime leaves. A sympathetic lady, Kitty, had warned me of the difficulties facing actors returning to the theatre after years of absence. Promising to 'get me started again after the war', Kitty kept her word and wrote suggesting I look up Gielgud during my next leave. Gielgud was in fact auditioning young hopefuls for a theatrical tour of India, and I grasped the opportunity to meet him at the Haymarket Theatre, where a few years earlier I had tried to flirt with Vivien Leigh. That day, I was one of two hopefuls who sat in Gielgud's dressing-room waiting to see the great man. The other was a shy young naval officer who was later introduced to me as Alec Guinness, and who sat with his face buried in Dostoyevsky's *The Brothers Karamazov*.

John Gielgud was the soul of kindness. Though surely more impressed by Alec's talents than by mine, he nevertheless expressed a desire to take both of us to India and enquired as to the earliest date upon which we could join the company. In the event neither Alec nor I was able to get a release from the Navy in time. To cheer myself up, I went down to the Old Vic. Led by Laurence Olivier, Ralph Richardson and Sybil Thorndike, the company was in the midst of the second of their legendary post-war seasons. Having applauded a sparkling performance of Shaw's *Arms and the Man*, I went backstage to look up Michael Warre, my old friend from Eton, who'd been cast as a Russian officer in the play. Michael heard my tale of woe, swept me out of his dressing-room and announced that we were off to see Laurence Olivier.

Though I was desperate to get back into the theatre, I felt sure Laurence Olivier would remember my attempt to flirt with his wife and, panicking, I tried to run away. Michael ignored my cascade of protestations, however, saying that Olivier might well offer me employment once the Navy had released me. Trying to free myself from Michael's hand, which was now grasped tightly around my left arm, I accidently pulled some frogging away from his jacket. At this, even the usually gentle Michael swore. While he examined his torn jacket, I seized the opportunity to make my escape and tore down a corridor, my old friend giving chase. Rounding a corner, I slithered to a halt in front of another Russian officer, who just happened to be Laurence Olivier. Michael caught up with me, and explained to the great man who I was and what I wanted.

Laurence Olivier ordered me to march along the corridor and back. I tried to imagine that the corridor was the parade ground on Horse Guard's, and strode out as though carrying the colour before our reigning sovereign. Laurence Olivier was not impressed. 'No. Nothing for you now,' he announced briskly. 'Come back in another ten years.'

I returned to Torquay where I spent the next couple of months in a more or less drunken state. From there we were billeted at Leigh-on-Solent and Gosport, where I continued to booze and keep up the tedious appearances of naval life. I was bored to the teeth, and I prayed that my days in uniform were numbered.

Within a month I'd been ordered to appear before the Royal Family in a British Legion concert at the Royal Albert Hall. Booked to do a solo recitation, such was the thoroughness with which Barbara had coached me in my lines, that the two of us were convinced I'd give a masterly performance.

A fanfare of trumpets opened the show. After the National

Anthem, the Band of the Royal Marines belted out several numbers before a squad of sturdy sailors pranced on stage to show off their drill routines. My flirtation with a well-upholstered blonde from Queen Alexandra's Imperial Military Nursing Service was interrupted when a pint-sized commander with a pansy purple nose warned there was a minute to go before I went on stage. I glared at him, he glared back, and with the tone of our relationship set, I marched out to face thousands of people.

A sharp object of some strength and determination prodded my loins. About to snap at the pint-sized commander, I then realized I'd somehow hitched myself on to a pipe jutting out from the Albert Hall's giant organ. Unhitching myself from this cruel fistula, and clutching my hat in both hands, I shrilly announced:

'THE WHITE ENSIGN'
BY
ADMIRAL RONALD A. HOPWOOD, C.B.

'Farewell, White Ensign, battle-scarred and torn,' I began. 'We know . . .'

'Put your hat on,' hissed the pint-sized commander.

'Oh, sure love.' Plonking on my hat, I continued: 'We know at last the magic of your spell.'

Several lines on, I decided that wearing the hat was discourteous to both Their Majesties and the Ensign, so I took it off.

'St George, St Andrew and St Patrick,' I continued, my voice now at soprano pitch.

'Put your hat back on,' the Commander growled.

Come the finale when I was rambling about sea salt and sea brotherhood, once more I decided against wearing the hat and removed it. Finishing my recitation in a voice that had soared to falsetto, I tore off the stage and found my way barred by the pint-sized commander. He threatened to have me cashiered.

Desperate to wriggle out of the Navy, I'd no objection, but was mildly chastened by Barbara's view of my narration.

'Really, darling,' she sighed, 'there were times when you bore a close resemblance, visually and vocally, to one of the organ pipes in the treble section.'

While my professional life continued to meander from misfortune to disaster, sadly my domestic circumstances were running a similar course. Like so many of our contemporaries, Barbara and I had married very young, and at a time when no one could be certain of living to enjoy another day. We had spent most of our time apart, and this enforced separation had rekindled my roving spirit. I was fond of my wife, but I could no longer endure the restrictions and sacrifices that marriage demands. I knew that if I continued to live with Barbara, I'd only make her unhappy, and concluded that a divorce would be for the best.

An invitation had arrived recently from Evelyn inviting the two of us to visit Rooksnest. I hadn't been near that unhappy old house for years and didn't particularly wish to return; but with my emotions so confused I accepted, and decided it would be there that I'd ask Barbara for a divorce. Rooksnest seemed an appropriately gloomy place to end another sad chapter in my life. After several years of occupation by the American Army, the place had a battered air. The lawns were strewn with junk, the rose gardens turned into vegetable plots, and the house itself required a complete face lift. The old girls were in a foul mood, having spent the entire war quite drunk, though two of the harem's more enterprising members had gone as volunteers to Italy, where they had driven ambulances at speeds that had terrified even the daring, car mad Italians.

Mama's days were obviously numbered. Though saying nothing, Evelyn stared with resentment at her erstwhile favourite as she flirted during dinner with a more recent addition to the harem. Aurea, the object of Mama's attentions, was an Irish aristocrat with a penchant for auburn wigs and dresses some twenty-five years out of date. After a fifteen-year affair with her benefactress, Mama was about to lose all.

Putting off the awful moment when I'd have to broach the subject of divorce with Barbara, I escaped for an hour to College House. By now my father had become a complete stranger. He was greatly embittered by the fact that his horses had been put down at the declaration of hostilities, and had spent the war improving his considerable talent for drawing cartoons and for insulting passers-by from behind the safety of his gate. That night, still highly nervous about mentioning the subject of divorce, I borrowed a bottle of Evelyn's gin and lay in the bath swigging liberally, before crashing onto the bed. A few hours later, our first child was conceived.

With a baby now on the way, I was forced to re-consider divorce and my career. Now demobbed, I found myself unemployed. Our neighbours in Cranleigh Gardens, Kensington, included Donald Houston and an old friend from drama school days, Ian Carmichael. Each Sunday morning we'd all meet up for drinks in the nearby Drayton Arms, where the main topics of conversation were our impecunious circumstances and our uncertain futures.

Yet again, Kitty Black came to the rescue with financial loans and offers of work. For several weeks I was employed as an understudy before being cast as Lieutenant Baker in a play called *The Assassin* at The Lyric Theatre. The play was a dramatization of Abraham Lincoln's death from his assassin's point of view. Cast as the assassin was Peter Glenville, who finished the show dying in my arms. Peter adored the death scene, and how my arms ached as he prolonged that scene by a few more seconds each performance! Staggering home one night, I collapsed on the sofa. 'God!' I complained to a concerned Barbara, 'tonight Peter Glenville took seven minutes to die.' Within days, the play followed suit.

The Assassin did not transfer to the West End, and once

again I was out of work, this time with the added responsibility of a pregnant wife. It was also the worst winter of the century. We shivered over a two-bar electric fire, and the post contained nothing but bills and offensive letters from the bank. Eventually I had to surrender my cheque book, and I left the bank with snow and starvation staring me in the face. Then I ran into Michael Benthall. An old friend from Eton, Michael had very quickly become a successful theatrical director. On hearing my tale of woe he promptly offered me a part in his forthcoming production of an Elizabethan tragedy called *The White Devil*. Such was my ecstasy that I squandered half my ration coupons and money on a pound of steak from a butcher with reputed black market connections. By necessity, Barbara and I had been vegetarians for months.

The White Devil had a colourful cast. Foremost was Robert Helpmann, the legendary dancer, waspish wit and outrageous practical joker. On the first day of rehearsals, he singled me out for special attention. Encouraging my talents and allaying my fears, Bobby began a friendship between us that would endure until his death some forty-one years later. I felt most flattered, especially as I'd only one line to say. The actresses included Martita Hunt and the gorgeous Margaret Rawlings.

Martita was reputed to have taught Alec Guinness everything he knew in the bathroom. She never took me there, and as a most junior member of the cast I found myself quite ignored, except when she found me offensive, which was frequently. Margaret, on the other hand, who'd done what she could to gain me entry into RADA before the war, proved most warm and helpful. Another member of the cast was a rampant Welsh actor with saturnine good looks and a mellifluous voice. A darling man from the Isle of Anglesey, Hugh Griffith had an unrivalled record as a bacchanalian.

'Patrick, dear boy,' he'd always begin as a prelude to a request for crates of liquor to be collected. Since there was a quid to be made, I'd always oblige.

After some initial rows, tantrums and faiting fits, rehearsals settled down into a comfortable routine, and we soon had the beginnings of a potentially excellent production together. Given my one skimpy line, there wasn't too much for me to do except look useful and behave.

As rehearsals progressed, so the day of my child's birth grew nearer. Although well satisfied with the care Barbara received under the newly formed National Health Service, I nevertheless pawned a silver snuff box in order to employ two gynaecologists, should Barbara require their services. These gentlemen were named Dr Pink and Dr White. Leaving Barbara immersed in the Dick Read Theory of Relaxation, I went off to dress rehearsal.

The dominant feature of my costume was a huge codpiece whose size was further accentuated by my black tights and semi-transparent shirt that completed the outfit. I'd been dressing when messages came that both Miss Hunt and Mr Griffith wished to see me. Teasing the codpiece into place and checking my tights for holes, I gave Hugh preference over Martita and visited his dressing-room. Although a magnificent sight to behold, dressed as Cardinal Monticelso, Hugh could have passed for a turkey cross-bred with a red-headed woodpecker.

'Patrick, dear boy,' he began.

'For God's sake, love,' I protested. 'I can't go down to the local dressed like this.'

Largesse was pressed into my hand. Given my growing domestic responsibilities, I chanced a run. As the pubs hadn't opened, I sneaked into the back yard of our local, and knocked up the landlord who readily struck a cash deal without commenting upon my appearance. After a return journey that was mercifully devoid of incident, I dumped the crate with Hugh before venturing into Martita's dressing-room.

Martita came to the point. Talking at me, she announced

that, 'one of her athletic friends' would be attending the dress rehearsal and she'd be keeping an eye on my loins. Scrutinizing my legs, Martita suggested I loosen my tights to allow a minimum of flexibility into their stretch. On that, I was ordered out and left quite bewildered by the entire interview. Forgetting Martita, her 'Athletic friend' and the tights, I was overjoyed when, that night, Barbara presented me with an adorable baby boy who wrinkled his face and blew a raspberry as I kissed him. Filled with elation I felt convinced that, given more effort on my part, our marriage could endure, and we named our baby, Rupert.

Norman Parkinson and Michael Warre accepted my invitation to become Rupert's godfathers, and Norman's wife, Wenda Rogerson, became a godmother. Still a godmother short, I gave the matter some practical consideration and contacted Rooksnest. Given Mama's reckless conduct, there could be no doubt that Gussie, her old rival, would inherit the entire estate upon Evelyn's demise. Gussie agreed to become Rupert's second godmother, but refused outright my request for a loan. She did give her word, however, that she'd put her godson through public school. As I walked on to the stage that night for the first performance of *The White Devil*, I was in a state of euphoria.

The critics were in a good mood. Since I had only one line, I hadn't expected a second glance from anyone and I could only read the words of the great Harold Hobson with surprise, pleasure and disbelief: 'Then treading on silence, a page whom I had not noticed before, and was not to notice again, quietly says these five words: "This is not true, Madam." That is all. As this play counts noise, it is hardly more than a whisper. Am I right in thinking that the name of the actor who plays the page is not even mentioned on the programme? Yet for me it was the most striking moment in a performance in which such moments are now few.' With a new son and a rave review, surely my star was in the ascendant? Brimming with confidence, I flung myself into the second performance with possibly too much enthusiasm. From that night on, Bobby Helpmann did a quite wicked mimicry from the wings of me uttering that one line, which he kept up every night for weeks on end.

Having been summoned to Martita's dressing-room for a second time, I assumed this bidding was related to her athletic friend. This assumption was correct. A glowering Martita trilled, 'Patrick, dear, do you have to breathe so often and so heavily? And my athletic friend has again complained that she can't see the ripple down the back of your tights. Do something about it.'

'The breath or the tights, Miss Hunt?' I trembled.

'Both.'

Martita managed to combine Lady Macbeth, Lucretia Borgia and Lady Bracknell into that one retort. She was a truly terrifying creature.

Margaret Rawlins played 'The White Devil'. In her youth it was reported that she had danced naked on tables all around the West End. Whether or not this was true, I don't know, but by now she was Lady Barlow and conducted herself with elaborate decorum. Dressed in a deliciously low-cut gown, it was her misfortune to be murdered by a bunch of thugs towards the end of the play. One night, up went the cry to head for the wings. Pushing my way through the crowd, I saw Margaret lying 'dead' on the stage with her gown ripped to the waist while her upstanding naked breasts faced the brightly lit stage like two magnificent pyramids of alabaster.

Given that this was 1947, the audience sat numbed with shock. Unable to move, Margaret had to lie there until the curtain came down, but if the audience was shocked, we actors feasted our lustful eyes on this opulent sight. Clutching the shreds of her torn gown around her, Margaret glared at us and left the stage. We never had the good luck to see so much of her again and it was strongly suspected that the bunch of thugs were deliberately carried away.

The White Devil had kept Barbara and me in groceries for months. Then I landed the part of Laertes in a BBC Television production of *Hamlet*. John Byron was well-cast as Hamlet, for he was a young man torn between the stage and evangelism. After having attended a Billy Graham rally at Earls Court, John settled for the latter and spent years in Africa trying to convert the natives to Christianity.

Barbara and I moved to a modest flat in Chelsea. Given our limited resources, I couldn't help but admire Barbara's talent for interior decoration. Her imagination, keen eye for a bargain and feeling for colour transformed the flat into something stylish and elegant. It was amid this tastefully inspired mock-up of affluence, with its echoes of my privileged childhood, that I saw Evelyn for the last time. With Mama surprisingly still in tow, Evelyn took tea with us. She was obviously dying, but nevertheless she chose to sit on the floor, something I'd never seen her do before. After an hour or so of small talk, the two ladies inspected a sleeping Rupert and left.

By now the Press were describing me generously as 'one of the most promising Shakespearean actors in the West End'. While all this was very heady stuff, it was the lure of hard cash, and not the possibility of theatrical glory, that sent me chasing up to the north of England to play Mark Antony in the Sheffield Repertory Company's production of *Julius Caesar*. Since this was the company's first Shakespearean production for some years, the local papers wrote nostalgically of their last venture into Shakespeare, when Alec Guinness had played an outstanding Macbeth.

I didn't even bother to attempt a comparison with Alec Guinness, who reputedly observed that if you can't say eleven sentences of Shakespeare on one breath, you shouldn't be doing it. I settled for a sustained shout throughout the funeral oration. The length of Shakespeare's soliloquies and declamations have always filled me with paralysing fear and I rarely attempt them, preferring to read them. A bad admission for an actor, but my admiration is unlimited for those who can, on stage, make modern audiences understand the words, thoughts and cadences of the daunting poetry. My favourites are Judi Dench, Anthony Hopkins, Alan Howard, Barbara Jefford and Ian McKellen.

Michael Benthall made contact and offered work. Poised to accept, I had to withdraw when told of my wages. Such earnings would have scarcely kept a single man, left alone a family. He then, most generously, made a second offer. At that time Paul Scofield was playing Young Fashion in Vanburgh's *The Relapse* at the Phoenix Theatre. As Michael wanted Paul Scofield to do *Hamlet* at Stratford, he invited me to take over from Paul, and join them at Stratford when *The Relapse* came off. But even a brief West End run wouldn't, in the long term, cover the cost of Rupert's nappies.

Through the further good offices of Michael, I was offered a small part as a courtier in a film version of *Hamlet*. The star, producer and director was Laurence Olivier. I was still a little nervous of this remarkably gifted actor, and did what I could to remain unobtrusive, cowering behind a false beard and the delicious shape of the eighteen-year-old Jean Simmons. Such was the magnetism of Laurence Olivier that, once he appeared in the studio, a hush settled over everyone.

My main position, as a glorified extra, was to stand behind Sir Laurence and Jean Simmons in the 'Play' scenes. To see him rehearse Jean Simmons like a magician – to see the beauty and revelation of the perfidy of Claudius in the hands of this master – and, one day, to see, because of the lights, right through Jean Simmon's diaphanous dress when she forgot to put on any knickers, were memories I'll always treasure!

During rehearsals, a female voice hissed into my left ear, 'Can you ride a horse?' It was Doreen Hawkins, wife of Jack. She then mumbled something about the French Revolution, and invited me down to 'The Moore Arms', a public house in Chelsea where Jack Hawkins was part of the furniture. A glass of gin in one hand and a cigarette in the other, Jack asked about my horsemanship. Given my background and the recent rides I'd enjoyed with Dennis Price in Rotten Row, I thought my riding well up to standard. Nodding, Jack said he'd put in a good word for me with Michael Powell, a gentleman who would shortly be co-directing *The Elusive Pimpernel*, a film requiring numerous actors who could ride with Sir Percy Blakeney's band of daredevils.

A letter arrived from Mama. The letterhead was that of a public house in Cheshire called 'The Bear's Paw'. As I read it, the realization dawned that Mama was not simply staying there, she had become the landlady. She had at last been thrown out of Rooksnest, along with Aurea. I contacted Gussie at Rooksnest. Ostensibly, Mama had fallen from grace for watering down the drinks, but I suspected that Aurea had been the final straw for Evelyn. She altered her will, making Gussie the beneficiary rather than Mama, and three months later she died.

The filming of *The Elusive Pimpernel*, a co-production of Sam Goldwyn and Alexander Korda, opened with a fanfare of trumpets, firework displays and the biggest blaze of publicity given to a movie since *Gone With The Wind*. It starred David Niven, Jack Hawkins, Maggie Leighton and Bob Coote, and among those actors chosen solely for their equestrian skills were, apart from myself, Terry Alexander, John Fitzgerald and Hugh Kelly. Shooting began in Marlborough and Bath, and during the first few days a coach race was staged in the Savernake Forest, stunt men doubling for David and Jack.

Up to now, David had made no attempt to introduce himself to me. I assumed unkindly that he had become a little grand. I decided the time had come for him to at least acknowledge his less illustrious relation, and approaching him, I shook his hand and announced, 'How do you do. I'm Patrick Macnee, your cousin.' After what seemed an interminable length of time, David drawled, 'Oh, really?' I gave him a brief explanation of our relationship, upon which he brightened considerably and invited me to a party. It was very soon all over the set that I was a cousin of the star, and attitudes towards me changed overnight. I was even asked for my autograph by one of the camera crew, though my ego came crashing down when this 'fan' asked if, after my name, I'd add in brackets 'David Niven's cousin'.

At that time, David seemed very happy. After the tragic death of his first wife, he'd recently married the lovely Swedish model Hjordis Tersmeden. Never a man to break a date with a beautiful lady, he'd staggered into his second wedding running a temperature of 104 degrees.

Upon discovering I was too poor to run my own car, David insisted upon giving me a lift back to London after a day's shooting at Bath. He had offered the same hospitality to several other people, and I found myself seated on the knees of other actors. David started up the engine, the shiny monster trundled off, and out came the bottles. We laughed uproariously as the shiny monster meandered across main roads and scattered anything and anyone that dared to obstruct its way. The mirth increased with our speed, and the monster often lost its way, wandering off the main road and on to some farm track. They were such carefree, not to say downright irresponsible, weeks and I found myself reminded of those carefree days of youth I'd known so briefly in the summer of 1939.

On a wage of ten pounds a day, I could afford to launch into a spree. I bought new dresses for Barbara, teddies for Rupert, and a pair of silk cami-knickers for the nanny. Perhaps the cami-knickers were an imprudent move, since Barbara stared at them frostily when I unpacked them. In an attempt to mollify her, I told her to splash on the paint and wear her prettiest dress: we were off to David's party. Since Barbara had a streaming cold, she mixed herself a hot toddy, and chose to take an early night.

If only Barbara had attended that party. I got terribly drunk, and through the alcoholic mists spotted a well-stacked brunette who was an extra on the *Pimpernel*. The inevitable happened and very soon, racked by guilt, I came out in spots. I went sheepishly to what was then called 'The Special Clinic' of a London hospital, where to my relief I was told I had a nerve rash. Deeply mortified, I swore that from now on I'd behave like a responsible married man.

Sam Goldwyn was in a dangerous mood. Having seen some of the rushes, he pronounced them as 'Goddam awful' and ordered a re-shoot. Given the kind of money Mr Goldwyn was paying, I'd no objection to repeat performances. With much of the shooting in England completed, the *Pimpernel*'s band were shipped over to France where, two of them, including me, faced the daunting prospect of swimming the River Loire on horseback. As the *Pimpernel*'s band selected their nags from the cavalry school at Tours, producers and directors were battling with the owners of several chateaux. Although proud that their ancestral homes would be immortalized on celluloid, and ready to accommodate some of the film crew's more adventurous whims, the owners expressed concern when Mickey Powell outlined his major plans.

As he explained so cheerfully to Monsieur and Madame François Carvallo, the owners of the magnificent Château Villandry, a mob of peasants would advance upon their home and smash it up, having previously ransacked the grounds. Given the shock with which such a proposal must have been received, the Carvallo family recovered and explained their point of view.

Never mind the château and its treasures, but one hundred years of work was responsible for the ground's present splendour. Perhaps Monsieur Powell could modify his plans? Following protracted negotiations it was agreed that the maximum effect of carnage could be obtained if the camera used a wide-angle lens to obtain a long range shot of a mob of peasants poised to storm the château, before doing a close up of just one peasant savaging just one hedge. As for the shattering of statues, Mickey promised to provide his own and send the bill to Sam Goldwyn.

With that problem solved, Mickey prowled the French countryside on the look out for a mob of peasants. Cheap labour came when he was inspired to visit local old people's homes and when he promised to make the inhabitants stars. Inundated with offers, Mickey left some underlings to fix a deal on his terms, while I trembled at the thought of my forthcoming journey across the River Loire.

I wandered down to the river bank with John Fitzgerald who'd be riding alongside me. Dismayed, the two of us stared at the surging waters. Then Mickey ordered us to mount our steeds and start crossing at the widest point of the Loire. Initially, I allowed my horse to swim ahead while hanging on to its tail. A sharp kick in the groin sent me swiftly to the saddle crupper where I should have been in the first place. As the horse pawed frantically in the fast-flowing torrent, stinking water flooded through my nostrils and swilled around in the top of my nose before pumping its way out through my mouth. I longed to throw up, but swallowed a litre of the Loire as my horse plunged briefly beneath the waters.

'Cut,' yelled Mickey.

In our drenched hats and long black wigs, John and I resembled a couple of old Welsh witches, but this didn't deter Mickey.

'Alright, dears. Back in the river,' he said between clenched teeth. Mickey had set his heart on doing some close-ups.

When that day's filming was completed, John, myself and the horses staggered back to the river bank. To their credit, Mickey, the crew and the rest of the cast gave us a round of applause and two enormous brandies. We bathed in the glow of our achievement, but those who've seen the film say that scene was cut.

The critics panned the *Pimpernel* and Sam Goldwyn was said to be behaving strangely, but for me it was back to a diet of beer, baccy and beans. By now our position was so precarious that I even gave serious consideration to leaving the theatre and embarking upon a sensible career. I continued to consider during a seaside holiday sponsored by a charming old sculptor of independent means who'd taken a shine to me and my family, and whom I had dubbed Roly-Poly. At the end of our holiday I had to tell Barbara that we could no longer afford to live in London.

Mercifully, Barbara took this news calmly, and thanks to the Roly-Poly, I was put in touch with a wealthy artist called Edward le Bas, who owned a cottage called 'Harbour Lights' in the enchanting old Cinque Port of Rye. Together we visited Edward in his Cheyne Walk home. He readily agreed to let 'David Niven's cousin' have the use of the cottage. What's more, he said, there'd be no rent to pay. The sole condition the kindly Edward imposed upon our tenancy was that we pay the cleaning lady Mrs Almond one pound ten shillings a week.

Chocolate box pretty to look at, 'Harbour Lights' had a pokey interior whose upstairs could only be reached by a ship's ladder that had been placed in a small hole cut out of the downstairs ceiling. When the redoubtable but plump Mrs Almond tried to negotiate this ladder she got stuck in the narrow cavity, and once Barbara and I had succeeded in freeing her, she announced that doing upstairs would be out of the question.

Rupert loved his new environment. Showing a preference already for one of his father's favourite haunts, he quickly took to playing in puddles outside the 'William the Conqueror' pub, where he became a great favourite with the local fishermen. As I left Rye to do some radio work in London, I recalled the advice of Sebastian Shaw, with whom I'd worked during the BBC television production of *Hamlet*. Seb had remarked that the country air was good for a family, and that a little absence really did make the heart grow fonder. In my case such absences contributed towards the break-up of what might otherwise have been a fairly successful marriage.

I had come to know Dennis Price well. With his saturnine good looks and impeccable manners, Dennis was a highly sought-after movie star. He was also prized as a dinner guest, and leading society hostesses would compete to have him seated at their dinner tables. Certainly his eccentricity gave rise to much comment, but such was the sweetness of his nature that Dennis became one of the most loved human beings I've ever known.

At that time, he was living in Egerton Gardens in an elegant home conveniently close to Harrods. Dennis spent a lot of time poring over wallpapers, fabrics and furnishings with the aim of decorating what would be for him and his guests the ideal home. Upon hearing that I'd been forced to give up my London flat, with typical generosity, Dennis offered me a room and invited me to move in at once. What Dennis didn't tell me, but which I quickly discovered, was that I'd be sharing it with a brood of chickens, who used the bathroom as their nest and provided us with breakfast every morning! From my new base in Knightsbridge I scribbled a mountain of correspondence to producers, directors, casting agents, rich friends and anyone else who I believed would be impressed by my expensive new address.

I received a reply from the London Gate Theatre Company, which was scheduled to tour Western Germany with a production of *Hamlet*. I auditioned for the part of Horatio and was duly given it. But shortly afterwards I received a telephone call from Jack Hawkins. He told me to go at once to Claridges, where my presence was required by Orson Welles. Orson wanted me to read Cassio for his own production of *Othello*, which was being filmed in Morocco. I was dazzled by Welles's glamour, the lush setting of the film and the prospect of wages fifty per cent above those being offered in London.

Pouring pre-audition cocktails, Orson asked whether I'd

mind also reading Desdemona. Not wishing to offend I agreed. Diverse as I flattered myself my talents were, even I blanched when he asked me to read Cassio's mistress, Iago's wife, a clown and the Duke of Venice as well. Downing a third cocktail, Orson announced that he'd be playing Othello and the other roles. He then suggested we get started, and heaved himself on to the top of a sideboard.

Come the beginning of Scene Two, Orson interrupted my lines and told me to climb on to the sideboard since he'd be lying on the table. I obliged, but was soon forced to take Orson's place as the table was too small to accommodate his bulk. With Orson now sprawled on the sofa, we continued reading, before going down on all fours. Orson read a herald's speech and then instructed me to follow him into a bedroom.

There, he asked me to give him a leg up and clambered on to the top of an enormous wardrobe from where he called down: 'You are welcome to Cyprus, sir. Goats and monkeys.'

Whether that Shakespearean line is a subtle insult, I wasn't sure, and I just concentrated on the remaining text until we came to Desdemona's smothering.

'Say, where do you want me to do you in?' Orson yelled, departing from the text.

I thought the bath might be novel. Orson agreed, and following another round of cocktails, he 'smothered' me in the bath with one of Claridges' pillows.

The role of Cassio was mine provided I didn't tell my agent. The news leaked out, however, and already committed to *Hamlet*, I was forced to turn Orson down. I even had a telegram from the Foreign Office forbidding me to join Orson, since the FO were putting up some of the money for the trip in the cause of improving Anglo-German relations. I was desolate, but was later consoled by the news that the cast of *Othello* didn't get paid until some six years after the film had been shot.

The German tour was a horror story. The country was

literally one great heap of rubble. Clustered around these pyramids of debris were wretched groups of people faced with the unenviable task of clearing and re-building their country. The few Germans employed by the company worked as stagehands and dressers, every one of them looked worn and gaunt. Women of all ages offered me and my fellow-actors the use of their bodies in exchange for cigarettes or a bar of soap. Those three months touring Germany greatly saddened me, especially when, at the end of performances given in English, grateful German audiences rose to their feet applauding and cheering. So these were the people against whom I, and so many more, had wasted years of our lives fighting.

On returning to England I went straight down to Rye and sat up half the night pouring out my feelings to Barbara. Like me, she hoped the world had learnt from a most harsh lesson and that the new generation would be blessed with sufficient wisdom and vision to avoid future hostilities. We decided to have another child. Not only would this baby be an expression of our confidence in the future; we also hoped, I think, that it would bring the two of us together again.

When working in London I continued to stay with Dennis Price, but his chickens were becoming tiresome flatmates. Having asked whether they'd be staying long, I was sharply told that the birds could stay as long as they wished.

'But Dennis,' I protested, 'it's not as though they contribute towards the rent.'

'No, but their loyalty to me is remarkable, and can you lay eggs on a daily basis?'

'Well, no.'

'Right, well give credit where credit is due.'

Very soon, Rupert had a quite adorable little sister, whom we christened Jenny. She arrived during a period when I hadn't worked for months. Our poverty had now become so acute that I would travel from one destination to another by jumping on and off buses every few hundred yards, thus

Left: Already looking concerned about Mama. *(From the private collection of Patrick Macnee)*

Above: Pa and Mama at a meet of the Craven Hunt in 1928. *(From the private collection of Patrick Macnee)*

Below: Rooksnest. *(Sotheby's of London)*

Uncle Evelyn. *(Mrs. M. Johnson)*

That accursed kilt. *(Mrs M. Johnson)*

Gussie. *(Mrs M. Johnson)*

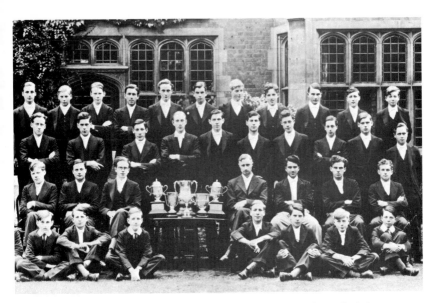

Eton, 1939. Patrick Macnee is in the top row, fifth from the left.

Claude Aurelius Elliott v. Daniel Patrick Macnee. *(picture of Patrick, courtesy of Mrs J. Williams; picture of Claude Elliott, courtesy of Peter Lawrence and Moholy-Nagy)*

With Barbara in 1942. *(From the private collection of Patrick Macnee)*

At war. *(Lieutenant Commander Eric Archer RD, RNR, RTD)*

Appearing in *Hamlet* (1947) with
Muriel Pavlow and Arthur Wontner.
(*BBC*)

Another production of *Hamlet*
(1948). Laurence Olivier (at the
front), Jean Simmons seated behind
him, and me standing third from the
left. *(National Film Archive/Stills
Library)*

The Elusive Pimpernel (1949). Seated next to David Niven, 'my cousin'. *(National Film Archive/Stills Library)*
Playing The Prince Consort to Margaret Wedlake's Queen Victoria. *(The Theatre Royal, Windsor)*

Still learning my craft in *Mansfield Park* (1951). *(The Theatre Royal, Windsor)*

With the late Joan Benham in a disastrous production of *A Midsummer Night's Dream*. The critics disliked both my acting and my costume! *(Copyright – Old Vic Productions?)*

Three Cases of Murder, with Orson Welles and Helen Cherry in which Orson took over the production! *(National Film Archive/Stills Library)*

The Battle of The River Plate. Seated next to Anthony Quayle who did so much to help me. *(National Film Archive/Stills Library)*

Listening to Lord Mountbatten. *(R. G. McFarlane)*

With Kate in the early 1960s at Malibu. *(Copyright unknown)*

Beginning to avenge. Ian Hendry and myself. *(National Film Archive, London)*

Honor Blackman, the leather and I.

Advising Linda Thorson, but why should she look so sceptical? *(Weintraub Entertainment Group)*

Diana Rigg and I. *(Weintraub Entertainment Group)*

With Susannah York in *The Importance of Being Earnest*.

Pissed in Paris. *(Marc Cinello)*

Divorce, Divorce. Trying to sort myself out alongside Fenella Fielding.

Richard Burton and I prior to the start of his eighteen-vodka air passage. *(The Press Association)*

The Return Of The Man From UNCLE. David McCallum, Robert Vaughn, Patrick Macnee.

Jordie Christopher was a joy to act with in *Sleuth*.

Joanna Lumley, Gareth Hunt and myself in *The New Avengers. (The Avengers Film and TV Enterprises)*

The Sea Wolves. Happy days with Gregory Peck, David Niven and Roger Moore.

A visit to West Berlin with my old friend Lorne Greene. *(Axel Springer Publications)*

Samantha Eggar played my wife in *For The Term of His Natural Life*, and by then the booze had begun to show. *(The South Australian Film Co.)*

A View to a Kill. Tibbet (Patrick Macnee), a British Secret Service Agent and thoroughbred expert disguised as a chauffeur, taking orders from James Bond (Roger Moore). *(Eon Productions)*

The London Premiere of *A View To A Kill*. Meeting HRH The Princess of Wales.

Above left: With Marie Cameron (centre). *(PIC photos)*

Above right: Wedding of Rupert and Heather, with Jenny in mandarin's coat.

Left: With Baba, my darling wife. *(John Westo)*

avoiding the ticket collectors. Then it was back to the West End for a part in *The Family Honour*, by Laurence Housman. The play was given a Royal Command Performance. I tried not to look at the formidable Queen Mary who, wearing pearls and one of her famous toques, sat upon a huge armchair of crimson velvet in front of the front row surveying us gravely. Shortly before I was to be presented to Her Majesty, an actress in the play complained loudly that I smelt of onions. The Queen was far too polite to refer to this. 'Very nice, Mr Macnee,' she said, and presented me with a silver tie pin decorated with a gold fox's head.

I just hoped that I wouldn't have to pawn it.

On a wage of three pounds a week, I couldn't afford to give up the room Dennis was letting me for a peppercorn rent, but my relations with the chickens deteriorated. I was further intrigued by mankind's fascination with fowl and feather when Nancy Price, the octogenarian co-producer of *The Family Honour*, had confided to me that her closest confidante was her parrot. Shortly afterwards, the chickens triumphed when I fled Dennis's flat in a whirlwind of feathers. Now occupying a minute room off Draycott Avenue, I waited for offers of work that never came.

The Christmas of 1950 promised to be a lean one. My brother James turned up quite unexpectedly, just back from Palestine, where he'd had 'such a fun time avoiding Arab bombs'. It was James who saved our Christmas Day after a stray dog had run off with the mangy turkey I had left hanging on the washing line. While Barbara burst into tears, and the children howled with hunger, James disappeared. When he reappeared he was caked in mud and clutching a huge replacement for our stolen Christmas lunch. He absolutely refused to say how and from where he had obtained this splendid bird, but it still had its feathers on and was still warm to the touch!

A rare letter arrived from Pa. The old boy wondered

whether I had any money to spare. But this was evidently no begging letter. If I had a few bob, he wrote, then I should back any horse being ridden by a fifteen-year-old called Lester Piggott, who he was sure would become the greatest jockey to ride upon the English turf since the fabled Fred Archer. This would be the last piece of advice my Father was to give me.

Once again, I was poised to quit acting. Not only was there a dearth of work, but the parts being offered me were positively humiliating. Having just played the Demon King in a radio play, I seriously considered joining John Byron as a missionary in Africa. Then Kitty Black called. She was throwing a party and would I like to come? There I met John Counsell, who ran the prestigious theatrical company at The Theatre Royal, Windsor. John asked whether I'd be interested in joining his company on a permanent basis, and looked a little surprised when I didn't reply. Overcome with disbelief at this sudden turn in my fortunes, I eventually managed to nod in acceptance.

A week later, Pat Marmont, an actress friend, invited me to another party. As I walked into the main reception room, I caught sight of an actress whose sylphlike figure, long black tresses and widely spaced green eyes had already caught the attention of a major British film studio. And I fell madly in love.

— 9 —

The Windsor Theatre Company had been founded in 1938 by John Counsell. Having failed in his previous attempt to establish a company in Windsor, John's ambitions were revived when he met a quite lovely young actress named Mary Kerridge. Determined that Mary would have a splendid background against which to show off her considerable dramatic talents, John worked his persuasive charm on Lady Iris Capell, who willingly became the theatre's lessee. John's stock soared overnight. Offers of financial assistance flooded in, the company opened to great success with a production of *Dear Brutus*, and John talked Mary into standing alongside him at the altar.

John's company grew quickly, both in popularity and prestige. Importing many unknowns who would later go on to great theatrical glory, John fused these talents and staged crop after crop of vintage productions. Very soon the next-door neighbours in Windsor Castle were taking an interest, and the royal seal of approval was finally given when King George the Sixth and his beloved consort visited the theatre for the first time to watch a production of *The Rose Without a Thorn*, an account of King Henry the Eighth's fifth matrimonial fiasco. Not only was the show a smash, but George the Sixth made his own theatrical history by becoming the first British monarch to watch from the stalls, stumping up three shillings and six pence for the experience.

I arrived at Windsor brimming with optimism. After years of haphazard employment, at last I had a secure position that might well lead on to West End success. Perhaps Harold Hobson would someday reward my work with the same praise he'd lavished upon my one line in *The White Devil*. I was now earning a regular wage of twelve pounds a week, and the ever open beaks of Rupert and Jenny could be properly fed. Barbara and I might even treat ourselves to a new pair of shoes apiece.

With financial stability came emotional turmoil. I struggled to balance domestic considerations against the genuine love I had developed for the sylphlike actress I had recently met whose name was Tamara. Rehearsing for *The Wind and the Rain*, the first production in which I would appear at Windsor, I shuffled across the stage with head bowed, preoccupied with thoughts of divorce. If I had any sense, which I hadn't, I should forget the long black tresses and widely spaced green eyes of Tamara and concentrate on what had sadly become the shell of a marriage. I decided to compromise, or rather to come to no definite decision. I would continue to visit my family in Rye, chase up to London to see Tamara, and while in Windsor, I would for the time being reside with my former Classics tutor, Richard Martineau, at Eton College.

It was twelve years since I'd been thrown out of Eton. Apart from the generous hospitality of my host, I didn't enjoy this return visit. I was surrounded on all sides by boys who embodied what I myself had been years before. Many of them seemed like peacocks, strutting through the streets of Eton in their embroidered waistcoats, while I, a man of twenty-nine, would cross the street to avoid them. One person I failed to avoid, however, was my former headmaster, Sir Claude Aurelius Elliott, who was now the Provost of Eton College, and whom I bumped into one day by accident. Sir Claude did not recognize me. It was time, I decided, to bid my old school and its memories farewell and I took to commuting between London and Windsor during the week.

Given the complications of my private life, I couldn't have been cast in a more conscience-provoking role than that of Charles Tritton in *The Wind and the Rain*. Like me, Charles found himself entangled with two ladies, and the play's theme was that age old struggle between sense of duty and illicit love. I was always grateful for encouraging notices, but in this instance I couldn't be sure to what extent my dramatic abilities had prompted *The Windsor, Slough and Eton Express* to note that 'Patrick Macnee plays the part of Charles Tritton with deep feeling and sincerity'.

Chasing between Windsor, London and Rye, I did not pause to consider the potential maelstrom of disaster into which I was whirling, very likely dragging other innocent parties with me. After each performance I would jump on a train from Windsor to Paddington, briefly see Tamara, and then chase across London to Waterloo from where I'd get a train to Ashford, from where I would change for Rye. Having arrived at Rye I would spring onto the saddle of my parked bicycle and pedal off to our cottage. Throughout all this frenzied activity I would have a French's Acting Edition stuck underneath my nose.

I spent very little time at home in those days. I was a stranger to my children, and domestic life held no charm. I fled back to London. From now on, all my efforts and emotions would be concentrated on reaching the top of my profession. But there was still the distraction of Tamara. Up to now we'd done nothing more than meet for an occasional discreet tea or a walk in the park. Given her extreme youth and complete lack of worldliness, I became convinced she was a virgin, a rarity in the theatrical profession. I was now obsessed by a determination to mould Tamara into the model woman of my fantasies and possess her solely for myself, though the thought of robbing her of her innocence made me uneasy.

I was in turmoil, and sought refuge in Windsor, where, away from the distraction of Tamara, I could concentrate upon improving my craft and advancing my career. But Windsor had become another Bedlam. Cast in a play called *Harvey*, I found myself acting out a tale about a mad rabbit and a drunk. A more straightforward role came in *The Heiress*, about which *The Windsor, Eton and Slough Express* observed, 'If there is to be a criticism of Mr Macnee as Morris Townsend, the scheming young lover, it is that he is altogether too charming and not nearly quite nasty enough. We nearly felt sorry for him – and that would never do.' To which John Counsell added, 'It's time you behaved like a first-rate shit.' The irony was inescapable. I could be a first-rate shit in my private life, but not on stage.

We went on to a production of *The School for Scandal*, which developed into a riproaring production that most of my family came to see. Barbara brought Rupert, who endeared himself to everyone, even when running amok backstage. Then Mama appeared. She and Aurea had been thrown out of the 'Bear's Paw' for drinking away all the profits. After a tour of southern Ireland, where they'd fleeced some distant cousins of Aurea's, they were now residing in the Shires in a state of genteel poverty. I had to explain to them that I was in no position to finance their imbibing, and suggested they find employment. I was touched by Mama's dignity when, removing a shoe to straighten a cardboard lining she'd inserted, she remarked that no lady ever soiled her hands with manual work.

Though *The Windsor, Slough and Eton Express* had given me a good notice for *The School for Scandal*, I was privately beset with worry about my theatrical future. Nearly thirty, I was still an unknown actor. Like numerous fellow thespians I had to continually convince myself that the big break would soon be mine, but I was often beset by doubt. This doubt was more over the vagaries of luck than confidence in my ability, though my confidence took a battering when an actor remarked, 'You're a very handsome fellow, Patrick, but a lousy actor. I can't think why you stay here.'

I stayed at Windsor for several reasons. I was learning from John Counsell and from my fellow-actors Patrick Cargill and

Joseph O'Conor, who taught me so much of what I now know about the business of acting. Added to these advantages, Windsor gave me a tremendous feeling of domestic security without the attendant responsibilities. Along with other members of the company I crowded into local cafes for eggs, bacon, pots of tea and theatrical gossip. I was lucky to be with a group in which such a marvellous camaraderie existed. But when was I going to be a star?

I truly believed my hour had come when John Counsell announced his plans for a production of *Victoria Regina* in honour of The Festival of Britain. When Patrick Cargill was cast as Disraeli, I had thought I might get a look in as one of the Queen's lesser prime ministers. Instead I was asked to play Prince Albert, the male lead. Surely such a spectacular production would entice every critic of note? If I could give a fine performance then my agent's telephone would undoubtedly be jammed with calls offering me West End leads. The producer, Hugh Cruttwell, expressed concern about my accent, however. The Prince Consort, he explained, did not speak in a way that suggested an Etonian education. I was packed off to see Miriam Karlin, who at that time was earning a crust by giving instruction in foreign accents.

John Counsell arranged some dazzling publicity, including a procession through Windsor. Dressed as the Prince Consort and accompanied by Margaret Wedlake, my Victoria, I climbed into an open landau and led a procession of no less than seventy-five similar vehicles around the town. Crowds lined the pavements and cheered as though Margaret and I were the genuine articles. After some initial embarrassment, I quickly fell into the part and greatly enjoyed this adulation. The only threat came when some malcontent in the throng, roaring his allegiance to the Stuarts, yelled, 'Germans, go home.'

Thanks to this publicity we played to packed houses, although it was noticeable that none of the Royal Family turned up. This disappointment was offset by the reviews. The critics were ecstatic. Surely my hour had finally come? Shaking his head, my agent had to tell me there'd been not a single offer from the West End managements. There was nothing to be done but stay on at Windsor, and continue to learn and gain experience.

Tamara had remained resolute in her decision not to visit my single room off Draycott Avenue. Then she astonished me by saying she could come over for dinner. I was now determined to seduce her, and decided to overwhelm her with a macho image. In the event I went a bit overboard, however, for I wore a fishing jersey and wellingtons! I had bought two steaks, and, anticipating an evening of seduction, I was to be disappointed when Tamara showed more interest in her knitting than in me. Perhaps it was because I had a streaming cold, and whenever I tried to approach her had to back away sniffling. At any rate, my attempt at seduction failed miserably, and I felt more insecure than ever.

I was asked to audition for a good role in a film called *Something Money Can't Buy* but I felt highly nervous before my audition and confided these fears to Pat Jackson, the director. Leading me into a small room, Pat told me to forget the five hundred or so other actors competing for the part. It had already been decided that the role would go either to me or Anthony Steel, so why not relax and outshine my one rival? Pat left me to take a telephone call and I wandered around the building where the auditions were taking place. The five hundred or so other actors looked just as I had after the war, when regular work had been so hard to come by. They were all down at heel, tired and chain-smoking. I wanted to suggest they give up and find a sensible job with a bank, but how could I pontificate when, like me, they all longed to be stars?

Although the role was all but mine – if I didn't count Anthony Steel – my attack of nerves returned. To calm me down, Pat Jackson offered me a drink, told me to relax, think straight and use the camera to my advantage. I nodded and asked for another drink. After a third drink, my nerves were soothed, but just to give myself that extra boost, I had a fourth when no one was looking. It was a sad Pat Jackson who told me after the audition that the part had gone to Anthony Steel. Though he'd wanted me for the role, Pat pointed out not a little astringently that no one was going to employ an actor who auditioned smashed out of his mind, even if the part was that of a drunk.

Then came a big break. My agent called to say that a part was available in a production of Jean Anouilh's play *Ardèle*, which was running at the Vaudeville in London's West End. Ronald Howard had been forced to drop out, and his role as Nicholas was mine for twenty-five pounds a week. With my name in lights and a wage more than double my pay packet at Windsor, I announced I'd be leaving the Theatre Company. Unfortunately, no one bothered to mention that *Ardèle* only had another six weeks to run. I was too embarrassed to face John Counsell who I knew I'd let down very badly, and it was clear that he had felt most hurt by my day's notice. Indeed, for the time being he could scarcely bring himself to mention my name.

During my stay in London, I ran into Tamara. She was most kind but made it quite clear that she was now involved with a gentleman she intended to marry. I still loved her deeply and became intensely jealous of my rival, I took to loitering within the vicinity of her flat and following her around. I was determined to discover this fellow's identity, though what I'd do with him I hadn't quite worked out. On discovering that it was someone of my acquaintance, I nearly reached for a shotgun. As the penalty for murder at that time was still hanging, I went to see Dennis Price instead.

The ever imperturbable Dennis Price said there was little I could do bar talking the girl into a divorce. Dennis assured me the marriage wouldn't last the month. He also suggested I give up my ridiculous pursuit of a quite unobtainable lady and look to my own marriage.

Within the month I was back on the telephone to Dennis. He'd been right. The couple had separated, and there was already talk of divorce. I wanted to rush round to Tamara's home, tell the girl I still adored her and would happily still give her my name in marriage. Realizing that Dennis's advice had been sound, I played a rejected Romeo to the full and imposed my miseries upon anyone who'd listen.

I was out of work once more. John Counsell relented and took me back, but any trust he'd had in me was understandably gone, and from that time our relationship, although polite and not completely devoid of pleasantry, lacked the basic faith John had once had in me as an actor who could be relied upon. I continued to be given a series of good leading roles in productions as diverse as *The Holly and The Ivy*, a drama of christian ethics, and *Mansfield Park*, a stage adaptation of Jane Austen's novel.

As always, *The Windsor, Slough and Eton Express* were most supportive with their notices. Even the prestigious *Stage* referred to my 'considerable eloquence of bearing and beauty of voice-inflection'. But none of this praise could console me for my lost friendship with John or convince me that I had any future as an actor. I had a premonition that my days at Windsor would be few, and that my career would wane, the name of Patrick Macnee becoming a foot-note in the vast annals of British theatrical history.

I poured these miseries out to Katie Blake and an actor in the company called Michael Yannis, who later received international acclaim as the director of *Zorba the Greek*. Though sympathetic, the two of them had no idea what they could do to help. Then Katie sugested I should go to Canada where David Greene, her husband, would undoubtedly give me permanent and lucrative work with the newly founded television section of the Canadian Broadcasting Corporation.

'Canada?' I exclaimed.

Appreciative as I was of Katie's suggestion, there was no way I could go. It was a long journey to undertake in 1952, added to which, a departure would create further complications in an already complex domestic situation. Though I didn't doubt David's kindness, given the instability of the business and the circumstances in which David had obtained his own position, what assurance was there that he wouldn't be out on his neck by the time I hit Canada?

My financial and personal situation was by now extremely desperate. Faced with a stack of bills, a marriage that had long since died but had never been buried, and a career that was walking down a dead end street, I swept these problems to the back of my mind, rehearsed for a production of Sheridan's *The Rivals*, and whooped it up at a party in Hampstead where Noel Coward played the piano, Judy Garland sang and Peter Ustinov impersonated everyone and everything from the Tsar of All the Russias to a herd of stampeding elephants.

Mickey Powell re-entered my life. Richard Brinsley Sheridan was a great man to be sure, Mickey argued, but he had a play lined up for me whose dialogue made Sheridan's words seem clumsy. Marching me up Piccadilly, Mickey all but talked me into accepting the part on offer. I'd be working with Raymond Massey. What more could I, 'a rising star', as he so generously called me, want out of life?

I was just on the point of accepting when what must have been my forty-second bank manager in ten years informed me there was no money in the Macnee account. Just as I was thinking of shutting myself in the oven and switching on the gas, Bobby Helpmann telephoned. He was producing a play called *The Wedding Ring*. Rehearsals were to begin the following week, a factor which I translated into instant money in my pocket. I'd be working with Peter Cushing and Irene Handl, and we'd open at Manchester Opera House before going to the West End. I was bound to accept, but it meant turning down Mickey Powell's offer. Mickey called me a fool, was a little uncharitable about the play and its producer, and said he'd never use me again. My designated role went to John Byron who, bored to the teeth with bringing Christ to Africa, had folded up his mission and returned to the British theatre.

Bobby Helpmann was, as always, a most able producer, and the rehearsals went well. There were unspoken reservations about Irene Handl, who kept her pet Chihuahua fastened to her breast, but she explained that her barking brooch deterred would-be gropers.

The Wedding Ring opened to disastrous notices. We played in Manchester for as long as we dared, but instead of the planned triumphal entry into London's West End, decided to test the water in Worthing. While Mickey Powell's production played to capacity houses, we were hissed off the stage, and in desperation Bobby called in Noel Coward for a rescue attempt. Having watched a run through of the play Noel, with his characteristic brevity of language, came elegantly to the point. 'If I were you, Bobby, I'd take the fucker off.'

I was out of work again, I had a starving family, and an ever diminishing belief in my own ability. In such a situation, one can either be positive and practical, or hit the bottle. Down at the Buxton Club, I must have been into my fourth gin when Katie Blake swept in. This time Katie all but ordered me to go to Canada. She'd just heard from David who'd be delighted to have me working for him in Toronto, where he'd pay me an undreamt of fortune of thirty pounds a week and give me sufficient work to keep five actors in employment.

Having decided to leave England, I had the painful experience of breaking the news to Barbara. A practical woman, she discussed the matter with me long into the night. Certainly the money was sufficient incentive to go, but she feared my absence might place a further strain upon a marriage she wished to continue, if only for the sake of the children. In retrospect, it might have been sensible to divorce at that time but, overwhelmed with guilt about leaving my family, I told

Barbara that I'd send for her and the childen once I was sufficiently established in Canada.

I was so hard up that I didn't even have enough money for my air fare. My landlord, Edward Le Bas, generously gave me a loan, then died before I had a chance to pay him back. I arrived in Toronto with less than ten pounds in my pocket. Booking myself into the first of the many YMCAs I'd inhabit over the following eight years, I spent that first night in Canada feeling cold, homesick and utterly despondent about my future.

In the morning I joined the queue for the washroom. As one man emerged from a matchbox of a cubicle having finished his ablutions, another would take his place. I was jammed between an Indian and a Jamaican. Thanks to the influence of the British Empire, we all spoke the same language. I yawned. Sleep had been impossible. Crammed as we were into dormitories, I'd been kept awake by a chorus of snores and grunts, and a gentleman of far eastern extraction who had attempted to climb into my bunk. He gave me his most honourable word that he'd only been sleepwalking, an explanation I accepted until a friendly West Indian let on that my bunk was the latest in a very long line of bunks into which he'd tried to sneak, looking for unattended wallets. I was again reminded of Eton and my early naval days when a repellent hash which passed for breakfast was slapped on my plate. From then on I boycotted the YMCA's haute cuisine, and survived on a diet of coffee and buns in a chain of seedy cafes.

Given the Canadian Broadcasting Corporation's majestic title, I'd assumed its studios would be a cross between Buckingham Palace and Versailles. I was directed to a building barely larger than a chicken shed. David Greene greeted me enthusiastically. 'You son of a bitch. I love you and I'm gonna make you a star,' he trumpeted. Uncertain as to how I should handle him, I just let him give me a bear hug and a kiss. Then he introduced me to a group of strangers.

'Okay, this is John Colicos, Chris Plummer and Kate Reid.'

These were just a few of the most remarkable collection of talented people just beginning their careers in Toronto at that time.

'Oh, and that's Lorne Greene. No relation of mine and he reads the news bulletins.'

CBC had come about through the Canadian National Railway. Since the railroad had brought regular communication to the many states that made up Canada, when radio was invented, the Canadian Government entrusted it with the task of bringing the broadcast word to this vast country. The BBC in London was asked whether they could spare anyone with the ability and vision to run the newly founded radio service. The person chosen was Tyrone Guthrie, who was sent out from the BBC's Belfast studios. After a year, the organization became known as The Canadian Broadcasting Corporation. It continued to expand, and by the time I arrived in Canada the country boasted eighty television sets.

I began to enjoy Toronto. By now I'd gone up in the world, having fled the YMCA for an apartment in Prince Arthur Avenue which I shared with Herbert Whittaker, the drama critic of the *Toronto Globe and Mail*, and no bad ally to have.

These were golden years, for me and everyone else involved. As Canada was something of a cultural wilderness, its embryonic television service didn't have to compete with either a movie industry or a thriving theatrical community. With what was still a fairly raw radio service as its only rival, Canadian television began as a quite fresh innovation in the world of Canadian entertainment. Not having the experience and the unlimited financial resources of the film industry, the television service had to rely upon brains, talent, taste and energy.

Seeing an outlet for their creative talents, some of the most gifted people I've known headed for Toronto in the early and mid nineteen-fifties. They included Leonard White, a great burgher of a man who later switched from acting to produce many episodes of *The Avengers*; Sydney Newman, a gentleman who would do so much to get *The Avengers* off the ground, and who made CBC-TV the most important drama outlet on the north American continent; Hank Caplan, a director whose favourite expletive goaded his actors, upon the completion of one production, to present him with a box of lavatory paper; and Paul 'Nutty' Almond, a producer of enormous ability who had the good taste to marry Geneviève Bujold.

I thrived in this heady atmosphere. True to his word, David gave me more work than I could handle. There existed a camaraderie not unlike that I'd so enjoyed at Windsor, and the opportunity arose to further improve my stagecraft when I was invited to appear in several productions at Toronto's Jupiter Theatre. Some of the guilt I'd felt over leaving my family was alleviated, for I was now in a position to send them regular payments of money. But during that first Christmas in Canada, I did feel very far away from them. The radio station played 'Jingle Bells' incessantly. For some reason I associated this tune with my family back in Rye, and to this day I can't hear it without feeling quite wretched. Yet it was during that Christmas that I knew I'd have to raise the question of divorce with Barbara when I returned to England.

I became embroiled once again. Gina was the result of a brief liaison between a French Count and a Thai hooker. A cloud of black hair framed a perfectly shaped oval face whose apricot complexion glowed with robust health and youthful enthusiasm. What I did know was that her husband was a very powerful Canadian businessman of a vengeful nature who would, if he so wished, destroy the career of any man foolish enough to risk playing around with his wife. Nevertheless, I continued to play around with Gina, and also to involve myself on the fringes of another gin-smuggling racket. Toronto, like Letchworth, was 'dry'.

Then Barry Morse hit town. Wearing a dirty mack and looking generally down at heel, he's brought his family along and, like the Macnee tribe, the Morse clan knew about living rough and existing on a diet of bread steaks. With this, and so much more in common, it was inevitable that Barry and I would go on to enjoy a friendship that still endures.

Along with Lorne Greene, Barry and I were cast in a production called *Ebb Tide*, a tale of three beachcombers who'd found themselves stranded in a Tahitian port. According to the CBC press release, 'These beachcombers have sunk to the lowest level of human degradation,' which, in those days, was a daring statement. David Greene, our director, was beside himself with excitement. If we drew upon our own experiences, he advisd, we'd surely sink beneath the sewers. Given David's excursions into fantasy, none of us took this as a personal affront.

After the show, CBC's switchboard was jammed. Filthy, disgusting and obscene were just a few of the adjectives that crackled down the wires. Then, General Motors, the show's sponsors, blasted in. What were we doing, for Chrissake? *Ebb Tide* should have been a family show. After this, they'd never sell another automobile. When *The Toronto Star* described the show as, 'Physical filth and alcoholic excess', we did what we could to calm everyone by following up *Ebb Tide* with a religious play called, *The Vigil*. Though, this production was nearly cancelled when the Virgin Mary got drunk, tripped over and smashed her front teeth.

I dashed off to a party given to celebrate Queen Elizabeth the Second's coronation. My host was a rising Canadian politician, and I was also having an affair with his wife. The party ended with a firework display. Joining in the chorus of 'Oohs' and 'Ahs', I was horrified when a firecracker whizzed up my girl-friend's dress. I ripped off the dress and doused her with bottles of lemonade. Surrounded by shocked guests, she scampered across the lawn wearing nothing but her singed

underwear. 'You bastard,' she snarled. 'You did that deliberately.' Our affair was over.

The news arrived that Pa had died, and I took the first
opportunity to return home. Taking a boat up the St Lawrence river I drank and danced the night away with a crowd of
students. The girls, many of whom were still in their teens,
were so friendly and we had a lot of fun. On the flight to
England I dwelt on the pleasures of that night, and I realized
how desperately I needed to have my freedom. I now felt I had
the strength of character to ask Barbara for a divorce.

Upon arriving in Rye this resolve abandoned me, for draped
over the porch of the front door to our cottage was a huge
banner that read: 'Welcome Home Daddy'. I was overwhelmed with emotion and tortured by renewed feelings of
guilt, and I couldn't bring myself to speak as Rupert and Jenny
tore down the garden path and into my arms. How on earth
could I now ask Barbara for a divorce?

Pa had left me two thousand pounds in his will. I gave half
to Barbara, paid off some outstanding debts, and was left with
a few hundred pounds for myself. Pa had also made small
provision for James, my half-brother, who immediately left
for India to become a tea planter. The rest of the estate went
to Mama. In the few months since her husband's death,
Mama had moved into 'College House', squandered her
six-thousand-pound legacy on wild parties and costly gifts for
favoured lady friends, and had now mortgaged 'College
House' and sold off most of its contents. I arrived just in time
to salvage two tiny pictures painted by my great-grandfather,
Sir Daniel Macnee, before they went under the auctioneer's
hammer.

My agent asked whether I wanted to do a film with Orson
Welles? Since the money was tempting and my previous
encounter with Orson interesting, I accepted, and joined
Orson and Helen Cherry in *Three Cases of Murder*.

Orson's presence dominated the film. It took him only a few

days to decide that in addition to acting he'd also handle the lighting, and within a week he was running the entire production, having ordered the director, George More O'Ferrall, into a far-off corner.

A cable arrived from David Greene urgently requesting my presence in Toronto. CBC-TV would be filming *The Duke of Darkness*, which would be shown under the title of 'General Motors Theatre'. I was keen to do *The Duke*, since I'd missed a previous production with Michael Redgrave when I'd been called up. Before I left, Barbara asked when she and the children would be joining me in Canada. My equivocal reply undoubtedly convinced my wife that I was either stalling for time or being unfaithful, two convictions that were both sadly true. I did promise to continue the regular financial payments, as though that would compensate for emotional distress. I'm sure Barbara must have known what I wanted to ask but lacked the nerve to do so. Admittedly I was confused, wondering whether staying with my family or leaving them again would be the better course to take; but certainly I departed from England feeling quite furious with myself for having balked over the subject of divorce.

The work continued to pour in, more Canadians bought televisions, our fan mail began arriving in sacks, and true to his word, David Greene had made me a star – within the city limits of Toronto. But my love affair with Gina began to go wrong. I'd discovered, somewhat belatedly, that I wasn't the only man in the lady's life, a fact that became apparent when one day I entered her home through the back door and collided with a fellow-actor coming out. Being liberal in outlook, Gina, the fellow-actor and I settled down for a drink. But if the lady was piling them in like this, surely everyone's day of reckoning would arrive when this conduct came to the attention of her husband, who was backing many of CBC-TV's commercials.

Canada had been marvellous for me in so many ways.

Admittedly, I was now on a bottle of Scotch and eighty cigarettes a day, but the relaxed attitude I'd encountered among numerous people had pierced my English upper-class crust, and I felt more cosmopolitan in outlook. I was less formal, and had developed an accent that might be described as mid-Atlantic. Although I did miss England and would have enjoyed resuming many lost friendships of my early youth, I had no overwhelming desire to return to London, where a precarious life as an actor was all I could look forward to. But I still desperately wanted to be a star, and felt a little irked that, as yet, Tyrone Guthrie had not invited me to appear in one of his prestigious Canadian theatrical productions.

Then a rumour went around that a quite spectacular production of *A Midsummer Night's Dream* was being planned, one scheduled to be shown both in Britain and the United States. The rumour turned out to be true, and it was evident that whoever was lucky enough to be given a part would be playing to audiences that included some of the most important names in the business. A telegram arrived from London. 'Doing a production of "The Dream". Hear you've become a fat lush. Lose weight and you're in.' *Bobby Helpmann and Michael Benthall.*

— 10 —

Rehearsals for *A Midsummer Night's Dream* began in a dusty room above the Old Vic. It was there that Michael Benthall as producer and director, began moulding Shakespeare's comedy into what he and Bobby Helpmann had promised would be a Hollywood-type spectacular brought for the first time to live theatre. I played Demetrius, and along with the play's other dewy-eyed lovers, Joan Benham, Maggie Courtenay, Anne Walford, Terry Longdon and Anthony Nicholls, began to create a tableau. Michael immediately took me aside, and asked in an agitated whisper whether I couldn't create what he termed a more fluid posture with those agile limbs of mine?

Back in the tableau and doing what I could to follow such vague directions, I began to fidget. Having creaked my agile limbs into a pose most appropriately described as a 'squat', I then raised a hand and asked to be excused. Taking me aside a second time, Michael issued waspish instructions as to how my role should be interpreted. When Shakespeare created the part, said Michael, he envisaged Demetrius as a Grecian heart-throb and not some tiresome juvenile who whiled away his time hanging around lavatories.

Before we broke for lunch, in whirled Bobby. A streamlined creature in a black leotard, tights and ballet pumps, he performed a cabriole or two, spun himself into a whirligig and, gliding to a precise halt, clapped his hands for silence. He told us that high standards of professional conduct would be expected throughout the production. How we behaved privately during the tour was our concern, provided it didn't give the company a bad name. Bobby settled a hostile eye upon the heterosexual actors and those he had yet to make a decision about. He issued a strict edict that his fairies were not to be molested. Dear old Stanley Holloway raised a tired eyebrow to Heaven. At his age, he told me, he'd rather sink his teeth into a chunk of steak and kidney pie.

After this pronouncement was made, Terry Longdon sought me out. A muscular blond, Terry was a great ladies' man. Since we'd be working together for some time, he explained, it only made sense to avoid arguments by settling an important matter at once. Within minutes, the two of us were casting lots for those female fairies over the age of consent.

By now, my family had moved from Rye and were living in Melbury Road, Kensington. In spite of our differences, Barbara and I agreed that London offered a broader range of educational facilities for the children. Whatever Rupert's view on the matter, he declined to confide them, preferring to ignore me. As Barbara later explained, the child had been most aggrieved at having to say good-bye to his heavy-drinking fishermen friends at the 'William the Conqueror'.

Barbara now suggested actual separation. The moment I'd so longed for and yet dreaded had come. How different it was from all the horrors I'd envisaged. No screaming, shouting or recriminations. Just two sad people discussing what they both realized had become a quite impossible situation in a quiet, resigned manner. It was agreed that I'd move out of Melbury Road, complete the tour of *The Dream*, and see what professional offers resulted. Then we would re-consider our marital circumstances.

Before the final rehearsals I was invited to audition for a part in a forthcoming film to be called *The Cruel Sea*, an adaptation of Nicholas Monsarrat's novel.

'Sorry Patrick, but you're not what we're looking for,' the casting director said tersely. Perhaps he could be a little more precise as to what he was looking for, I asked. 'You're not the naval type,' he replied. I pointed out that I'd spent four years at sea during the war and demanded that Michael Balcon, the producer, hear my case. This request was refused and remaining quite unimpressed by my protestations, the casting director gave the role to Donald Sinden who made a considerable success of the part and just about everything else he's done since.

A Midsummer Night's Dream opened in Edinburgh. With Bobby playing Oberon and Moira Shearer cast as Titania, the show was a sell out. Kilted Jocks jumped the long queue of fans which had snaked its way around the Empire Theatre. Clustered on street corners, the more commercially minded did a roaring trade in black market tickets and what they labelled 'Souvenirs from The Fairy Grotto'. Even I was offered some exotic hosiery that was described as 'the Fairy King's coronation tights'. 'Och man,' the vendor exclaimed, sliding both his arms into the tights to show off their perfection. 'There's not a ladder to be seen. Wear these and you'll have all the lassies chasing you down Princes Street.'

The Scottish capital was caught up in 'Dream' fever, and come the first night the cast found themselves sucked into this whirlwind of frenzy. There'd been a few last minute traumas to be sure, including a bloody row between Bobby and Freddie Ashton, who were jointly handling the choreography, but the entire cast went on that night believing they were poised to appear in one of the most enchanting productions of 'The Dream' that had ever been staged.

At the interval, part two of the Helpmann/Ashton row erupted. No one dared ask the cause of it, but the row soared to such a crescendo of venom that at one point I heard Freddie threatening to pull off Bobby's wings. I turned my attention to Maggie Courteney who, in her role of Hippolyta, was staggering around quite burdened down by one of her weighty and over-ornate costumes, which flaunted trains twenty-three feet in length. When actors weren't stepping on these trains, the fabrics invariably hooked themselves on to some of the nails jutting out from pieces of scenery. Had it not been for the timely warnings of stagehands, an entire set might have tumbled down. Muttering Anglo-Saxon expletives not usually associated with Hippolyta, this glamorous lady gave me a weary look that indicated the show might not be running to form.

Stanley Holloway, who was playing Bottom, ambled into the wings immersed in a copy of *Variety*. Having just concluded part two of his bloody row with Freddie, Bobby flounced past Stanley, paused, and turning on this quite innocent party, knocked off his wig. Quite unmoved by this outburst, Bottom yawned, put his wig back on and continued to read *Variety* until his call came.

In the second act, Bobby and Moira were to float across the stage suspended by wires and embrace each other. Rehearsals had been a little tricky, tangled wires causing these fairies to shoot off in unscheduled directions. But we told ourselves that it would be all right on the night. It was not to be. As the wires holding Bobby and Moira were released, not only did they sail straight past each other, but swung back again, and resembling a couple of human pendulums, continued to float back and forth in a regular 2/2 tempo. Eager to grab Moira and bring some professional competence to a show that was quickly declining into a third rate pantomime, Bobby broke into a mid-air backstroke, and lurched towards her. Just missing his fairy queen, he went careering into the scenery. The two wires then entangled and sent Bobby and Moira spinning into a giddy whirl.

The notices were not what we'd hoped for. One critic wrote 'This dream turned out to be a nightmare.' 'The cast must have been chosen for their inability to act,' wrote another, and 'A beautiful comedy mishandled under the heading of culture.' Each member of the cast scanned these vitriolic columns to see whether their own performance had warranted a special mention. They were better left unread. I felt quite humiliated when one critic described Terry and myself as looking 'disastrously funny in their costumes', adding, 'If only their performances had been as funny.' Only a liberal swig from a hip flask imbued me with sufficient courage to crawl into that outfit again.

Our sufferings did not end there, for a mob of enraged Scots besieged the theatre demanding refunds. Michael, Bobby and Freddie spent hours trying to work out a grand plan that might rescue the show. In the event it was decided to get out of town as quickly as possible and try our luck with our transatlantic cousins. Though it wasn't quite a moonlight flit, the cast and their accoutrements were hastily spirited out of Edinburgh and on to the first plane bound for the United States.

We opened at the Metropolitan Opera House in New York in a state of abject terror. Given our batterings in Edinburgh, we were astonished when both audience and critics went wild. The takings swelled to around $380,000. The box office was swamped with demands for tickets, and my address book was bulging with some most inviting telephone numbers. Amid all this optimism and fun, Bobby Helpmann was becoming increasingly outrageous. He even had the words 'Sod Off' written in gold sequins on his eyelids, which he would flutter at the slightest provocation.

The entire cast was feted by New York and there were even rumours of a ticker tape parade. This didn't come off, but we were invited to represent our country at Bloomingdale's 'British Week'. Standing against a background whose centre-piece was an M.G. balanced on Coalport cups and saucers, we didn't have very much to do except chat with the customers in our most pronounced British accents and extol the delights of Harrods and Madame Tussaud's Chamber of Horrors.

We went on a whistle-stop tour of the States. While Bobby and Moira travelled by aeroplane, the rest of us were given the run of an entire train. Maggie Courtenay bagged the prime compartment by virtue of the size and volume of her costumes. Having secured a couple of spacious rooms for ourselves, Terry and I settled down to enjoy a lengthy party. After several weeks of chasing women and boozing together, Terry and I made a resolution. The whole point of appearing in this production was to emerge as big stars, and by now Hollywood was only a couple of stops down the railroad. The two of us renounced all vice and embarked upon a rigid routine of body-building, sensible eating, early nights and abstinence from booze, baccy and birds. In Hollywood the world's most important movie moguls and casting directors would be turning out to size up the best of British talent.

We opened at the Masonic Temple Auditorium. With everyone convinced that the fabled 'Big Break' was just around a corner, we went on that night in a state of mild hysteria. Sadly we had all overlooked the fact that the Masonic Temple Auditorium was not in Hollywood at all, but in downtown Los Angeles. Far from having the power to attract the big names from Beverly Hills, it just about managed to fill itself with a responsive and enthusiastic crowd of locals. Apart from David Niven and Greer Garson, who came to cheer on their countrymen, not one big name arrived that night. The disappointment was heartbreaking. For me there was worse to come, for afterwards Michael Benthall told me I would never make a Shakespearean actor. 'You've no poetic imagination,' he said caustically.

With this remark still stinging me, I was grateful when David Niven called and offered to show me Hollywood. Picking me up from my hotel in a colourful old Buick car, David grinned and said, tongue in cheek, 'Hello, cousin.' He was undoubtedly amused by something, though what it was I felt too abashed to ask. I happily allowed him to show me around Malibu and Topanga, where I would later live, and then it was on to David's exquisite home in Pacific Palisades, where I drooled over Hjordis and marvelled at the house's marble floors.

David was very good about introducing me to agents, producers, directors and just about anyone else he believed would be useful to know. While no one had me marked as the heir apparent to Clark Gable, I was offered a lot of work. It looked as though my appearance in *The Dream* might, after all, indirectly lead to stardom. But there was no way I could appear in any American production until I'd gained a work permit.

The Dream's final performance was given on an ice rink in Toronto, where Maggie Courtenay and one of her cumbersome trains caught themselves up in a set of revolving doors. Not surprisingly, I ran into David Greene. He was doing a television production of *The Harry Lauder Show* (as *Macbeth* is known in the trade). I readily accepted his offer to play Macduff. Barry Morse, who'd been cast in the title role, gave me a warning. 'Beware,' he groaned. 'David's going through his Japanese period.' David had seen a film made on Mount Fuji, and had left the cinema quite spellbound and convinced he was the West's answer to the entire Seven Samurai. It was probably Sidney Newman who talked him out of doing a production of *Macbeth* with the cast wearing kimonos, but nevertheless David was adamant that Barry and I must pretend we were Sumo wrestlers when acting our armed combat scenes.

Altogether it was quite a family affair, with so many old friends from Canadian Television appearing in the production. Even Barry's young son was roped in to play the part of the child apparition. In spite of this conducive atmosphere, I had distinct reservations about the reception it was likely to get. I don't doubt that David had managed to fuse the tartans of Scotland with the Shinto shrines of Japan, but I felt sure that his imagination and creative powers would not be recognized by the still comparatively unsophisticatd audiences of Toronto.

On the day of transmission there were three rehearsals

before we went out on the air that night. Equipped with huge poles and David's version of Japanese flails, Barry and I stared dismally at each other's thighs, most of which were bared to the world, dressed as we were in mini-kilts. Before our major combat, Barry had a 'killing' to act his way through and prior to going on was waylaid by David.

'I want this to be rough,' he insisted. 'Remember, Macbeth was a murderous psychotic, so none of the gentle stuff. Heavy action, else this show will bomb.'

With their mini-kilts flapping about their hips, Barry and his adversary lunged at each other with convincing violence before the entire studio echoed with an agonized howl. Up in the control room David kissed whoever was fortunate enough to be standing next to him, then flung himself into that routine of agonized spasms which many directors adopt when expressing bliss.

'Oh, my God,' he raved. 'I wanted action, but never expected this. I mean, there it is for the world to see. Human blood. The real thing. Can you believe?' I could. Barry had accidentally injured his adversary who, by now, was spouting blood. Uncertain as to whether he should continue, Barry floundered momentarily, then remembering that the show was live, got back to work. As Barry's unfortunate adversary continued to be saturated with his own gore, David continued to enthuse over what he now called his 'Grit' production. With the scene completed, he immediately turned his attention to other matters leaving a minion to handle the more menial task of calling for an ambulance.

Grunting away like a couple of those Sumo wrestlers who'd so impressed David, Barry and I glared at each other with homicidal intent. A large pole whacked me on the head. Growling, I swung my Japanese flail between Barry's legs and hitched up his kilt. Although he said nothing, Barry's eyes hinted at revenge that came when I was chased around the studio and battered with the pole. Utterly exhausted and semi-blinded by sweat, the two of us squatted in the Sumo manner and continued our fight to its vengeful conclusion. Now quite blinded by sweat, neither of us could see a thing. Thumping what I assumed was Barry, I was alarmed into reality when a voice hissed, 'Watch the bloody scenery.'

Resembling a tartan Jack-in-the-box, I sprung into action, brandished the flail, kicked up my legs, and prancing over the squatting Barry, managed spectacular mid-air splits. Tumbling on to him, I went for the kill, while Barry, with his dying breath, hissed, 'You'd be great playing a decapitated chicken.'

I believe a record of this historic encounter lies deep in the archives of CBC.

Back in England, Barbara and I regretfully decided to seek a divorce. During my absence she'd met a farmer who had proposed marriage. I was delighted for her. A man of the soil seemed a much steadier prospect than a vagrant mummer, and I felt quite paternal as I gave her my blessing. At last my family might enjoy a life of contentment. In those days divorce wasn't the walk-over it is today. Having decided to go for grounds of adultery, since I couldn't think of anything else, I then had to find a lady who'd be willing to stand up in court and delight the world with an account of her bedroom antics with me. In the event, a lady did oblige. Given her 'star' status, I was grateful for her courageous act. Together with Hugh Cruttwell, who had a bit part in this legal 'soap', we left the Law Courts for a badly needed drink. Thinking back, one tiny matter concerns me. Although the lady would later be generous with her favours, I'm not sure whether at that time the two of us had actually got around to committing adultery.

I stayed with Dennis Price again in London, and continued my attempts to get a work permit for the United States. Two of the most notorious old queens in the business called me up. They were planning a production starring Katherine Hepburn, and if I was interested one of the male leads could be mine. Conscious of my alimony payments and still longing to be a star, I accepted. They then explained that a certain condition was attached to my being offered the part. I would have to join the two of them in a sandwich. Regarding this as a not unreasonable clause in my contract, I agreed. Later I mentioned the matter quite casually to Dennis Price. It was the only time I ever saw his unflappability desert him. I spelt out what kind of sandwich the old queens were referring to, and Dennis begged me to decline at once. Once again a chance to 'make it' seemed to have eluded me. But I remembered some advice Robin Darwin had given me all those years ago at Eton. 'Never, never do anything you feel is wrong, though it may be a means of obtaining work – even if you're starving.'

Having changed his tune about using me again, Mickey Powell made contact. He was filming *The Battle of The River Plate* and had a part tailor-made for me, an upper-class twit called Medley who had all of seven lines to say. I leapt at the money and the opportunity to work with, among others, John Gregson, Peter Finch and Anthony Quayle.

It was during the making of this film that I got to know Tony Quayle. A gentleman of immense kindness, Tony often gave me lifts to and from the studio in his Bentley. Upon learning of my connections with Canada, he mentioned that he would be working there soon, and suggested that if I returned, I must look him up.

I finally obtained a work permit for the United States and raced over to Hollywood, only to discover that David Niven was out of town and no one would give me a job. I must have gone on a binge, for there are about three months of my life for which I cannot account. The next thing I remember is ending up in Chicago, where, desperate to do anything that would earn me a dime, I landed a job washing dishes in a clip joint.

I checked out my contacts on the East Coast, got some offers of work and headed for New York, thumbing a lift from a truck driver. Most of the journey I spent sleeping, and awoke to find myself on the Canadian border. The truck driver had forgotten to drop me off in the vicinity of New York. Quite unmoved by my irritation, he shrugged and gave me the choice of getting out or staying put until he finished his journey in Toronto. I opted for the latter, where I cadged a room off Lorne Greene and looked around for work. I made contact with Tony Quayle, who was in New York. 'If you can get here in forty-eight hours,' he said, 'there's a job waiting for you.'

The job was a part in the forthcoming television production of *Caesar and Cleopatra*. Tony was a joy to work with, as were Jack Hawkins and Sir Cedric Hardwicke. Someone who saw this production was Archer King, one of New York's top agents, who apparently roared, 'I want that young man'. He meant me, and once more I believed my career was in the ascendant as an escalator took me up to his plush suite. Archer appraised my physical appearance, considered my work record – such as it was – checked my work permit, and I was away. Television work streamed in, my alimony payments were sent on time, and there just remained the question of moving out of a seedy hotel and into more salubrious surroundings.

After a couple of run-ins with somewhat voracious women, I went for the peace and privacy of an apartment of my own. Just as I'd begun to enjoy my own company, however, an ivory skinned blonde I'd salivated over for years, blew into town, and within days she had moved in.

Along with Claude Rains and a cast of thousands, I was given work in a television version of *A Night To Remember*, a well-documented account of the *Titanic* disaster. This play had been included in the repertoire of 'The Kraft Cheese Television Theatre', whose generosity kept me in hampers of malodorous curds for months. Playing the *Titanic*'s architect, a Scot by birth, I naturally adapted my native accent and instead of sighing resignedly, 'The ship must go down,' groaned, 'The ship must go doon.' 'No, no, no,' grumbled George Roy Hill, our director. 'Less of the Irish, please.'

A little while after the film was released, I was accosted on Lexington Avenue by a lady of uncertain years. In what must be the capital city of eccentrics, even this one stood out. Marcel waves tinted in ochre formed the crowning glory of an ensemble which comprised a diaphanous plastic mac worn over a waspie, and little else. In spite of this garish costume, the lady possessed an indefinable dignity. She asked me quite calmly whether I'd been the gentleman who'd designed the *Titanic*. Not wishing to spoil her fantasy, I nodded affably, a nod that was returned with seeming gratitude for this information. Suddenly she breathed into my face and let it be known that a murderous bastard such as I deserved to have his liver split open, and there'd come the day when as a service to humanity she'd do it herself. This was to be my first experience of the mad public.

Archer King quickly proved to be the kind of agent most actors dream about. Archer was always loath to take 'no' for an answer, and after half an hour with him, some of the most cynical and stubborn directors in the business would agree to employ actors they'd previously dismissed as quite unsuitable, a prime example being Patrick Macnee! Thanks to Archer, I was scarcely ever off the television screens of New York, and with offers still coming in from Toronto, I bought an old car and began commuting between both cities. Back in New York, I found myself rehearsing for a television show with a stunning Swede called Viveca Lindfors.

Viveca decided I needed kissing lessons, and invited me over to her flat. I knew she was married to a volatile producer, George Tabori, but nevertheless, I took this invitation as something of a come-on. When I arrived Viveca was looking ravishing in an outfit of tight black leather, and I lost no time in dragging her onto the sofa. My efforts were interrupted by the sound of applause. Covered in confusion, I got up to see

George and his children standing at the other end of the room. 'Well done, Patrick,' said George. 'You seem to have given Viveca a lesson or two of your own!' 'How would you know?' I spluttered. 'Oh, me and the kids were watching through the door.'

Tony Quayle invited me to take over the lead from Christopher Plummer in Jean Anhouil's *The Lark*. I accepted immediately. *The Lark* was playing to capacity houses on Broadway, and with my name in lights I'd be noticed by many important people in the business. My excitement turned to acute disappointment, however. I'd forgotten to update my work permit in time for the first night, and the role went to another actor. Thanks to my characteristic carelessness I'd missed a rare opportunity.

Hollywood beckoned. George Cukor was preparing for his forthcoming film *Les Girls*, and I was invited to audition. As my old car was wrecked and now lay in a swimming-pool after I'd driven it backwards at top speed through a friend's garden, I packed my belongings into a new secondhand car, kissed my girl-friends good-bye and headed west. Somewhere in the middle of America, while I daydreamed of working with Gene Kelly, Kay Kendall and Mitzi Gaynor, I discovered that the brakes didn't work. The car skidded across the road and finished up on the edge of a field. Leaving it for another sucker to pick up, I retrieved my luggage and hitched a ride to California. The first Good Samaritans to stop were a fleet of motor cyclists. With me riding pillion on one bike and my luggage strapped on several others, I rolled into Los Angeles with this crowd of early Hell's Angels as my escort.

I was unable to afford one of Tinsel Town's more plush hotels, and the Hell's Angels dropped me off at lodgings just along Sunset Strip. They had given the place a four-star rating. It turned out to be a quite appalling doss house, infested with fleas. That night, my wallet was stolen. When I went to audition for *Les Girls* all I had left was the hope that my big break had finally arrived. But I got off to a bad start when the casting director screamed that he'd wanted Leslie Phillips, not Patrick whoever he was, for the role of Sir Gerald Wren. Surely I hadn't crossed the continent in vain? Fortunately George Cukor stepped in and, suggesting I audition for a smaller part, sent me for a reading with Kay Kendall.

Kay Kendall was the personification of glamour. Sitting elegantly upon a high stool and draped in mink, Kay crossed a pair of slender legs and smiled. In my tired looking clothes, I looked like a wino compared with this chic actress. Sensing my discomfort, Kay slipped down from the stool and came across to squeeze my hands and reassure me. Just before the audition, Kay very sweetly fibbed, 'You're the image of Laurence Olivier,' thus restoring much of my confidence. We completed the reading, and the part was mine.

Shortly after the filming of *Les Girls* was completed a top agent named Hugh French asked me to look him up. Hugh had once been a singer in a trio called 'The Three Screws', and had sung and danced his way around the globe until his bunions began playing up. Donating his clogs to a museum, Hugh looked around for a new career. He bore an uncanny resemblance to David Niven, and sensibly he discounted acting as a profession, taking the view that all the parts he was suited to would probably go to Niven. He settled for being an agent and began on an exciting, if nerve-racking note when he was asked to look after the young Marilyn Monroe. Graduating to Burton, Taylor and many more of Hollywood's most glittering names, Hugh became a star agent. When the call came, I tore around to his office.

Hugh said he believed I had 'star' quality, and promised me a succession of plum roles if I could remain in town. Such praise and encouragement gave my battered ego a much needed lift. There was no reason why Hugh would waste his efforts on an actor who'd hit hard times. He got me started at once with a part in the film *Until They Sail*. Adapted from one of James Michener's novels, the script contained a good role for me as a soldier from New Zealand, and I would be working alongside Paul Newman and Jean Simmons, of whom I had such fond memories during Olivier's *Hamlet*.

I attended the premiere hoping that my performance would attract a few kind words and numerous big offers. First nights are usually an orgy of insincerity, but for me this one proved to be especially memorable. To my dismay I discovered that my entire part had been cut. As they say in the movies, I had ended up on the cutting-room floor. But this did not stop a dumb blonde from saying afterwards, 'Oh darling, you were so wonderful.'

Whilst playing Mr Rochester in a televised version of *Jane Eyre*, I received sad news from England. Barbara's marriage plans had, through no fault of her own, been cancelled. Still feeling deeply guilty about my own conduct, I now took on the additional burden of feeling personally responsible for this latest misfortune in Barbara's life.

Hugh French called. He'd lined me up to work with Eva Gabor, then gave me a dressing down. Unless I remained in California and was immediately available for auditions, he said, there was no way I'd pick up any plum parts. I responded by explaining my financial position. Hugh was sympathetic, but stressed that unless I took his advice star billing would not be mine. I didn't listen, I'm afraid to say, because soon a small matter of some embarrassment arose in my private life. Believing she was pregnant and that I was the father, an old girl friend I'd kissed good-bye to in New York had arrived in Hollywood, announced our wedding plans to a bemused film colony, and sent out a posse to look for me. I decided it was time for an engagement in Vancouver, and it was only Hugh French's frantic telephone calls that lured me back to town, where I skulked for days in the murkier recesses of the doss house. It was there that my 'intended' finally ran me to ground.

By now, the lady had decided she wasn't pregnant, but for reasons best known to herself was still determined to marry me. Not wishing to hurt the lady's feelings, I pondered how I could wriggle out of this situation with delicacy. When she went on an extravagant shopping spree for bridesmaids' dresses, wedding cakes and other nuptual gewgaws, I called a brilliant writer friend and implored him to produce a script which I could use to gently discourage the lady. 'Listen, Macnee,' this candid drunk bawled down the telephone. 'Tell the broad to beat it.'

By now I was on the bottle, biting my nails and twitching nervously. During rehearsals for a television show an irate director reminded me that I was the romantic lead and not someone afflicted with St Vitus' Dance. With the wedding day only a couple of weeks away, there seemed no way out of this predicament. Since the lady had now announced that she was genuinely pregnant, to run out could well have had a deleterious effect upon my career – though I might have eked out a living playing English cads. Even Hugh seemed pleased about the forthcoming nuptials, since he believed they would lend some respectability to my name. Middle America adored clean living family men, added to which, with a wife in tow, I'd be reasonably safe from the malicious whispers of the notorious gossip columnists Hedda Hopper and Louella Parsons.

My 'fiancée' dragged me off to some dreary party where show business and big business drank, flirted and conducted nefarious deals. I must have been there a couple of hours when I noticed that she had vanished. A few days later a cable arrived for me. Having picked up an oil millionaire, the lady I'd been due to marry had fled with him to Mexico, where they'd become man and wife. Some months later, the proud couple announced the birth of their first child to the world.

My career continued to shuttle me back and forth between Hollywood, Toronto, New York and Vancouver. Hugh French alternated between fury and despair, but I told him I simply could not afford to hang around town waiting for parts to come in. Given my alimony payments and general living expenses, it was imperative I took everything that came along, whether the location be California or The Republic of Outer Mongolia.

Shaking a mildly exasperated head, Hugh remarked that my life style and continual mishaps had all the makings of a black comedy. He offered me financial assistance, and begged me to stay in town since there could be a suitable part coming up in a new Glenn Ford movie. I was deeply touched by such kindness, but felt it only fair to decline Hugh's financial assistance, since I couldn't be sure when he'd be reimbursed. I drove up to Canada in another old car for some television work, hoping I'd make it back to Hollywood in time for the Glenn Ford movie audition. But my bad luck with cars returned, and on the way back a wheel rolled off. I dumped it somewhere in northern California, thumbed a lift into Los Angeles and chased around to Hugh's office. Hugh shook his head sadly. The part had just gone to another actor.

In spite of Hugh's continued efforts on my behalf, work suddenly became scarce. With so little money in my bank account, I had to vacate my doss house, where life had anyway become horrific. The place was heaving with drunks, many of whom were failed actors, and I'd finally decided to quit when someone was knifed outside my bedroom door. I found a tiny shack on the beach at Topanga, and slipped easily into the role of beachcomber, taking long walks along the Californian coast, regretting so much of my past and contemplating my future.

At that time Topanga Beach was a thriving colony of actors, writers, artists, directors, drunks, drop-outs and general eccentrics. Many of these people would later become part of cinema history, but in those days we avoided starvation only by chipping in to buy enormous steaks, wholesale, from a Los Angeles warehouse. I soon became part of this colony, where all-night barbeques and bathing parties were frequent events. While we continued to struggle on the beach, many of our more prosperous fellow thespians resided in splendid mansions that stood on the surrounding cliffs. It wasn't uncommon for many of them to treat their less fortunate colleagues to a decent meal.

I was one of many famished actors who scaled the cliffs to their up-market soup kitchens. I bumped into Bob Coote, who I hadn't seen since the filming of *The Elusive Pimpernel* some ten years previously. We quickly became drinking chums, and he gave me some marvellous introductions, one of which was to Gladys Cooper. The divine Gladys was still quite lovely, and proved the soul of kindness to many an impecunious actor. I became a permanent fixture at Gladys' dining table where, squeezed between Robert Morley, her son-in-law, and Robert 'Tim' Hardy, her son-in-law to be, I passed salt and pepper while these talented and highly successful individuals strove to out-wit each other.

In this celebrated company I felt terribly conscious of my poverty and lack of progress. Gladys quickly sensed this, and one day she suggested we took a stroll in her gardens. Gladys was not one to flatter, and I found it surprising that she should express the utmost confidence in what she termed my 'successful future'. Trying to cheer me up, she suggested I come to her next party, where the guest of honour would be Montgomery Clift. Gladys had become a little concerned by the conduct of some of the many invited and uninvited guests who streamed into her 'open house', and had decided to ban the riff raff and lend some tone to her parties by including many of Hollywood's biggest names on her guest list.

Kay Kendall, Gary Cooper, Rod Steiger and the very young Steve McQueen were safe bets, but I worried for Gladys' sake when she mentioned Monty Clift. He was certainly one of the cinema's biggest box office draws and a sweet man, but he was known to be drinking heavily and to have become rather unpredictable. He turned out to be exactly that. The party was in full swing when he appeared at the top of the staircase clinging to Gladys' arm and swaying a little. The couple's descent began, with Gladys inclining a regal head to favoured friends. Given her dignity, I felt inspired to lead a rousing chorus of 'God Save the Queen'. Suddenly Monty lurched forward, announced he was Kirk Douglas, changed his mind to Ava Gardner, and proclaimed that the war with Japan was over. He then crashed through the banister and landed on top of me. I glanced at Gladys. She resembled a wrathful Valhalla.

The Hollywood Depression lifted and once more work was plentiful. Finally I earned Hugh's approbation. I remained in town, directors were showing interest, I had an exemplary record for learning lines and showing up punctually, and the future looked assured. I vacated my miserable shack and moved into a house owned by a colourful lady whose steady date was a sea captain who had once been Marion Davies' lover. He had a tiresome habit of crawling into my room most nights demanding that he be allowed to sleep underneath my bed. That apart, he was a decent chap with whom I spent many absorbing hours discussing seamanship. Since I couldn't afford the entire rent for my portion of the house I advertised for a couple of flat-mates, one of whom turned out to be the irresistible Claire Bloom. I quickly realized that any overtures from me would be a waste of time. All I could do was eat my heart out and feed beached seals with tuna fish from a tin as, walking with her on the beach, she told me of her love for Yul Brynner, with whom she'd been filming.

Then I met Shalimar. Half Mexican and half Iranian, Shalimar soared to a magnificent six feet which, given her perfectly proportioned figure, made her all the more sensational to look at. A veil of blue black hair tapered off at the base of her spine, and her saucer-sized dark brown eyes expressed a sensuality that ignited my passions. Shalimar and I drove away to the rambling old house she owned by the beach at Malibu. After a night of bliss, I stared out across the Pacific watching the great breakers crash on to the white sands of Malibu Beach, and realized that this lady was no one night stand. Fortunately, Shalimar felt the same way and invited me to move in.

An academic by profession, Shalimar was the mother of a quite adorable baby whose father had vanished. Happily stepping into the role of step-father, I worked regularly and came home early at nights thoroughly contented with the stability of my newly acquired domestic environment. I sold my latest ancient car and replaced it with a gigantic station wagon. I'd begun to dream of settling down and filling the wagon with the many babies I'd give Shalimar. Hugh greeted news of this development paternally, wished me well and advised me to keep my goddam ass on the straight and narrow.

It was around this time that I renewed my friendship with Larry Harvey whom I hadn't seen since the 1940s. Now a big star and with his amorous sights set on Maggie Leighton, he promised to call if anything suitable for me should arise in any of the productions he was doing. With so much to look forward to, I ran amok in a car showroom, bought a swish sports model I couldn't afford, and took Shalimar and her baby for a hair-raising spin around Malibu. We'd barely got home when the jangle of a telephone bell echoed through the house. 'Pat. You gotta do something,' a hysterical friend screamed down the line. 'Arturo's on fire and his animals are going wild.'

Arturo was a volatile Italian who had a vast ranch that sprawled across the Malibu Hills, from where he supplied the film studios with beasts of every description. King Kongs, Christian-eating lions or swarms of mad bees – telephone Arturo and he was your man. Under Arturo's auspices, even a circus of centipedes had been licked into shape for a German princeling who'd nothing better to do than sit in his schloss and watch the insects perform acrobatics. When my hysterical friend had screamed that Arturo was on fire, what he'd actually meant was that the ranch was ablaze.

I must have been some three miles from Arturo's when I first spotted the flames, which were eating their way into the verdant hills. Swerving the car to avoid crashing branches from blazing trees and gigantic boulders that were rumbling down slopes and on to the freeway, miraculously I arrived at Arturo's without a single singe. I jumped out of the car, but found myself overwhelmed by the intensity of the heat. Swirling clouds of smoke stung my eyes, and with tears streaming down my cheeks, I broke into a bout of coughing as Arturo rushed up and thanked me for coming. 'Okay, Pat. Can you manage the elephants?' he pleaded. I inclined my head towards the sports car, and the point was taken. I finished up driving away with a car-load of eight chimps, who cowered together in the back and whimpered with fright.

I headed for Santa Monica, and soon the inferno was far away. I began to relax, and then realized that the chimps had crept up behind me and were grinning. Not one to be unsociable, I grinned into the mirror and lifted a hand in a friendly wave. Then just as the car approached a hairpin bend, a furry hand clamped itself across my eyes and an arm curled around my neck. Releasing the steering wheel, I used both hands to wrestle with this friendly arm, while the car zigzagged its way across the road at an ever increasing speed. The vehicle headed straight towards a heap of rocks on the edge of what I knew to be a ravine, and I grabbed at the steering wheel again. The car ground to a halt alongside the rocks just as flashing lights came into view and the wail of a siren cut through the still air.

The two policemen stood with arms akimbo and stared at me in disbelief as I lay there being cuddled by eight chimpanzees. When they'd separated me from the chimps they came abruptly to the point. Was I a deviant or had I just been drinking?

News of Arturo's fire had reached them, and when I explained what had happened they took the chimps into custody and followed my car to a warehouse in Santa Monica where Arturo had instructed rescuers to leave his animals. Although his eyebrows had been badly singed, all of Arturo's animals were saved. Streaked with black grime, I arrived home just in time for breakfast, which Shalimar served wearing a wet-suit. She had spent the entire night fighting another fire in a neighbour's house!

My domestic life continued to be idyllic until a lady producer invited me to lunch. She offered me a couple of lucrative roles in exchange for my body. I played at considering the deal while trying to figure out a method of getting the work without having to romp on her casting couch. In the end she dropped her carnal demand yet still gave me the roles. I announced the exciting news to Shalimar who merely shrugged and became morose, something she'd never previously been during our time together. She was sure I had slept with the producer, and refused to believe my protestations to the contrary. Shalimar's eyes became heavy with distrust, and from that day our mutual affection began to cool.

Since marriage and a family seemed to be an unattainable dream, I sold the gigantic station wagon and drove up to Toronto in the sports car. A glut of television work awaited me, work I needed badly to pay off the money still outstanding on the car. With Paul Almond as my director, I began to relax a little, but in private quite despaired of ever forming an enduring relationship with anyone. Back in Hollywood, Hugh French had all but disowned me, while Shalimar now accused me outright of being unfaithful. I pleaded and cajoled, but all to no avail. Feeling utterly disconsolate, I went out on the town, hit the bottle, picked up Elizabeth Taylor's children's nanny, and, returning to Malibu in a mood of recklessness, announced that the accusations of infidelity now had substance.

Back in the bowels of my old doss house, I had plenty of

time to regret my hotheaded behaviour and to take stock of my position in Hollywood. I had appeared in over three hundred productions on the North American continent, but I hadn't become a star. Should I remain in town? Perhaps I ought to move back to Toronto? What were the chances of steady work in Great Britain? While I posed these questions to myself, Shalimar dropped by, said we'd both behaved rashly, and asked if I would return with her to Malibu. I was delighted, but I felt instinctively that what days we might have together would be tempestuous and few. Indeed, Shalimar's distrust increased when she announced sulkily one day that some English woman had telephoned from London and wished to speak to me. God knows how she'd tracked me down, but it was Barbara.

Bringing me up to date on events, my ex-wife reminded me that Rupert was now twelve years old and Jenny coming up to ten. Having kept her word, Gussie, who had inherited Rooksnest, would be sending my son to public school, but since Eton was too pricey, the boy would have to settle for Bedford College. Feeling grateful, I didn't argue; then Barbara asked whether Rupert could spend a holiday in California. I agreed at once, and scraped the air fare together. Not having seen my son for years, I could only guess at what might appear in Los Angeles.

It was a white-faced little boy who shook my hand gravely at the airport. Although he didn't say as much at the time, he'd been badly sick during the flight, and I immediately noticed a rare dignity in one so young. The ensuing six weeks were a joy. There was so much I longed to show him, much more I wished to give him, but most of all, I ached to know my son. I took him up to Gladys' for lunch, gave him a tour of Disneyland, grinned as he squealed with pleasure in the great breakers that rolled up Malibu Beach, and took him down to one of the studios where he watched his idiot father audition for a part.

Dressed as an eighteenth-century Redcoat, I had to speak with a Scottish accent and canter around the set on horseback. When he heard I'd got the part, Rupert seemed most impressed and asked, 'But why can't you do that kind of thing in England, Pa?' When eventually I saw Rupert off on a flight destined for London, I could barely fight back the tears and knew my return to England was inevitable.

Shalimar now having acquired a new lover, threw me out. My successor arrived just as I was leaving, and passing each other in the drive we both nodded and murmured 'Good luck'. I was resigned to a further term at the doss house, but I was rescued by a British actress who'd just breezed into town. I explained I'd soon be heading for England, but the lady didn't care. We could always meet up in London at a later date, but in the meantime let's have fun.

Shortly afterwards I was flattered to receive a telephone call from Ben Hecht. Would I help him put a new play together at a theatre in Laguna, Southern California? Having accepted, I found myself involved in a sixteen-act production called *Winkleberg*. It had been written for Robert Newton, but another actor took over when Bobby got drunk and fell through a shop window. *Winkleberg* received what the trade refers to politely as 'mixed reviews', but as I was well paid, I ignored the critics and began saving up for my fare back to England. Then Ben asked me whether I'd like to make a little extra cash on the side by acting as his chauffeur. We must have stopped at every girls' school in southern California so that the 82-year-old Ben could ogle the teenage beauties. Terrified of being done on one of America's numerous morality laws, I raced out of town. 'Come on, Patrick,' Ben moaned. 'Let me have some fun.'

Larry Harvey urged me to return to Los Angeles. He was doing a television play for Alfred Hitchcock and had wangled a part for me. Ben Hecht asked if I'd give him a lift into Hollywood. Having warned the old boy there'd be no detours to girls' schools, I obliged and the two of us headed for town. He was mildly annoyed when I stopped off at a car pound, sold my motor for a profit, and bought a clapped out old van. It wasn't in keeping with his dignity, he complained, to enter the world's film capital in this way.

'Hitch' resembled a pork chop on two little legs. A producer who lusted for his leading ladies, he was fairly peremptory with actors, except for Cary Grant and Larry Harvey. He was slightly in awe of Cary Grant, while the witty Larry could easily top 'Hitch's' rather bad jokes. I asked Hitchcock for his advice on how I should play my part. Looking straight through me he replied, 'I don't know how you should play it, dear boy. Just get on with it and make sure you know your lines.'

Whilst rehearsing for the play, which was called *Arthur*, another opportunity arose for me to work with Ben Hecht. He invited me to help on the production side of a new show he'd planned, and tempted by the money, I agreed and put more effort into Ben's show than Hitch's. Consequently, I turned up to work on *Arthur* having learnt my lines on the way. I trembled in front of the camera, then completely dried up. Shaking his head sadly, Hitch said, 'You don't know your lines, do you, my boy?' I tried to make an excuse, but I was cut off. 'It's no good. You don't know your lines,' he repeated. He repeated this accusation to me many times, and with my head bowed I slunk out of the studio. This was something I've never done before or since. Amazingly, Hitch was kind enough to feature me in his next production.

It was time to leave Hollywood. Paul Almond had called from Toronto with an offer of work. Deciding to return to England via Canada, I promised to meet up with my English girl-friend in London, and went to say good-bye to Hugh French. Hugh was very kind, but his eyes registered intense disappointment as we shook hands. He asked me to look him up should I return to town, but although he occasionally telephoned, we never met again.

With my latest old van playing up there was no way it could complete a journey back to Toronto. Out of kindness I drove it into the Pacific and left it there to rest in peace. Paddling back towards the beach, I found myself surrounded by a crowd of concerned small boys.

'Excuse me, Sir, but your automobile's drowning,' one of them informed me politely. I nodded and explained I was a sea captain who'd been the last to leave his sinking ship.

After working with Paul Almond I appeared with Dame Edith Evans in a televised production of *The Importance of Being Earnest*. By now it was mid-February and Toronto was submerged in ten feet of snow. With taxis and cars in hibernation and public transport on strike, those who dared brave the elements had to skate, ski or slide around town. After the show Dame Edith swept into my dressing-room, and asked what arrangements I'd made to transport her back to her hotel. Having rounded up Eddie Mulhare, I then 'borrowed' a stretcher from the props department, wrapped Dame Edith in several blankets and tied her to the stretcher. A hostile-looking policeman eyed the two of us as we skidded through the snows of Toronto. Not wishing to be done for attempted kidnapping or any related offences, I explained that Dame Edith was my mother and had just broken her ankle. The officer said the hospital was in the opposite direction, and we eventually reached the hotel after a circuitous detour. Curious as to how Dame Edith had arrived at the television studios, I asked her. In those famous quivering tones, she replied, 'I walked, dear boy'.

With sufficient money to return to England, I arrived at the airport with minutes to go before take-off. Racing across the tarmac with a girl I'd been passionately in love with for five months, the two of us were almost sucked into the jet-stream, but made it aboard and arrived at Heathrow in April, 1960. After a television play with Diana Dors in which I played her husband, a sculptor, made love to Evie Bricusse and was battered to death by Ian Hunter with one of my own sculptures, I waited for further offers to come in. Several months later I was still waiting and, again desperate for money, I decided to give up acting and find a regular job with a steady income. For a man of thirty-eight, this would be no easy task.

Walking down Piccadilly, I heard a voice call my name and recognized the tones of a highly gifted if explosive producer called Edgar Peterson. Loaded with goodies from 'Fortnum's', Edgar peered at me between two large carrier bags, one packed with pineapples and the other overflowing with onions. 'Pat,' he began, 'How would you like to be the associate producer on a western I'm doing about Winston Churchill?'

Why Edgar thought a film about Winston Churchill would be categorized as a western, I'm not quite sure. But that was Edgar Peterson! There was further alarm when Edgar gave a press conference. Even the jaded hacks of Fleet Street were astonished to hear that a western starring Sir Winston Churchill was in the making. Edgar remained undeterred. 'Churchill', he stressed, 'had all the immediacy, urgency and understanding of a classic western,' an explanation that caused a furore. All the old admirals, generals and air vice-marshalls called emergency meetings in London's clubland where they were later seen penning outraged letters to the London *Times*.

It transpired that Sir Winston had given permission for his books on the last war to be televised as a series that would be entitled *The Valiant Years*. With Johnny Schlesinger as my boss, I started work, and thanks to Carl Foreman was given offices in Jermyn Street. Having switched overnight from actor to businessman, I interviewed and employed a team of highly competent secretaries, many of whom had worked for Churchill, got our office into some kind of order, and helped set up the London Production Unit. With a steady wage of fifty pounds a week, I could look after my family and live reasonably well myself. Having just been re-joined by the English actress I'd left in California, I moved into her Mayfair mansion and, for the time being, life looked good.

It was decided to use Laurence Olivier for the narration, but we settled for Richard Burton since he was cheaper. A flat rate of seventy-five pounds would be paid to everyone we interviewed for background. Field Marshal Lord Alanbrooke was delighted, since he could now afford to thatch his cottage, while Field Marshal Lord Alexander refused to have anything to do with us. Matters were perhaps predictably tricky with Viscount Montgomery, who declined to be interviewed for a sum under five hundred pounds. We conceded, since the money would be paid to one of this distinguished gentleman's favourite charities – the gifted offspring of indigent clergyman – and also interviewed Field Marshal Lord Slim, and Lord Mountbatten.

We feared that the most emotive and tricky interview would be that of Odette Churchill. This brave woman was tortured most horribly by the Gestapo, and later accused by some of lying about what had taken place. In view of such malice, it wasn't surprising that Odette was reluctant to discuss her war. I was put in touch with a courageous gentleman called René Burdet. Head of the Marseilles Underground during the war, René had also taken a physical battering. He understood Odette's apprehension and our nervousness, and had arranged a lunch for Odette, himself, Johnny and me. Instead of firing direct questions at her, René would pour a little wine and say things like, 'My God, do you remember when . . .?' Odette gradually opened up, and I was quite overwhelmed with admiration for her heroism. Frankly, I don't know how she endured her sufferings.

The series was highly successful. Even the military men barked with approbation. As I watched it, I began to realize how lucky my war had been. I seemed to have done so little, and I doubted whether my courage would have been up to that of the brave European resistance members who contributed so much towards ultimate victory. But the war had been over since 1945. I must forget the past and turn my thoughts to the future.

11

I was christened Daniel Patrick Macnee, and in 1960 I could scarcely imagine that I was on the brink of becoming known in one hundred and thirty countries around the world by a completely different name, that of John Steed, 'The Avenger'.

After the success of *The Valiant Years*, my resolve to quit acting hardened. Producing had rewarded me with satisfaction, an enormous sense of achievement and a comfortable living. After so many years on the stage and in front of the camera, I longed to enjoy a steady career with a lucrative income. Apart from enabling me to pay my bills, regular wages would also afford me the financial freedom to pursue those pleasures enjoyed by my sensual eighteenth-century ancestors. I dreamt of squiring beautiful ladies to grand dinners and riding thoroughbreds through the English countryside. It hadn't occurred to me that the producer's life is just as precarious as that of an actor.

Paying my alimony courtesy of public assistance, I was much obliged to the English actress I'd met in California for the generosity she lavished upon me. Upon the resumption of our relationship, she offered me the indefinite use of her Mayfair mansion, showered me with tokens of affection, and generally pampered me like an overgrown schoolboy. Indeed, as our association progressed, she seemed to take the place of the caring mother I'd always craved, and I began to detect hints of possessiveness.

I was striding down Curzon Street one evening when a delicious looking teenage girl approached and asked whether I was Patrick Macnee. I nodded guardedly, wondering how on earth she'd even heard of me. Preening myself, I enquired suavely as to how this teenage temptress could know who I was. She explained that I'd worked with her mother just before the war. I remembered her mother. Close friends we'd certainly been, but I knew that this little girl wasn't mine. I invited the girl to a bibulous dinner, after which the two of us also became close friends.

Within days I'd been thrown out of the Mayfair mansion. Having nowhere else to go, I moved myself, my diminishing bottles of Aloxe-Corton burgundy, a pair of riding boots, an oil painting of Eton and the pathetic remnants of the family silver into the girl's sleazy Pimlico bed-sitter. This situation became something of a rehearsal for the role I was to become best known for.

The girl was known by the name of 'Stockings'. By day she occasionally turned up for a typing lesson at a fashionable West End secretarial school. By night, she supplemented her income with a spot of nude modelling. Lavish as she was with her affections, and with a sweet nature, Stockings had one problem. She could not stay out of trouble. Within a month, I'd seen off a potential blackmailer, smuggled her out of a politician's bedroom, all but bribed a police officer not to report her for speeding, and cleared her bank overdraft by arranging one with my own bank. I still adored her sufficiently to continue playing Sir Galahad, but felt I had an exclusion clause when the bed-sitter was invaded by Gaston and his Huskies.

Gaston was a twenty-year-old French criminal whose scarred face was a sad testament to his lack of skill with a knife. We loathed each other on sight. For some unfathomable reason, he accused me of insulting his virility when I jokingly presented his Huskies with a sledge purchased from an out-of-work actor. In a fit of vengeful temper, Gaston smashed the sledge, swigged my Aloxe-Corton and pawned the oil painting of Eton. Trying to explain away Gaston, Stockings purred that she still adored me, but added that she was at an age when a girl needed a bit of fresh. Remembering her mother, I sighed. She would never have made a remark like that.

Given the bed-sitter's lack of privacy, I took a temporary vow of celibacy and cleared off to the theatre whenever the awful Gaston began the preliminaries of his love-making. One evening, I returned to find that the Huskies had chewed my riding boots into a mound of minced leather. I placed the silver and my other possessions in a suitcase along with the empty Corton bottles and the mound of minced leather. Stockings was in tears. I explained with considerable regret that the questionable advantages of her bed-sitter were no longer in keeping with the life-style of a gentleman.

This well-meaning if muddled girl asked whether we could remain good friends, a request I readily acceded to, though the back of my neck began to prickle when she enquired whether she could rely on me if further trouble arose. I gave my word, but suggested that Gaston might also care to help out. Shaking her head, she expressed reservations about my suggestion since, in her opinion, Gaston was rather dim. Unable to fault this view, I advised her to be grateful for what compensations the wretch could offer and cleared out.

What remained of that night I spent at the home of a retired stunt man whose wardrobe boasted a unique collection of rubber masks. Then I found a flat in Kensington High Street which I couldn't afford and moved in to contemplate how I might pay the rent. This, coupled with bills from Harrods and my tailor, meant that I desperately needed work as a producer.

Eventually the telephone rang. The caller was a brilliant producer friend from my Canadian days, Leonard White. He invited me to the theatre and dinner, and I accepted with forced gaiety, since I'd been hoping for an offer of work. On 9 September 1960, Leonard, myself and a couple of very dear Canadian friends went to see the stage version of *Passage to India*. From there we went to another theatre to catch the second act of *A Man For All Seasons*, agreeing to catch up on the first act the following night.

Over dinner Leonard mentioned a series he was working on. It was called *Police Surgeon*. It hadn't made the ratings, but whenever its star Ian Hendry appeared, women cuddled their television sets. The television bosses had decided to re-shape the show. That re-shaping would include changing the title from *Police Surgeon* to *The Avengers*, as well as introducing a side-kick for Ian.

'The side-kick's called Steed. John Steed,' Leonard informed me. 'Interested?' I shook my head and replied that nowadays I worked only as a producer. Leonard asked me what I'd done since the Churchill series, and I was forced to admit that I'd done nothing. Leonard said that any decision obviously had to be mine, but that he would advise me to consider Steed. I had to: Christmas was coming up.

Reluctantly agreeing to accept what I assumed would be a short-term contract, I was then put in touch with Sydney Newman, who I'd also known in Canada. Sydney's credits include putting hockey on the air in Canada for the first time, creating *Dr Who*, and originating the idea of the mini-series. Alternately charming and explosive, Sydney reminded me of a vacuum cleaner salesman, which is why I dubbed him 'Our Man in Havana'. He also wears glasses whose lenses resemble giant reflectors. Deliberate or not, it's an ingenious ploy. Talking with Sydney is like talking to a one way mirror. Those lenses, coupled with a cigar the size of a factory chimney, an ear-splitting voice and a passport stamped 'Secret Agent', contrive to make Sydney an awesome figure. But this awesome figure didn't always get his own way. There's a story that during a business meeting in a Montreal skyscraper, Sydney became difficult, and the eminent director Ted Kotcheff opened a window, picked up Sydney and dangled him over twenty storeys above the pavement. I'm told that Ted prefers playing his fiddle to juggling with humans, added to which he's directed some damned good films, and as for

Sydney – he's still alive and well, and puffing his giant cigars.

'Okay. So ya wanna play John Steed?'

'Who's he,' I said.

'A sidekick to the lead.'

'Oh all right,' I agreed flatly.

'What's your price?' Sydney growled

'Would you be agreeable to one hundred and fifty pounds?'

'You gotta deal.'

I had meant one hundred and fifty pounds a week, whereas Sydney thought I'd meant one hundred and fifty pounds an episode, which took two weeks to film. A scene ensued. With increasing debts to settle, I needed to stand firm. On the point of losing, I casually threw in a humorous reference to the Montreal skyscraper. Sydney emitted a stream of obscenities, called me a crook and we were in business.

When we started work, Ian Hendry and I sniffed each other cautiously. Ian's looks, energy, youth and masculinity had already made him one of the most popular actors in England, especially in that genre known as 'kitchen sink drama'. *Police Surgeon* had been re-named *The Avengers* on account of the first episode's story line. Ian played a doctor whose fiancée was gunned down by a syndicate of drug barons. My own entrance into the story came as he left some consulting rooms, when I sprung out of the shadows, tapped him on the shoulder, and offered to help avenge the girl's death. Thank God Ian agreed. His acceptance gave me nine years of work avenging some of life's more outrageous crimes. The part of the fiancée was played by Katherine Woodville. In real life she would become the second Mrs Daniel Patrick Macnee.

I had some initial difficulty in establishing a sound working relationship with Ian, and the show was beset with problems of all kinds from the beginning. Ian thought of me as an 'aristo', and it was only when we discovered our shared passion for Scotch whisky that we broke the ice. From then on we became firm friends. Among Ian's innumerable gifts was an ability to write. Suggestions from actors regarding script changes may sometimes be treated sympathetically, but there is understandable distress on the author's part when an actor not only re-writes a script but tells him that the original might have been concocted by a Barbary Ape whilst scratching its seat.

The very first episode of *The Avengers* was called 'Hot Snow'. I spent so long puzzling over the title of the script that Ian told all and sundry that Macnee was attempting *The Times* crossword puzzle. With half the cast listening he shouted, 'Just because you were grovelling before Lord Mountbatten the other month, don't think you're an intellectual.' Then, putting an arm about my shoulder, he asked whether eight across was giving me trouble. I explained I was studying the script and not a crossword puzzle. A little exasperated, I pointed to the title, 'Hot Snow'. What did it mean? If snow was hot it would melt, so wouldn't it be logical to call the episode 'Hot Water'?

'Add "bottle" and we'll all have a laugh,' replied Ian. 'Wherev'yer been? Snow is cocaine, you dope.'

The television bosses sent us their tablets of stone. Mercifully, there were only five instead of the expected ten commandments:

1. You are contractually bound to shoot just six episodes of *The Avengers*.
2. After the conclusion of the aforementioned episodes, unit and cast will be out on their necks.
3. Don't be late for work.
4. Know your lines.
5. Behave.

A barrister chum expressed concern over clause five, since what the big bosses regarded as bad behaviour hadn't actually been specified.

'So good conduct could be construed as bad conduct?' I asked.

'Patrick, dear boy, from what you've told me of this lunatic series, everything apears to be back to front, upside down and inside out.'

With Honor Blackman I later christened *The Avengers* 'The Arse About Face Show'.

Ian was furious. As a highly disciplined actor he had no objection to punctuality and word perfect lines, but as a man who valued both himself and his work highly, he felt insulted by the way these commandments had been handed down. He raged at the bosses, sometimes directly, at other times to me. He confided to me exactly where he'd like them to shove their tablets of stone.

'Physically impossible,' I protested.

'Not for poofters.'

Fond as I'd become of Ian, I found his attitude towards homosexuals mildly wearing.

Much of our early location work was done around the sleazier parts of London's West End. In those early days our wardrobe seemed to consist of one dirty mac apiece. As Ian and I jumped over the walls and hid in the alleyways of Soho, we surely resembled a couple of dirty old men on the run from police officers who'd just raided a strip joint. In fact, we were the ones chasing criminals. I remembered my barrister friend's words while tearing through such a back to front, upside down and inside out situation.

That day we were after some crooks disguised as MI5 men. In other episodes the suspects included seedy Spanish retainers and a Communist madman called Zibbo the Clown. Despite my initial doubts I began to enjoy playing Steed. What, Ian wanted to know, was the attraction, apart from being in work of some kind? I wasn't certain, but found many of the show's characters quite fascinating, related to them and relished my new-found confidence as I developed the part of John Steed.

'Don't get too involved,' Ian warned. 'It'll play hell with your private life. Oh, and another thing.'

'Yes?'

'I'm the star.' Ian looked at me sternly, and then he winked.

Stockings re-entered my life. After having rid herself of Gaston, she'd run off to Madrid with a Moroccan who claimed he was an illegitimate son of General Franco. Within a month she was back in London, penniless and fuming. The Moroccan's family ran a fairground booth in Fez, and if Stockings was to be believed, the Moroccan wasn't really a man. What she quite meant, I decided not to probe.

She quickly acquired a horde of new admirers, typed the odd letter for the then Marquis of Bristol, and stayed with me. Rehearsals didn't start until 10 a.m. in the show's early days, and this gave me time to rise at dawn, enjoy a brisk walk and prepare an old-fashioned English breakfast. Conscious of her divine figure, Stockings declined the kedgeree, preferring black coffee and cigarettes. On the mornings she worked, I'd drop her off in Belgravia, and then drive to the rehearsal room at Hammersmith. By now I'd accepted that she would not be a permanent fixture in my life, a realization that made me very sad.

The rehearsal room was always jam-packed with people yelling orders, chalking out positions and arguing over everything from lines to the exact measurements of various actresses' vital statistics. Ten days after the first rehearsal the director would at last allow cast and crew into a studio, where he'd run through a final rehearsal before filming.

One evening I arranged to meet Mama at The New Theatre where Lionel Bart's hit musical *Oliver* was running. Mama's increasing vagueness and her constant use of the royal 'We' were giving me cause for concern.

'We suspect you are about to have us confined,' she accused me in ringing tones, as we stood in the bar.

Several hundred people stopped talking. I suggested Mama lower her voice, and several hundred people strained their ears to listen.

'We are not mad,' she announced. 'Barman – drinks for all.'

I hastily changed her order and downed a Scotch, while she demolished her first gin.

Having started on her second she proclaimed, 'You will find that we are very difficult to get rid of.'

A highly competitive spirit began to develop between Ian and myself, though we remained friends. Ian believed that *The Avengers* had the greatest potential he'd ever seen in a television show, potential of global proportions. He felt that the show had an elusive quality which neither he nor anyone else was able to pinpoint. I wondered what direction Ian saw the show taking in the near future. He said that if things continued as they were the show would end up as just another boring cops-and-robbers routine. If only the two of us had more freedom to experiment, then together we could make it the most original and popular entertainment since . . . and on that, just for once he appeared stuck for a comparison.

Much of *The Avengers*' original innovation, wit and sheer lunatic brilliance emanated from Ian and the two of us were downright lucky in having an outstanding back-up team of exceptionally creative individuals, comprising many of the foremost madmen in show business. Then there were the writers, such as Philip Levene, Richard Harris, James Mitchell and Brian Clemens, and the directors and producers Leonard White, Don Leaver, Peter Hammond and many more. Bobby Fuest's designs and Johnny Dankworth's zippy jazz theme added to its distinctiveness. *The Avengers* began steering towards world-wide fame.

'Jesus!' Ian shouted, as I arrived one day for a rehearsal. 'The show's taking off.'

The Avengers was originally scheduled for showing only in The Midlands, where our Birmingham cousins gave it a thumbs up. I had sweated through and survived some twenty years of anonymity, occasionally punctuated by an odd minor theatrical success, and it took time for this good news to sink in.

'What did I tell you?' Ian enthused. 'I always knew the show would make it.'

We were signed up for another six episodes, and even cautiously encouraged to submit ideas.

Peter Hammond was an extraordinary director, with the ability to make the camera his slave. His vision on graphics and design veered towards the maniacal, but that suited me. Peter adored bizarre story lines, and appeared to be highly influenced by the decadence of the early German cinema. Peter asked Ian and me to contemplate some more interesting things to do with women. For example, couldn't we see a woman sitting on a chair in the middle of a field and dressed as one of Napoleon's marshals?

'So long as the chair's a Chippendale,' I murmured.

'Such elegance,' Peter replied, sighing. 'I love it, darling.'

The Avengers quickly became a new form of popular entertainment. For me, it brought long-overdue security. On one hundred and fifty pounds a week, my long suffering-family were being properly looked after for the first time in their lives, and I could afford to enjoy the life-style I'd been brought up to expect as part of my birthright. Patronizing the merchants of St James' and Mayfair, I took delivery of assorted delights which were sent to the Jermyn Street flat where I now resided.

Mama preferred not to notice my modest success. Over lunch in Wiltshire, I teasingly asked her whether she wasn't proud of her son. With a disdainful sniff, she pointed out that people of our background did not draw attention to themselves in this way.

Stockings left me. Her newly acquired friend turned out to be a sturdy Suffolk farmer. After Barbara's bad luck with a man of the soil, I worried for Stockings, but my fears were unfounded. A sensible man, he was a widower, a year younger than me and obviously deeply in love. I was less certain of her feelings. Essentially an honest girl, she was just a little fickle when it came to men. I asked about her feelings and she told me she truly loved him. Her reply hurt, but I was nevertheless genuinely pleased and relieved for her. I wished her luck, kissed her good-bye and prayed that it would endure for both their sakes. Stockings and her husband recently celebrated their Silver Wedding.

Back on the set of *The Avengers*, Sydney Newman was on the loose. He felt the show had a problem, and that that problem was John Steed. Sydney surveyed me through the enormous lenses of his glasses while I shifted about on a chair in front of him. 'Okay, Pat,' he said gently. 'Relax.' He began by saying that the two of us went back a long way, and I wondered whether this was a prelude to firing me.

Sydney came quickly to the point. He knew me very well and was puzzled that I, a man of such extraordinary imagination, should opt to wear such boring clothes for my role as Steed. What the devil did he mean? John Steed was more than a part to me, he was an extension of myself. And that 'self' had been shaped by eighteenth- and nineteenth-century influences. It was Mickey Powell who had said, 'Patrick, you're an eighteenth-century man'. My clothes were elegant but in such a conventional way as to make them thoroughly uninteresting. Steed's daring conduct had to be complemented by his clothes. I decided that Sydney was right, and decided also to take my cue from that supreme boulevardier, George 'Beau' Brummel. I gave away my clothes and instructed my tailor to measure me for a new wardrobe.

A short time later, dressed as an updated version of the 'Beau', I twirled on to the set. Ian goggled and took the name of the Lord in vain.

'What do you think?' I asked, desperately needing reassurance.

'That bowler . . .'

'A devil to iron.'

'You iron it?'

I nodded. 'No common bowler. One flat irons it on the side.'

'And where does the brolly fit in?'

'I prefer umbrellas to guns.'

'Listen Macnee, you might be adding a little style, but go easy on the high camp.'

Sydney strode in, spotted me and stopped dead. I thought I'd gone too far and, expecting instant dismissal, decided to go out on a pleasant note. With a gracious incline of the head, I raised my bowler to him. After a considered pause, he remarked, 'Well, it's sure as hell different.'

We filmed further episodes, and the ratings continued to rise. Ian still teased, but I knew that his banter was quite devoid of spite. By now I'd even been invited to design some of the clothes for the part of John Steed.

The bosses commissioned further scripts and the regular cheques paid into my bank encouraged me to enjoy what was now a profligate standard of living. Unfortunately John Steed was developing into a porker. A nutritionist put me on a diet of lentils, crushed oyster shells and prune juice supplemented with its pulp. She was adamant that the pulp should be taken several times daily since that was the only way I could hope to purify my system.

After I'd been on this diet for a few days Ian invited me out for a drink. We met up in 'The Grenadier' in Wilton Row. This pub's hallmark is its ceiling, which is plastered in paper currency of many denominations. It had always been an ambition of Ian's to pinch the lot. He asked what my poison would be, and I asked for a glass of prune juice. Ian looked pained, and I explained my weight problem. I don't think Ian understood, for he asked for two double Scotches. Shaking my head, I insisted upon prune juice. 'Prune juice?' the earthy barman queried. 'Never heard of it, squire.'

Ian asked what the hell I was up to, since the two of us had become such good friends. I failed to see the correlation between my diet and our friendship, and explained that although I hoped to remain on excellent terms with him, I had to lose weight. Ian still failed to understand, since he drank heavily but remained slim. When I launched into a lecture upon differences in metabolism, he just looked bewildered.

Realizing I was serious, Ian drank his Scotch sulkily, then ordered another. I had to settle for pineapple juice, which Ian sarcastically suggested I should tart up with a cherry on a stick. He was a man who felt he'd been betrayed. 'I've lost a good boozing mate,' he muttered, more to himself than to me. I asked him to try and understand. He retorted that I thought he was a lush and this was my way of trying to wean him off the bottle. Certainly I thought he was downing to excess, I said, but that had nothing to do with it. Ian and I never became enemies, but that evening the special camaraderie we had began to die.

In 1961 Equity, the actors' union, called a strike over pay rates and put the clamps on any of its members appearing in film work. Naively unaware that this would affect *The Avengers*, I turned up for work one day to find no one else on the set. When the politics had been explained to me by Dennis Price, a very elementary, but important thought came to mind. If there wasn't any work, there would not be any money. Heavily overdrawn at the bank, I sniffed about for a loan. Would the bosses pay me in advance for the next few episodes? This suggestion was received with several attacks of heart failure. I sounded out Mama, but, as always, she was on the verge of bankruptcy.

Returning to the bosses, I laid on the charm and tried for a straight loan. What, they asked, could I offer in the way of collateral? I brazenly suggested my talent. After much moaning and muttering, they handed over five hundred greasy oncers. With so much money to spend, I went berserk. Grabbing a highly surprised Barbara and Rupert and Jenny, I whisked them off to Portugal for the first decent holiday I'd been able to afford, and two weeks later returned to England quite penniless. What's more, for the next nine years I was never allowed to forget this act of charity.

Mama telephoned. It was one of her Joan of Arc days. Augustus John, an old chum of Mama's back in the thirties, had died. I shuddered and recalled the meeting I'd had with him at Rooksnest, where he'd grabbed me by the throat before warning me against catching the pox. With her erstwhile chum pushing up the pansies and periwinkles, Mama was outraged that the old boy hadn't been knighted, and was planning what might be described as a posthumous protest. She announced that she'd be chaining herself to the railings of Buckingham Palace and Number Ten Downing Street, and asked if I could arrange national press coverage. I decided to humour her by pointing out that she could not be chained to both sets of railings at once. When the physical impossibilities of such a feat had been digested, she informed me that she'd alternate.

The actors' strike lasted for many months. When a return to work was imminent, Ian informed us that he wanted to leave the show. There was pandemonium among the bosses, whose panic and discomfort delighted me. But privately I too was aghast at Ian's decision. His departure would assuredly mean the end of *The Avengers*. I gave Ian lunch and during those all too brief couple of hours, a little of the old warmth that had once existed between us flickered into life. Ian asked me to try to understand in the same way that I'd asked him to understand the business of the prune juice. Frankly, he was bored with the show. He wanted more freedom to do things his way, but was convinced that such licence would not be permitted. The lure of film contracts had finally proved too irresistible.

Ian certainly couldn't be blamed for that, but we would need a replacement for him. Ian smiled and suggested me. I shook my head. There was no way I wanted to carry the responsibility of having the show succeed or fail. Ian, very kindly, thought I'd be great with someone else as my sidekick. 'The crown and sceptre are yours, Patrick,' he said, 'though I suppose they have been for some time in the shape of that bowler and brolly.'

'Ian,' I pleaded for a final time. 'Please stay on. Without you, the show will be finished.'

He was not to be persuaded. 'Good luck, Patrick,' he said, 'and for God's sake, lay off the prune juice.'

12

The familiar pattern of my life continued to repeat itself. The Equity strike dragged on and again I descended from well-heeled gentleman to vagrant actor on his uppers. I just hoped the strike would end with all sides smiling, and that we thespians could return to earning a humble crust and the odd crate of Château-Latour. Added to the worry of industrial strife were my continued fears about the future of *The Avengers*. Given these combined concerns, I concluded there wasn't a future, and I confided my insecurities one evening to an Old Etonian chum who'd stopped by for a drink. Noting my impecunious circumstances, this affluent Honourable made a quick shopping trip to Harrods, where he generously purchased some class hooch for my empty wine rack.

The Honourable decided a stay in the country would do me good. A day or two of mud, tweeds and horses and I'd emerge refreshed and optimistic with all anxieties forgotten. I wasn't convinced but, too pre-occupied to argue, I accepted his invitation to stay with a lady who 'trained horses and gentlemen'. My anxieties faded a little as we drove through London's northern suburbs, up into Essex and on towards Constable country. Stopping his car in a lay-by, the Honourable made a bolt for a clump of bushes to answer a call of nature.

As my chum staggered out of the clump, I thought he looked in some pain. Perhaps he'd passed a stone. Noting my concerned look, he twisted his face into a gargoyle smile and drove off. From that moment on his driving became increasingly erratic. Eventually he pulled over again. What, I demanded to know, was the cause of this reckless driving? Easing himself out of the car, the Honourable dropped his trousers. I now understood both the reckless driving and the gargoyle smile. My friend had squeezed himself into a pair of tight black leather combinations whose seat was studded with an intricate pattern of drawing pins. This made-to-measure lingerie had been a Christmas gift from the lady with whom we'd be staying. By now, I'd a fair idea about our hostess with a reputation for 'training horses and gentlemen'.

We were welcomed by a large and supremely polite lady; the kind of woman one usually encounters at the Badminton Horse Trials. Childhood experiences had long ago taught me that many an odd female lurked behind the camouflage of baggy tweeds and sensible boots! Not unreasonably, I assumed that my host would be a mouse of a man. Instead, I was surprised when a tall gentleman of some authority welcomed me to his ancestral pile. Incongruously, he was wearing a silk topper perched some way on the back of his head. The tilt of that topper revived memories of my own headwear during my days as Eton's leading bookie and pornographer. I endured the predictable conventions of a weekend in the country as the clink of glasses intermingled with the tinkle of polite chatter and the incision of cut-glass accents. In some ways England hadn't changed since Mama's heyday. Then the guests were ushered into a great dining hall where my host took his place at the top end of a refectory table, still wearing that silk topper. Everyone sat down, dinner was served, but that silk topper remained in its vantage point from where it had a peerless view of upper-crust chompers.

The soup was evil. When no one was looking, I poured it away underneath the table where several Labradors prowled. Regrettably, the soup trickled down the leg of an ancient general seated on my right. The veins in his beetroot coloured face wobbled with indignation and for an unnerving moment the old boy glared at me through his monocle. 'Bloody dogs,' he muttered.

The fish that followed had obviously fled the world's ocean

some years previously. Resigned to a bad case of salmonella, I awaited the meat dish. The butler entered, blew a bugle and announced, 'The arrival of the swine.'

A vast haunch of an Oxfordshire porker made its debut. As a concession to culinary window-dressing, the porker's head, festooned with a collar of frilly paper trimmings, had been placed before the haunch. Recalling my brief career as a swineherd of Evelyn's estate, I felt certain pigs didn't have tusks and assumed we'd be dining off wild boar. My hostess later confided that it was a pig, while the tusks of an elephant shot by her father in Africa, had been added for effect.

Rising to his feet, my host, with the butler's assistance, slipped off his dinner jacket, rolled up his shirt sleeves, removed his silk topper, saluted the pig, and began to carve.

'Do yer see the brute?' snarled the ancient general. I imagine he meant the pig. My fellow-guests seemed to take this rite in their stride, except for the Honourable who fidgeted with increasing discomfort. The rite was concluded, my host rolled down his sleeves, was helped into his jacket and replaced the silk topper.

Looking directly at me, he then boomed, 'Mr Steed.'

Not wishing to disappoint a fan, I inclined my head.

'You, Sir, are one of us. It therefore goes without saying that you're a man who'd remove his bowler for a carving.'

This little episode was to have some significance, for on our return to London the Honourable launched into a lengthy critique on *The Avengers*. If the show continued to run, he suggested, a strong injection of black leather and more than a hint of sexual deviation would arouse a population still shacked by Victorian morality and hurtle *The Avengers* into the ratings. For myself, the last thing I wanted was a series designed to appeal to every kink in the country, and I treated this suggestion as nothing more than the fantasies of another pervert. I had begun to wonder, however, whether some aspects of my background and social experiences wouldn't give *The Avengers* a more unusual slant.

The Equity strike was called off in May 1962. I was summoned to appear before a board of beady eyed lawyers whose hostility reminded me of the many call-up boards I'd dodged at the beginning of the war. They warned me that if *The Avengers* was resumed, I'd be out on my neck if I so much as asked for another pound. I could only wonder who'd emerged triumphant from this industrial punch-up. As I'd guessed, without Ian the death of *The Avengers* appeared imminent. I began searching for alternative work, preferably in the field of production. As this search continued, unknown to me, Sydney and Leonard had decided to forge ahead with another series featuring John Steed as the lead. With Ian's departure, his character, Dr Keel, had been neatly written out by being sent abroad on a scholarship.

I accepted this news with cautious relief, but until the bosses actually sanctioned the idea, I still remained out of work. Added to this, an outstanding problem still remained: who would play my side-kick? Sydney's answer left me astounded. Ever the daring innovator Sydney Newman wanted a woman to replace Ian. The bosses shook cynical heads. Sydney was asked to be reasonable – a quite absurd request to make of this unpredictable gentleman. Sydney and Leonard explained they'd come up with a new concept of what a woman should be. Cynical heads continued to be shaken. There was only one kind of woman, and if Sydney and Leonard persisted with this outlandish notion, then the show would not go on.

Undefeated, Sydney expounded his theme to the bosses. At the time of the Mau Mau insurrection in Kenya, Sydney had read of a redoubtable lady whose farm had been besieged by native insurgents. With a gun in one hand and a baby in the other, this lady had managed to survive the onslaught while her husband and other children were hacked to death in the sitting room of their bungalow. Greatly impressed by such courage and coolness, Sydney wished to introduce such a female character into the series.

The character would be called Mrs Catherine Gale. Added

to the outstanding characteristics of the Kenyan heroine, Mrs Gale would also be imbued with several attributes of two further real life ladies, Margaret Bourke-White, one of *Life* Magazine's leading photographers, and Margaret Mead, the eminent anthropologist. Sydney envisaged her physically as an ice cool blonde in the Grace Kelly mould. A woman of impeccable moral standards, Mrs Gale would combine intelligence with great strength of character. She would be an ace with firearms, a judo champion, and possessed of acerbic wit, great feelings of humanity and enormous resilience.

The bosses were dumbstruck. In their world ladies such as this simply did not exist. I too realized this was quite the opposite to the conventional roles written for actresses, but I had known many such women in my own life, Evelyn, Ella 'Kini' Maillart, and Odette Churchill to name but three — women who possessed purpose and a sense of adventure that was supplemented by imagination and sheer guts. The Feminist Movement was at that time still embryonic, but the early sixties opened a chapter of history in which many considerable women would make their presence felt in worlds that had previously been the bastions of men. Indeed, how could any of us have then guessed that the pretty blonde who had recently entered Parliament as the honourable member for Finchley would later become Britain's first woman Prime Minister?

Possibly realizing that Sydney and Leonard might just have a point, the bosses went into closed session. As they argued and dithered, I busied myself replying to fan-mail that had accumulated from the previous series. Many of these letters came from smitten teenagers whose correspondence was accompanied by a photograph of the writer in a bikini or negligee. But some of the ladies, though more mature, were equally enchanting. I was greatly touched when a devoted fan, a widow, sent me the obituary of Lenny, her dog. Having parted with a lifetime's savings to have the pooch stuffed, the widow rightly felt cheated when her taxidermist failed to capture what she referred to as 'that plaintive facial expression that was so very peculiar to Lenny'.

Yet again, Sydney triumphed. After a succession of rows, scenes and threats, he talked the bosses into accepting a woman to replace Ian. Sydney's boss, Howard Thomas, and Sir Robert Clark, the overall head of ABC Pictures, felt they had probably taken leave of their senses in giving in, but there it was. Against this background of male chauvinistic resentment, Leonard took on the enviable task of auditioning some of the loveliest actresses in Great Britain for the plum role of Mrs Catherine Gale. It wasn't easy, but he finally decided upon a peach of an actress called Honor Blackman.

One look at Honor and it was tricky concentrating on anything else. Possessing a magnificent bust and the lithe hips of a boy scout, Honor was also blessed with an English rose complexion, superbly chiselled bones and honey blonde hair. Casually, I asked Leonard whether this lovely girl had a man in tow. Sensing trouble, he growled that a Mr Maurice Kauffman had placed a ring quite firmly upon Honor's finger.

Honor and I immediately established an excellent working relationship, and set about discussing the kind of partnership that should exist between Mrs Gale and John Steed. Honor understood Ian's determination that the show had to be a cut above the average 'Cops and Robbers' routine if it was to succeed and endure. As the two of us considered innumerable suggestions, we decided to put the partnership of the two characters upon a strictly formal basis. We would refer to each other as 'Mrs Gale' and 'Steed'. Why did men and women always have to end up between the sheets?

The bosses were appalled, once again. This kind of relationship would not be commercial. While Honor and I could only express dismay at such a narrow view, Sydney and Leonard backed us to the hilt, insisting that Honor play a female version of Ian's role. Professionally, a highly charged rapport had developed between Honor and myself. Unconvinced, the bosses demanded a little light romance, but the production team stood their ground, and the demand for a little light romance was reduced to a request for an occasional kiss. We still held out and won. There was much wailing and gnashing of fangs as the bosses slunk away to their plush suites quite convinced they had a flop of potentially gigantic proportions on their hands. Thrilled as I was by our victory, I hoped Honor would not insist that this on-screen propriety should embrace our private lives.

As preparations began for the 1962 series, I found myself pestered by telephone calls from the masochistic Honourable who, upon the recent death of a distant cousin, had become an earl. Longing to hang up as he burbled away for hours about his beloved black leather and drawing pins, I resorted to holding the receiver well away from my ear and learning my script as he rambled on. 'MACNEE!' a voice boomed down the wires, as I mouthed some lines of an episode called 'Mr Teddy Bear', 'ARE YOU STILL THERE?' I replied that I'd listened, enthralled, to his every word. Then, lowering his voice, the earl mentioned with genuine surprise that he couldn't understand why his recent marriage was already giving rise to problems.

Back on the set, we had to contend with problems of another kind. It had been decided to further re-vamp my wardrobe, and this resulted in a more outrageous version of my previous clothes, and the addition of embroidered waistcoats and spectacular cuff links. As I twirled and whirled around the studio in my new frills and fripperies, I transported myself back two hundred years in time.

Serious consideration was also being given to Honor's wardrobe. Given the show's public relations pitch, which had boasted that *The Avengers* was ahead of everything, Honor's costumes had to be designed by someone who could envisage what women would want to wear in six months' time. This task was undertaken quite brilliantly by Michael Whittaker, the fashion expert, who designed a unique wardrobe for Honor. Comprising tailored suits, rakish hats and knee-length boots, the clothes were outstanding, and possessed a twentieth-century style that would balance my eighteenth-century elegance. But problems arose during discussions on the clothes Honor would wear for her combat scenes.

The original plan was to have Honor equipped with a tiny .25 calibre pistol, which she'd carry in a handbag. Since this proved impractical, not to say dangerous, in moments of attack, other methods of concealment were experimented with. An under-arm holster proved cumbersome since it tangled itself up with Honor's magnificent breasts, whilst tiny daggers secreted in the same geographical region only punctured her or shredded her bra.

It was then that an imaginative and sensual mind came up with the quite novel idea of what we dubbed a garter holster. On getting wind of this the bosses streamed on to the set to give their views. Rows of glazed male eyes ogled Honor springing into action. Nothing needed to be said. In obvious concord, the glazed eyes told me that not only was the garter considered highly feminine and downright sensual, but might just compensate for what, to an unsubtle mind, was a quite sexless series. Eventually it was pointed out, however, that whatever its other advantages, the garter holster forced Honor to walk bow-legged. So, that idea landed on the rubbish heap.

I remembered René Burdet, the former head of French Resistance in Marseilles, whom I'd interviewed for *The Valiant Years*. Honor and I were packed off to René's for a course in self-defence, and Douglas Robinson, a Judo Black Belt, was brought in to teach us the basics of his art. All appeared to be going well until I noticed that Honor seemed unhappy.

'It's all right for you, Patrick,' she said. 'When someone throws you over their head, the world doesn't see your stocking tops.'

I'm not sure what inspired me to telephone my old friend Peter Arne, but possibly thinking that Peter had the answer to some of life's more interesting problems, I explained the predicament to him. It didn't take Peter long to come up with a sound suggestion. For the combat scenes, why not put Honor in trousers? Black leather trousers with a matching jerkin and boots? Of course! Why hadn't I thought of it myself. My masochistic earl had been talking about nothing else for ages. Furthermore I remembered an encounter in New York with the delicious actress Viveca Lindfors, who treated me to a 'kissing lesson', decking herself out in tight black leather pants, jerkin and high boots, an ensemble which had resembled a second and highly erotic skin. I realized Peter's suggestion could well be a winner.

Although a daring girl who was receptive to many suggestions, Honor regarded Peter and me with suspicion as we explained this idea. Giving us the kind of look that suggested we seek urgent and highly specialized medical treatment, Honor shook her head doubtfully and said, 'Oh God. Don't the two of you realize what you might be starting?' Peter looked deeply wounded by this apparent rebuff, but I pondered on the masochistic earl. I knew exactly what Honor was hinting at, and I had no wish to be held responsible for bringing that particular fetish out of the closet.

Honor weighed up the disadvantages of unusual fan-mail against the disadvantages of flashing her stocking tops, and agreed to be measured for a combat suit. But instructions came down from above that black leather should be used only as a final resort. Honor had split a pair of cloth trousers, and was fitted for a suede suit. This had to be abandoned as it failed to 'light' well on television. Groaning and gnawing their finger nails up to the elbows, the bosses could only stand by and watch as the show got out of hand. Honor graduated from red to brown to green leather, which on a black and white screen came over as black. The public went wild.

My life became a new and highly challenging adventure. It seemed as though I'd been transported back to the lunatic years at Rooksnest and Eton as the scripts became increasingly outlandish. A colonel was murdered during a television interview; Venus Smith, the show's resident night club singer, struggled for her life with a giant squid; a peer of the realm planned to overthrow the British Government; and I counteracted an order to murder a divine French film star. And there was much more to come.

Bringing all of my enthusiasm, imagination, sense of fun, and talent, such as it was, to the show, I had more fun than I could ever remember having, even as Eton's leading bookie and purveyor of smutty books. The only difference between Macnee and Steed was one between a silk topper and a bowler. I thanked fate for steering the character of John Steed in my direction. Only two years previously I'd sworn never to act again, and but for that chance meeting with Leonard White, would probably be driving to an office instead of to a studio where a television camera made my face known to thousands.

My growing fame began to cause occasional trouble with those thousands! By now, I was on quite friendly terms with Barbara, and delighted in taking her and my children, whom I hardly knew, out to Sunday lunch. But I couldn't eat in a restaurant without being recognized and stared at, especially when I dribbled spaghetti and tomato sauce down my shirt-front. 'Mum,' Rupert queried, 'why are all those people watching us?' 'It's not us they're watching dear,' came the weary reply, 'it's your father.'

Fond as I still was of Barbara, who allowed me unlimited access to our children, I had to be pragmatic and accept that a reconciliation would be disastrous for the family.

I saw in the New Year of 1963 by attending a fancy dress ball. I went disguised as a broom, and my lady partner, swathed in layers of cotton wool sprinkled with a greyish powder, represented a piece of dust. I felt I could afford to welcome the year on a note of optimism since *The Avengers* seemed to be growing in popularity by the week. My confidence was inspired not only by the ratings but by Peter O'Toole's announcement that it was only Mrs Gale who could induce him to leave the pubs before closing time.

With my career temporarily secure, I began to relax domestically and pay long overdue attention to the children I yearned to know. The sixteen-year-old Rupert was now at Bedford College, where he proved a credit to his disreputable old Pa, but I felt deeply concerned about the thirteen-year-old Jenny. Though a fan of John Steed, she confided to me that she was a bigger fan of an up-and-coming group called 'The Beatles'.

Gussie invited me down to Rooksnest. Still the owner since Evelyn's death, and also my son's godmother, she had kept her word and was paying his school fees. It was with gloomy memories that I drove westwards towards my childhood home. Looking good for her years and still startlingly alert, she ran the estate ably, and whatever ill will I'd previously felt was softened by charity that embraced not only my son, but Mama. Although immersed in good works, Mama's legs were going, her imbibing was on the increase, and her circumstances were pitifully reduced. Perhaps it was a sense of guilt at having contributed towards her old rival's ruin which prompted Gussie to allow her a tiny pension, but it has to be said that my poor Mama had done much to bring misfortune upon herself.

Back on the set of *The Avengers* I was slavering daily for Honor. When it actually came to making a pass, I was uncharacteristically reticent. Eventually I summoned the courage and sent a message requesting 'Miss Blackman to call'. Honor came in, wearing that enticing leather, slumped on to a chair and asked for a drink. She'd just concluded a rehearsal, the going had been particularly tough, and she was dead beat.

Thanking me for the drink, she raised her glass, then asked what I wanted. Forgetting my carefully rehearsed scenario, I replied bluntly, 'You.'

Honor's eyes widened and her mouth slackened with disbelief. After a few moments she stood up, placed her hands on her hips and said, 'Oh, Patrick, come off it. This is neither the time nor the place. I'm sweating like hell, my feet are killing me, I smell like a polecat and the answer's "No".'

Deeply ashamed, I apologized, and prayed she wouldn't tell her husband. From that moment on, Honor and I enjoyed a friendship that could not have existed had we misbehaved. To this very day we remain great pals and she still bosses me around!

I ran into Kate Woodville, who had so captivated Ian and me when she appeared in an earlier *Avengers* show. One look into Kate Woodville's eyes and I found myself reminded of Vivien Leigh. Kate's deep green eyes had the same kittenish quality which, accompanied by a natural seductive smile, confronted men with a bold challenge that said, 'Dare you?' Deeply attracted by Kate, I dared, took her to a party, and awoke the following morning to discover that she'd moved in with her dog, a mongrel whippet named Sheba. This was a little sudden, but I had fallen in love. I felt Kate could give me my longed-for emotional security, and I knew instinctively that we'd become man and wife. Blinded by passion, I gave no thought to the difficulties that might arise from our seventeen-year age difference.

Life had arrived at that stage of perfection which is more usually found in sweet dreams. At weekends the two of us would flee London and head for East Anglia or West Sussex. It was Kate who introduced me to the stark beauty of Norfolk and Suffolk, whose level lands stretch on and on, their flatness ocasionally broken by church spires or windmill's sails. Down in West Sussex we'd stay with Kate's parents, two of the kindest people I've ever met. There, Kate and I roamed the

South Downs, a place which would come to mean so much to me in later life.

The success of *The Avengers* gave me financial security. Still on good terms with Barbara, and very proud of my children who were growing up so quickly, I was now in a position to make up for their earlier deprivations. I could even send money to my ageing Mama. In an impulsive moment I even bought Kate a horse. The first season starring Honor and myself had been a smash hit. After our Scottish debut, clans of drunken jocks had deserted the pubs to get home in time for the show; the 'Bright Young Things' of Mayfair and Belgravia sat riveted in front of their television sets to watch us; pictures of naked ladies were removed from office walls and substituted with pictures of Honor wearing black leather; and according to the *Sunday Times* we were 'the darling of the Primrose Hill Set', though who they might be I hadn't the remotest idea.

The Spectator described the show as 'trivial'; but added that they 'loved it without reservation because it was shrewdly calculated and played with great style'. The only sour note came from a jealous writer who, having described the show as being 'empty as a dry skull', pompously expressed concern about 'the effect it must have on the people involved'. It so happened that the people involved were having the time of their lives.

A fresh emphasis was planned for the next series. Since Leonard White had left the show to run 'Armchair Theatre', his place was taken by the multi-talented John Bryce, whose broad span of interests and lively mind would come to have such a strong influence on future episodes. The writing team still included Brian Clemens and James Mitchell plus so many more outstanding talents such as John Lucarotti and Eric Paice. Under the brilliant guidance of Richard Bates, our story editor, these writers were encouraged not only to submit more daring ideas, but to regard themselves as major contributors towards the final execution of each episode. Freedom on such a scale was a rarity, and it seemed that our public relations people had been accurate in their boast that *The Avengers* was ahead of the times in everything.

Plans were made for John Steed to vanish and for Mrs Gale to be chained to a railway track in the path of an oncoming train, and new wardrobes were planned for the two of us. Imperial China and Napoleonic France became major influences in the design of Mrs Gale's outfits, and she began a vogue for gold lamé boots. While the British leather industry enjoyed it's biggest boom in years, my own wardrobe now included embroidered cummerbunds to match my waistcoats, curly bowler hats and braided pin-stripe suits, these designs being put together by myself, Mr James — a fine cutter, and Mrs Frances Bolwell the wardrobe mistress at Teddington Studios.

By this time Kate and I had moved up to Hampstead, where we enjoyed a life of utter harmony. Not only were we infatuated with each other, but our relationship was based on deep trust and immense affection. I prayed that I'd learnt from my earlier mistakes, and that this relationship would endure.

Back on the set, another row was simmering over my professional relationship with Honor. The bosses were pushing for Mrs Gale to have an affair with Steed. I was appalled. Mrs Gale was a spy, a crusader and a friend. What the bosses didn't understand was that a sexual undercurrent existed in the relationship between Mrs Gale and Steed. If this were ever expressed overtly or consummated, then the whole basis of the relationship would be destroyed. The row continued to simmer and then finally blew up. John Bryce stood his ground, and yet again the bosses were forced to slink back to their plush suites as the 'Keep Cathy Clean' faction won the day.

The show returned to the air on 28 September 1963, beginning with an episode entitled 'Brief For Murder'. I found myself in the dock at the Old Bailey on a murder charge. The script directed that I be found 'Not Guilty'. Uproar ensued when, possibly afflicted with an attack of nerves or a wicked sense of humour, Walter Swash, playing the foreman of the jury, stood up and announced solemnly, 'Guilty'.

Having disgraced ourselves by making a record called 'Kinky Boots', which achieved immortality by being nominated one of the ten worst records ever made, Honor and I were invited to a Variety Club lunch at The Savoy, where we were to be named Joint ITV Personalities of The Year. Many people who would come to personify the 'Swinging Sixties' were present, including the Beatles and Julie Christie. The lunch was spoiled by the realization that I'd have to make a speech, a prospect which quite terrified me. Over coffee, Billy Butlin, the King of the Holiday Camps, blew smoke rings at me. He continually consulted his watch like the White Rabbit in *Alice in Wonderland*. Then he looked at me and murmured, 'Look, I've got a meeting at three o'clock, so no long speeches when receiving your prize.'

I stood on the podium alongside Honor, the assembled guests clapped and cheered, the flashlights popped, and a beaming Harold Wilson offered his congratulations as our awards were handed over to us. After so many years of waiting and despairing, the moment I'd craved had arrived. At last I truly felt that I, Patrick Macnee, was a star. I was overwhelmed with emotion. A man pushed his way through a throng of people who'd crowded around me and shook me warmly by the hand. It was Mickey Powell. 'Well done, Patrick,' Mickey said through his teeth. He still spoke through his teeth. 'I always knew you'd make it.' This must sound very sentimental, but by now I was close to tears. I was in such a state that I forgot to get the Beatles' autographs for my daughter. I fell even further out of favour with her a little while later when I met the Rolling Stones, and didn't get their autographs either.

My sudden fame brought both advantages and disadvantages. I was nominated one of the 'Ten Best Dressed Men In The World', and Pierre Cardin and Hardy Amies invited me to join them in a partnership that would design mens' clothes based on the wardrobe of John Steed. Kate begged me to accept, and I'd all but made up my mind when a telephone call came from Mama. Would I visit her that weekend? Since such an invitation implied she was down on her luck, I left for Wiltshire to replenish her dwindling funds.

Mama no longer had a bank account. I recalled my similar humiliation just after the war, and handing over a wad of notes, I realized that the time had come for me to make her a regular allowance. When I could get a word in, I mentioned the Cardin/Amies offer that could make this proposition a reality. Mama was disgusted. That her eldest son had become a vulgar player was humiliation enough, but that he should also become a bespoke gents' outfitter was an indignity she'd never live down. It's a tribute to my daftness that I allowed her to talk me out of the Cardin/Amies deal.

The Avengers had by now become part of Britain's national heritage. Wallowing in the luxury of a commercially viable television series that looked like running for at least another couple of seasons, the bosses hired Julian Wintle and his assistant Albert Fennell to produce a further twenty-six episodes. Backed up by Brian Clemens, who'd become the show's new associate producer and story editor, this able trio hired a brilliant line-up of directors which included Jimmy Hill, Roy Baker and Peter Graham Scott. Just as we were poised to begin our third series, we found ourselves flattened by a quite unexpected bomb-shell. Honor announced that she'd be leaving the show.

As I had been when Ian Hendry left the show, I was convinced that without Honor *The Avengers* would be finished, and I had nightmares of myself standing once again in the dole queue. I pleaded with Honor to stay, but to no avail. Losing my temper, I snapped that Honor must be insane to walk out of the most popular television series in Great Britain. 'Cathy Gale was a child of her times,' Honor explained. 'I feel if I go on too long, I will outstay my welcome.' If Honor felt she was already going out of fashion, then how much longer did I have?

What had happened was that Honor had signed a six-figure contract with Eon Films to make a series of films, starting with *Goldfinger*, in which she'd play Pussy Galore to Sean Connery's James Bond. Not knowing this at the time, I felt homicidal and told her I thought she'd let down the series that had given her such an enormous break. In fact I launched into a tirade of fury. As a result of this row, the two of us didn't speak to each other for a couple of years, something I came to regret deeply.

As Honor hung up her leather boots for the last time, *The Avengers* team were left with the problem of finding a replacement. But there was no one who could replace Honor. I despaired. Just when I'd achieved stardom, I looked destined to lose it. Once the news was out about Honor's departure, every actress in Britain, with the possible exception of Margaret Rutherford, wanted to play the new Mrs Gale. Even Kate, much against my advice, was after the role. While the actresses pestered their agents, the bosses were closeted away in their plush suites discussing whether it was really worth their while resuming the series now that Honor had left. How things had changed! So long as the talking continued, in strictly practical terms I was an out-of-work actor with a wife, two children, an ageing mother and a girl-friend's horse to support. Desperate to escape the sheer tension of waiting for positive news, I accompanied Kate to Yugoslavia, where she was filming.

While my professional future looked precarious, I received joyful news on the domestic front. Barbara had re-married. Her new husband, Graham Foulds, was an eminent psychiatrist attached to Edinburgh University, and one of the sweetest men I've ever met. After a series of bounders, led by me, Barbara had at last found marital bliss and went off to begin a new life commuting between Scotland and Minorca, where Graham had a villa. Not only did this delightful man turn out to be an excellent husband, he was also a kindly and loving step-father to Rupert and Jenny, who were now seventeen and fifteen respectively.

On returning from Yugoslavia, I appeared in 'Divorce, Divorce', an episode of a television series called *Love Story*. I played an ex-public schoolboy whose education had barred him from anything remotely female, excluding Nanny, and who in manhood married the first lady he met. Floundering in what proved to be an unsuccessful union, he then sought solace in the company of a mad woman with artistic leanings, played in this production by the divinely mad Fenella Fielding. Fluttering her outrageous false eyelashes, Fenella said that I kissed quite well for a stiff-lipped Briton, and expressed the hope that we'd work together again.

It was to be just a couple of months before we acted together in an Armchair Theatre production of *The Import-ance of Being Earnest*. Given the clash of temperaments and general confusion that plagued this particular production, I can only express bewildered surprise that filming even got under way. By now, my concern for *The Avengers* future was so acute that I'd begun drinking, a habit that did not ease the task of learning Oscar Wilde's witty lines. Indeed, such was my state of intoxication that over a bottle of Scotch I convinced myself that Wilde had written an extremely bad play, and decided to re-write it myself.

It took Kate to bring me to my senses. As she pointed out, I was no longer working on *The Avengers*, where my altering lines had not been an uncommon practice. This was Oscar Wilde, Kate reminded me, and like Shakespeare, he could not be re-written. She was quite right. There was nothing I could add to the genius of Wilde, and in any case to tamper with a dialogue would have been to incur the wrath of the British theatrical hierarchy at a time when I had more than enough worries to cope with.

My old chum Ian Carmichael, who was also in the production, quickly realized my lines were giving me trouble, and helped solve the problem with tact and kindness. Ian lived just up the road from me in Mill Hill, and he asked whether I could give him a lift to rehearsals, as his car had gone down with a mysterious virus. Delighted to oblige, I looked forward to a few early mornings of theatrical gossip with Ian. I found myself instead being coached by him in my role. Very soon my lines were word perfect. Later I discovered that Ian had only pretended his car was disabled, thus creating a relaxed opportunity, when the two of us would be alone, to help me out. I'm not sure I could express my thanks adequately, but such an act speaks for itself.

By now my depression over the uncertain future of *The Avengers* had turned to frustration and anger. After three years of labour that had made the series into the country's top show, I'd begun to feel, possibly for the first time in my life, a sense of achievement. That I should continually be kept in the dark regarding future plans seemed not only ludicrous but downright unfair, so I confronted Howard Thomas. Shrugging, Howard claimed not to know a thing. I found myself being passed from one boss to another, all of whom claimed to know nothing.

I refused to be fobbed off with blandishments. My tolerance of the bosses was beginning to wear thin, and I asked outright what plans had been made for the next series. I was invited to several meetings at Elstree, but they were a waste of everyone's time, since much was mooted but nothing of substance decided upon.

I was now convinced that *The Avengers* was a thing of the past. I confided my fears to Ian Hendry, whom I'd met up with again quite by chance. Ian asked me if I still had faith in the show. I nodded, adding that I had no faith whatsoever in the bosses. Ian's remark about them was unprintable, though it reduced me to giggles. Then suddenly the agony ended. It was decided at a meeting to which I was not invited to go ahead with another series, though a replacement for Honor still had to be found.

I felt for Kate when, along with a bevy of gorgeous actresses, she was rejected. The hunt to replace Honor began to take on the proportions of David and Myron Selznick's hunt for Scarlett O'Hara. Finally a superb actress with a university degree and a retired missionary father, Elizabeth 'Beth' Shepherd, was named as Honor's successor. She would play the newly created role of Mrs Emma Peel. Although she was not too different in character from Mrs Gale, and had a strong infusion of leather in her wardrobe, Mrs Peel was envisaged as being a shade softer in character, and would enjoy a more warmly witty friendship with John Steed.

After many months of sheer hard work the bosses had to admit they'd made a mistake. Having watched the rushes featuring Beth in what was intended to be her first episode, they decided that in spite of her many attributes she wasn't quite right for the part, and she left the series. Once more I resigned myself to the show's instant demise and a personal future that would include a weekly appearance in the dole queue. It was all very wretched and I dreaded telling Kate that her horse would have to go.

Then a buzz went around after our producers saw an actress who'd appeared in a recent Armchair Theatre production. I did a screen test with the lady and, to my delight, found that the two of us not only enjoyed an instant rapport, but shared a similar mischievous sense of humour. I invited her to join me for dinner, and the course of our enduring friendship was set when, walking into my flat, she announced, 'I'm the Mother Superior.'

'And I'm the Garter King of Arms,' I chuckled.

It would prove impossible not to adore Diana Rigg.

13

'From Shakespeare to Steed,' screamed the headlines. But it wasn't me they were talking about, it was Diana Rigg.

A tall girl with auburn hair, wicked brown eyes and the graceful limbs of a gazelle, Diana hailed from Doncaster, but had spent much of her early life in India, where her Father had worked for the Indian Government Service. Sent back to England to complete her higher education, Diana had never considered the theatre as a profession until she was forced to appear in a school play as Goldilocks. From that moment on she pursued her ambition with single-minded determination, while the Three Bears probably got married and settled down to rear their cubs.

After a stint at RADA Diana began her career 'resting'. Given her marvellous figure, she was inundated with modelling offers. This was followed by a stint with The Royal Shakespeare Company, where she gained a solid, if tough, grounding in the craft of acting. Walk-on parts led to small speaking roles, from which she graduated to playing some of the greatest characters Shakespeare ever wrote for women. After tremendous success in *The Dream*, *Lear* and *The Comedy of Errors*, Diana and her fellow-members of the RSC were invited to perform *Comedy* before the Royal Family at Windsor Castle. With her own regal future assured as queen of the Royal Shakespeare Company, Diana was tipped for the female lead in the Company's Marat/Sade production. Instead, she opted for the role of Mrs Emma Peel. Her place at the RSC was taken by another comparatively unknown actress, Glenda Jackson.

As was to be expected, there were a few teething problems with the new series. Having given Honor the kind of adulation usually reserved for the Virgin Mary, nearly everyone had decided in advance that Diana could never expect to achieve the same impact as her illustrious predecessor. For myself, I was convinced, having enjoyed a hilarious dinner with this down-to-earth Yorkshire lass, that the series would be blessed with an actress of rare talent, and a girl who would contribute a special quality to the show — a quality quite different from Honor's, but just as effective.

It was decided there'd be little change in the guidelines already set down for the interpretation of Emma Peel. To counterbalance John Steed's preference for living in the past, Mrs Peel would be strikingly futuristic. She would be assertive but feminine. With this in mind, the wardrobe team called in John Bates and Alun Hughes, who played down the leather and replaced much of it with a more feline yet still quite lethal look. Since uncluttered designs come across more effectively on a television screen, the new wardrobe was composed of simple clothes with stark lines. At a time when Carnaby Street dictated a change of wardrobe each week, it was to the designers' credit that Mrs Peel's outfits were not only retailed with extraordinary success but also remained vogueish for several years.

To complement these more feminine clothes, the judo would eventually be eased out and replaced by Kung Fu. Since hardly anyone had then heard of the art, Ray Austin, the show's fight director, found himself under siege from fascinated film technicians demanding demonstrations and explanations. Diana quickly mastered Kung Fu, and Tai Chi, one of its cousins, which comprised a range of graceful ballet-like movements. Pretending my umbrella was an epée, I practised advanced fencing techniques. With luck, they might save me from the league of villains who would plot against John Steed in the forthcoming series.

The bosses invited me to lunch on a yacht and announced that they were on the brink of signing a multi-million pound deal for *The Avengers* in America. The show was already shown in many countries, and this capped its success. Furthermore, they told me that from now on I would have a share in the profits. I was overwhelmed. It meant real financial security for the first time in my life.

By now the schedules on the show had become onerous. Gone were the days when rehearsals began at 10 a.m. Instead, we were picked up at 5 and driven to the studio so as to be on the floor by 8.30. Since Diana and I featured in almost every shot, there wasn't time to think about anything but our work – a factor which possibly contributed to the outstanding success of that particular series. We would eventually collapse at around 7.30 in the evening. Though our hours were long and hard, for me they were enriched by the delightful presence of the extraordinary Diana Rigg.

Watching this girl act, I quickly realized that I had nothing like her dramatic ability. And not only was Diana a superbly gifted actress in both comedy and tragedy, she was blessed with a startling personality and a feeling for words. Together we'd sometimes alter scripts to suit our shared and very private sense of humour. If I had to sum up my partnership with Diana, I'd say it was not dissimilar to being bewitched by an impish kid sister.

I celebrated the New Year of 1965 with Kate, whom I'd now decided to marry. Although aware of each other's imperfections, we were maturely in love, and I was beside myself with joy. I set about planning spring nuptials.

We arranged to marry at Hampstead Registry Office that March. The bosses were jubilant over the announcement, since it would give the show some first-rate free publicity. I assumed there'd be no trouble in obtaining a few weeks off for the honeymoon. In the event I was allotted ten days. A large crowd gathered outside the registry office, and many telegrams of congratulation arrived. There was a letter from Barbara which read 'You were always such a good father to our children.' I felt sure she must have been referring to someone else. She was very kind!

I returned to work after our honeymoon in Tunisia a happy man. I had an adorable wife and a marvellous co-star. Diana and I worked in such famous *Avengers* episodes as 'Too Many Christmas Trees', 'The Man-Eater of Surrey Green', 'The Cybernauts' and 'Honey for The Prince', and I returned home each evening to relax with Kate and partake far too liberally of her scrumptious cooking.

The Avengers' fourth season opened with an episode entitled 'The Town of No Return'. Apart from a couple of snide remarks about lunacy and leather, the critics seemed well pleased, and if our fan-mail was anything to go by the viewers seemed ecstatic. I became the recipient of suggestions to perform antics I'd never dreamt of, and Diana received more offers of marriage in her few months as Mrs Peel than she'd received in her twenty-seven years as Diana Rigg. I didn't know whether to feel flattered or mildly insulted when a critic referred to John Steed as the grandfather of James Bond. Chris Plummer had told me years earlier that I'd make a good Bond, and I decided to accept the remark as a compliment which could be stored away and savoured more appreciatively in the autumn of my life.

I often feared that this success could not endure, but in my more positive moments, especially when recalling Ian's faith and determination to succeed, I could believe that the show would continue to run. If so, it would be a tribute to us all, to my fellow-actors, the writers and to the entire production team, especially Brian Clemens and Albert Fennell, who guided *The Avengers* into extraordinary realms of fantasy and sophistication. For me, however, there still remained an occasional lingering doubt that, as with my war service, I hadn't contributed enough.

Bar a few unexpected hitches, an American deal now appeared to be nothing more than a formality. This, coupled with frantic planning for a second series starring Diana and myself, lulled me into a false sense of well-being. I had no inkling of the troubles looming ahead. Having heard in a roundabout way that the bosses were finally poised to invade the American continent, I assumed Diana and I would be called upon to do a promotional tour, and there the matter would rest. In the event, Diana and I were informed that *we* would be required to sell the show in America.

The two of us left for the States in a blaze of ballyhoo. Blinded by flashlights and squashed by throngs of pressmen, I held on to Diana, but lost Kate, who was coming along for the ride. Trying to sell to America was worse than living through the Seven Plagues of Egypt. The bosses back home were like Little Bo Peeps compared to the money men of the USA. Seated in a boardroom before a pack of fat cats, I longed to vanish underneath the plush carpet. Then a stentorian voice boomed, 'Okay, Patrick. So what exactly is *The Avengers* all about?' Given sufficient time I might have written a lengthy treatise on *The Avengers*, but how was I to condense its many brilliant ideas, experiments and ventures into fantasy into a sentence?

'*The Avengers* is about a man in a bowler hat and a woman who flings men over her shoulders,' I spluttered. And with these words the deal was clinched.

All looked set for a successful launch. I was told that the money men and distributors had enormous confidence in the show's future, and that Hugh Hefner, who'd been treated to a private viewing, had said that *The Avengers* was his favourite television series. With that priceless chunk of free publicity in hand Howard Thomas telephoned to offer his congratulations on my helping to sell the show to the States. I later discovered that while I'd been sweating it out in a boardroom before that American Inquisition, Howard had been loitering in a nearby corridor just in case 'Macnee did anything silly'.

Kate and I took off for Los Angeles arriving in somewhat

better style than I had on previous occasions. On the way to Topanga Beach I stopped off at several grocery stores to settle accounts still outstanding from several years earlier. Then it was on to the colony to look up old chums. 'My God,' everyone yelled. 'You're so famous. Say, we're really proud of you.'

I showed Kate the ancient shack I'd once called home. She looked a little shocked, but her shock wasn't as great as mine when I discovered that during my absence property prices on the beach had soared several hundred per cent. Half the beach bums and drop-outs I'd known back in the fifties were now on their way to becoming dollar millionaires. We stayed in a delightful cottage rented from Stephanie Powers, and it was from here that I drove into town one morning for a business lunch with several agents who'd suddenly become wildly enthusiastic to represent my interests in America.

After such a run of good luck, perhaps it was inevitable that the Gods should turn their backs on me to bestow favours elsewhere. I began to sense that all was not well with Kate. She suddenly announced that our marriage was over. My immediate reaction was to ask myself what I'd done wrong. Had I been unkind? Had I ignored or neglected her, my head turned by success? Had I bored her? Kate denied all this, but simply said that it would be in both our interests if we parted. She would not give any reason. Of course I didn't want to let her go. Not only was I still deeply in love with her, but we'd been married barely a year. We argued the matter until I realized it would be useless to try to prevail upon her to stay. It seemed she wanted to be on her own in order to begin a new life. I had often felt this way myself, of course.

On reflection I'm convinced that it was the seventeen-year age difference between us that caused the break-up of our marriage. It couldn't have been much fun for a young woman in her mid-twenties to stay at home most evenings to cook dinner for an actor who was reduced by exhaustion to a mute wreck, and whose idea of amusement was to 'die' in front of a television set. On the same day Kate left I got a cable from my son Rupert telling me that he had been accepted at Princeton University. It was a bittersweet occasion.

I returned to England to be met by a media circus. It appeared that half of Fleet Street had turned out to greet the arrival of Patrick Macnee – minus his wife. Like me, the Press have their own job to do, but the last thing I needed was to have personal questions about my private life bawled at me in public. The headlines of the next day's papers read 'AVENGER AND HIS WIFE HAVE PARTED'. Throwing the papers aside, I poured a large Scotch and pondered the price of fame. I blamed myself for the break-up of both my marriages, for what I still believed had been the desertion of my children years previously, and anything else that might increase the pain. The telephone bell jangled. It was not another reporter, but Honor Blackman, calling to ask if I wanted to pour out my heart.

To the delight of the world's Press, Honor and I fled to Spain. To their disappointment, it quickly became apparent that the two of us were not having an affair. After a couple of late nights, numerous packets of cigarettes and God knows how many cups of coffee, I poured out my life-story. Now familiar with my upbringing and subsequent conduct and attitudes, Honor begged me to try analysis. I reacted angrily to this wise counsel. I'd endured sufficient humiliation throughout my life without suffering the final indignity of lying upon a psychiatrist's couch. But Honor begged me to consider her suggestion carefully.

By now I had moved to a pretty flat in Swan Court, Chelsea, where regular visitors included some fine friends, my daughter and my son, who was on the point of leaving for America. They were of enormous comfort at a time when I was overwhelmed with a sense of failure and longed to slip into the Slough of Despond. Rupert, though sympathetic, became quite firm with his old pa. 'Dad,' he stated, 'You must face reality.' I made gloomy visits to a divorce lawyer, and then immersed myself in a new series of *The Avengers*, hoping it would relieve me of emotional distress.

One busy evening as I skimmed through a heap of recently delivered scripts, I was surprised by a visit from Diana Rigg. I regarded this as a delightful excuse to take Diana out to dinner. Instead I had to listen aghast as she told me that she would be leaving *The Avengers*.

Preoccupied as I was with my private problems, I wasn't the best person to give Diana the advice and comfort she sought. She said how utterly miserable she felt and how, apart from me, the one person connected with the show she could trust was her driver. Diana was being paid one-hundred pounds a week, which, in the mid-nineteen sixties, was not an inconsiderable sum of money. Thanks to her the popularity of *The Avengers* had soared, and in view of this Diana felt that a salary increase would not be out of order. Her request had been slapped down by the bosses and the thought of Diana leaving increased my own dejection.

I begged Diana to stay on. By the end of that evening she'd agreed, for my sake, in a roundabout way, but subject to a pay rise. She'd been called a 'greedy bighead' in certain quarters, but I regarded her as an actress who knew her worth. I quoted Roger Moore to her, who had once said 'Okay, somebody makes five hundred pounds a week, and is then out of work for three years. It averages out at a docker's pay.' But Diana's concerns were not simply financial. She felt she had been taken for granted. She had even given serious consideration to an offer from Peter Hall to return to the Royal Shakespeare Company at half her present salary. At any rate the bosses eventually gave way, Peter Hall continued to woo Diana, and she finished up by working on the next series by day and driving up to Stratford after dark to play Viola in *Twelfth Night*.

My deep commitment to the next series not only helped take my mind off Kate, but brought the added bonus of working with some of Britain's finest actors and actresses. I was later told that the prestige of *The Avengers* was such that many people bullied their agents into getting them parts in it. It was a joy to work with old chums such as Peter Cushing, Patrick Cargill, Charlotte Rampling and Jeremy Lloyd. I also met Christopher Lee for the first time since we'd left prep school, and we both expressed surprise at how much we'd grown. Anna Quayle, Moira Lister, Nigel Davenport and Roy Kinnear also joined the gang of assorted friends and foes I'd encounter in the series. I was also fortunate in continuing to work with some quite brilliant directors whose inspiration and advice was valued by even the most experienced players. Jimmy Hill, Charles Crighton, John Moxey and Sidney Hayers – to name but a few – were masters of their craft.

If the directors had a maggot in the brain, it goes without saying that the actors were not without a kink in their horn. It was just after we'd finished shooting 'The Hidden Tiger' under Sidney Hayers' direction that I began to wonder about Ronnie Barker. The episode had opened with a knight of the realm and one of his manservants being mauled to death by someone or something unknown. After a little detective work it became apparent that this anonymous creature possessed whiskers and claws, and with these first clues to go on, Mrs Peel and I began unravelling a distinctly feline tale of mystery and murder. Having devoted a fortnight to fighting a criminal organization called PURR (The Philanthropic Union for Rescue, Relief and Recuperation of Cats) Mrs Peel and I emerged triumphant, having outwitted a team of villains led by a fellow called Cheshire and his dastardly assistants Angora and Dr Manx.

With that episode in the can, Ronnie, who'd given a quite crazy performance as Cheshire, invited me to his place for a drink. But I was perplexed when he tiptoed into his kitchen, bade me follow him and gleefully pointed at the refrigerator. He would surely be the first person I'd met who kept his spirits on ice. But instead of Scotch, Ronnie produced a pint of milk. He poured some into a glass for me, and then poured his own measure into a saucer, placed it on the floor and, going down on all fours, began lapping it up. Looking up, he gave me one of his famous beams before purring, 'I'm a ginger tom'.

I was working impossible hours that allowed little time for socializing and so I made the most of my weekends, and decided to accept every invitation offered and plunge myself into a round of gaiety. I'd no desire to become emotionally involved with anyone, but I longed for some respite from my work and from the sting inflicted by Kate's departure.

By now, given the show's popularity, many doors were opened to me. I was photographed by Patrick Lichfield and Terry O'Neill, went to the theatre with Princess Margaret, posed for pictures with Twiggy and drank vast quantities of excellent Scotch with Francis Bacon and most of the customers in all the pubs on both sides of Chelsea's King's Road.

Whenever I regaled Mama with tales of my socializing, she adopted a wistful expression. My 'Swinging Sixties' were the contemporary version of her 'Roaring Twenties'. But Macnee tribal history repeated itself in a less glamorous way when Jenny was expelled from school. Bored to her back teeth with 'O' Level examinations, Jenny and some of her friends had broken out of school one night and headed for a local party. On the way they ran into a couple of their teachers, and after a spell in solitary confinement back at school, my daughter's academic career finished on an ignominious note.

'What are we to do with the girl?' Barbara wailed at me down the telephone line. 'She's rebellious.' I packed her off to Paris to improve her French, but before we knew it she had written to say she'd met a young man, fallen in love and was heading for Madrid. I could only wonder what the youth of the day were coming to. Surely I'd have never done that kind of thing when I'd been her age? Having shown a talent for cooking, Jenny was later brought back to England and, courtesy of Graham Foulds, her kindly step-father, began a Cordon Bleu course in London. She stuck it out and graduated with full honours, later becoming one of London's top professional caterers.

A joyous moment came very soon when Kate rang out of the blue and asked whether the two of us couldn't give our marriage another chance. It was marvellous to have Kate back. Even the horse was welcome. Once more I savoured domestic bliss and went to work a happy man.

By now I knew for sure that Diana would not be staying on to do a third series of *The Avengers*. Even her nomination for an 'Emmy' and her success in being voted Actress of the Year in eighteen of the countries where the series ran was not enough to persuade her to stay. With two seasons of the show behind her, Diana wanted to broaden her experience in other areas of the profession. On the day she left I sat in my dressing-room and cried.

I was due a few weeks' holiday and decided to take Kate back to Californa. Perhaps I was tempting trouble by heading for the place where we'd first parted. We went to Malibu, where the two of us lived in a pretty little house near the beach. Sure enough, our attempt at reconciliation was short-lived. It culminated in a massive difference of opinion during a car ride, at which I asked Kate to stop the automobile, got out and walked away. Standing alongside a freeway, literally in the middle of a desert wilderness, I thumbed a lift from a highly attractive redhead who asked where I was going. I'd absolutely no idea and in turn asked the lady where she might be heading. Her destination was Palm Springs. Since this seemed as good a place as any to go, I willingly accepted the ride. I had no idea then that this town would become the Lambourn of my later life.

After some enquiries I booked in at the Canyon Club, which at that time was one of the few places, even in the United States, to boast a colour television set. Having watched a tinted episode of *The Avengers*, I woke up the following morning to contemplate my navel and my future. I ended that first day in town at the mansion of a gentleman who was known in the region as something of a holy man, 'Bull' Moses. Having kissed me, given his blessing and warned against the dangers of carnal lust, Bull Moses invited me to choose from a selection of mango, guava and prune juices. Settling for the prune, I reclined on cushions to hear the life story of this extraordinary man.

A native of Tombstone, Arizona, Bull Moses claimed direct descendancy from Johnny Ringo, of *O.K. Corral* fame. After qualifying as an attorney in Tuscon, Bull Moses practised for a while but then, bored and saddened by divorces and debts, he began to seek inner peace. He renounced his worldly goods, donned a loincloth and sandals and, taking up his staff, made for a cave in Death Valley where he fasted and prayed. After he was moved on by the police, Bull Moses trudged west towards Morongo Indian territory. Sometimes living in caves, other times resting in the local hot springs, he cleansed himself of mortal sin and at last found what had been such an elusive inner peace. With his hair now hanging down to his waist, and still wearing the loincloth and sandals, Bull Moses thanked Almighty God for his deliverance, came out of the moutains, and swore he'd devote the rest of his life to the service of humanity.

As that first memorable evening with Bull Moses drew to a close, I thanked him for his hospitality, was blessed a second time and left him some dollars for the Bull Moses Foundation. I knew then that I'd one day return to Palm Springs where, under the influence of Bull Moses, I'd re-discover myself and settle into a new life of inner tranquility.

Shortly before I left Malibu a telegram arrived to say that of the two hundred or so actresses who'd auditioned to take over from Diana Rigg, a Canadian girl called Linda Thorson had been chosen to play John Steed's new assistant, Tara King. Having lost Kate a second time, and on the point of losing Diana, I returned to Britain in low spirits.

Linda Thorson was only twenty years of age, but she had already got through a couple of husbands before coming to London to study at the Royal Academy of Dramatic Art. She was an accomplished pianist, singer, rider, ice skater, swimmer and diver, but her acting engagements were limited to several end-of-term productions at RADA and a bit part in just one professional production.

There were those who said she was far too young and inexperienced to play Tara King. Whatever professional finesse Linda may have lacked was amply compensated for by an extraordinary comic talent. A great feeling for fun bubbled out of this girl and my intuition that she'd be adorable to work with would quickly be confirmed. Given her opulent vital statistics, Linda was immediately put on a diet. In spite of these magnificent proportions, there was something about the girl that reminded me of the petite Vivien Leigh.

Unknown to me, there'd be another newcomer in our next series. John Steed was to have a superior. I wasn't too happy with this innovation until the hilarious Patrick Newell, who'd been cast as 'Mother', my boss, wandered on to the set. Like me, he'd begun life as a bewildered child in the country. He had been at RADA in a year whose intake had included Albert Finney and Peter O'Toole, and in view of this competition he'd decided to corner the market in 'heavies'. Patrick munched his way up to twenty stone, and by the time he joined *The Avengers* had a criminal past of at least two hundred villains.

During rehearsals for what would be *The Avengers'* sixth season, I cracked a couple of ribs. In an attempt to throw Linda through a window, I'd folded up under the *weight* of this delicious *weight*. I was ordered to rest for a few days, and had little to do but learn my lines and daydream. My thoughts meandered towards the show and its future. By now *The Avengers* had been running for nearly eight years. For how much longer could the show continue to succeed, I wondered?

There'd already been criticisms of the show, succinctly summed up by a critic who remarked 'Isn't the world becoming a little bored with living in this leather-lined rut?' We'd certainly advanced in many different directions since then, but in spite of the continued infusion of many clever ideas, I had a sense that time might be running out. Many people in the business were now viewing *The Avengers* as a large iced cake, a slice of which would provide a comfortable living. Where, I asked myself, had so many of the original innovators gone? We were terribly lucky in that we still had Brian and Albert giving their considerable talents and working around the clock; but even this dedication could not, I felt, save a series that seemed poised to slide. Perhaps my feelings were influenced by a general feeling of fatigue.

Almost immediately, a message came down from the bosses. Terse and to the point, it informed me I was fat, and since I seemed unable or unwilling to care for my body I had an appointment, along with Linda, with a reputable Harley Street doctor who'd supposedly written a thesis on fatsoes. That this reputable doctor later went to prison was his problem. Scribbling prescriptions on demand for a drug called Durophet, the doctor told his patients to keep taking the pills and all would be well. The weight certainly tumbled off, but I found I couldn't stop talking. I ran into Roger Moore at a party, who stared with concern and begged me to lay off drugs. I furiously denied the allegation. 'Oh, come off it, Patrick,' Roger insisted. 'You should see the pupils of your eyes. They're dilated.'

As the pressure of work on the show seemed to increase, so did my uncertainties about its future. My mind strayed back to the calming influence of Bull Moses. In a way he frightened me, yet I felt a strong need to see him again. After telephoning around, I managed to get his Palm Springs number and called him up to seek advice in this time of stress. He asked who my favourite character in history had been. I was unable to think of anyone in particular. Probing further, Bull Moses tried to draw upon the more contemplative side of my nature. Having talked me into admitting to my fascination with the monastic life of Mediaeval Europe, he instructed me to acquire a monk's habit, which I should wear only when walking out late at night. I got a chirpy Jewish tailor to measure me up for one. ('My first habit,' he said thoughtfully.) Soon I was wandering the streets of Mayfair and Chelsea, taking the view that if people wished to stare, so be it.

After having drunk our way through nineteen gallons of champagne, administered one-hundred-and-ninety-two ka-rate chops and worn thirty bowler hats, we Avengers were at last scheduled for burial. For some months the show had been dropping in the ratings and, given the stiff competition from Rowan and Martin's *Laugh-In*, our last series had flopped in the States. After eight years of avenging, I felt immense sadness over the show's demise; conversely, after eight years of working in what had now become a factory, I longed to break loose and spend a few months just roaming the beaches of southern California.

The Avengers ended on a high note when Steed, Tara King and Mother were shot into space in a runaway rocket after Miss King had inadvertently pressed the lift-off button. At the last day party on the set everyone made amusing speeches, got drunk and burst into tears. Having lost count of the good-byes I'd said, my attention was caught by the sight of Kate. She wished to make another attempt at reconciliation and I held her in my arms and kissed her. Sadly however, this latest reconciliation did not last, and shortly afterwards, we were divorced. I resolved never to marry again.

I packed my luggage, passport, visa and work permit and went for a haircut and the removal of the seedy sideburns I'd inexplicably grown for the show. Looking forward very much to California, I lounged back in the barber's chair and thought over my years as an Avenger. They'd brought the fame and money I'd always longed for. I had met some extraordinary characters, and acquired an army of devoted fans whose letters and tokens of appreciation, which once included a box of stink bombs, had always been a comfort. On the minus side I'd had to sacrifice my privacy, and I sometimes felt a failure for never having been acclaimed for my classical roles. After all, Laurence Olivier had declined to employ me except as an extra.

My musings were interrupted by a quiet and courteous voice.

'I just wanted to say,' a gentleman continued in that same quiet and courteous voice, 'how very much I've enjoyed watching The Avengers.' I listened, enthralled, as both the show and my performance were praised. Overwhelmed by his kind words and recognition, I was barely able to stutter my thanks to a smiling Laurence Olivier.

Some twenty minutes later, one of the barbers announced there was a telephone call me for. It was Laurence Olivier. He explained that on arriving home, he'd told his wife he'd just seen me at the barber's. 'Joan insisted that I call you at once to apologize, Mr Macnee,' he said. Sir Laurence had mistaken me for the actor, Patrick Magee.

— 14 —

A battered face leered in my direction. It was Richard Burton who'd just treated Heathrow Air Terminal to a brilliantly bastardized version of one of the Chorus's speeches from Shakespeare's *Henry the Fifth*. Beckoning to me as I stood in a corner with my friend, Tony Morris, Richard yelled: 'Come here, Magee. I'm off to see my wife.' He told me to replenish my glass of whisky, then invited me to sit with him on the flight we were both taking to Los Angeles. Downing what would be the first of eighteen vodkas, Richard jabbed an elbow into my rib cage and began regaling me with pieces ranging from the Bard to Chaucer, Ogden Nash and Dylan Thomas.

He told me how Sir Winston Churchill enjoyed attending his 'Hamlet' at the Old Vic – all the while reading quite loudly along with the immortal text. Cuts of any kind never disturbed him as he continued to read and enjoy the words as writ! One evening, after an interval, Sir Winston did not return to his seat. Richard assumed that the great man had given up the struggle to follow this shrivelled version of the Bard, but no. Sir Winston had simply been caught short, and found his way into Richard's dressing-room where he relieved himself.

Also helping himself liberally to Richard's brandy and leaving a note of thanks on the dressing-room's mirror, Sir Winston returned to his seat and continued his accompaniment with increased enthusiasm. He concluded his recitation with:

> 'Good night, sweet prince,
> Flights of angels
> Sing thee to thy rest –
> And a very good brandy'!

Several hours and many vodkas later I was still listening, enraptured by what should have been a private performance, though by now more than a few fascinated fellow-passengers were pretending not to listen in.

We staggered off the plane at Los Angeles, swore eternal friendship and swopped most of the gibberish intoxicated people come out with when about to part. Suffering from the after effects of jet-lag, Richard Burton and alcohol, I headed for Palm Springs, where I could try to find peace under the guiding hand of Bull Moses. Disappointment was in store. With the summer season approaching, many of Palm Springs' residents, including Bull Moses, had left for the cooler climate of the Southern Californian coast. This information was given by one of the very many aides who worked for Moses. With their crew cuts, collars and ties, and impeccable courtesy, these youthful aides were the personification of clean and decent Middle America. Underneath the crew cut, collar and courtesy, however, lurked the fangs of a piranha fish. I began to have certain reservations about Bull Moses and these reservations were confirmed by those aides, who reminded me of the Ivy League men who made up Richard Nixon's Praetorian Guard.

All the same, Bull Moses was quickly becoming to me what Rasputin must have been to the Romanovs. I longed to sit as a disciple at his feet and hear those tranquil tones once more, and asked the aide for a forwarding address. He began to bluster, and denied this request. On an impulse, I asked whether Bull Moses had gone to prison or a lunatic asylum. I quickly found myself grabbed by the shirt collar, pulled up to the aide's height and asked how much I knew. Perhaps it was the plummy English voice, but he accepted my spluttered squawks of innocence, and simply warned me to keep my face shut.

An enchanting oasis nestling in the desert near the Morongo Valley, Palm Springs is flanked to the west by the jagged peaks of a proud mountain range, and to the east by sands that sweep all the way to Arizona and Wild West country. The suburbs of Los Angeles are an hour's drive north, and Mexico the same distance to the south.

Until the nineteen-thirties Palm Springs had been something of a ghost town. Alan Ladd had been obliged to open his own hardware store there finding himself unable to purchase such basics as hammer and nails. With the advent of the predatory gossip columnist, such as the vicious Hedda Hopper and Louella Parsons, Hollywood stars locked into 'morality clauses' with the big studios used it as a bolt-hole. At weekends a stream of besotted lovers, transients and misfits streamed to Palm Springs, where a thriving colony of drunks and fornicators had by now been founded.

By the time I hit town, Prohibition and the dreaded morality clause had been long since dispensed with, and Palm Springs had become rather sedate. I was invited to fine parties whose hosts welcomed a snooty looking British actor. Later, as I roamed through the delightfully named environs of Cathedral City, Indian Wells and Rancho Mirage, I had a strong intuition that this still untamed wilderness and some of its equally unrestrained residents would assuredly make Palm Springs the Lambourn of my later years.

I left town and headed north for Malibu, where I planned to spend a few quiet weeks back on the beach. A lady I'd met at a party offered to drive me to my destination. Though past sixty she was still an attractive girl, and with the bonus of being a rich and fancy-free widow, she indulged her taste for young boys whose age more often than not hovered somewhere just around the legal limit. Thanking the lady for her kindness and about to climb out of her Rolls-Royce, I found myself entrapped by a superbly sculptured set of scarlet talons raking their way through my hair. I was ready to make a run for it, when I remembered that all my luggage was stacked in the boot. That indecisiveness cost me my virtue. The scarlet talons teased open my shirt buttons, the front seats fell back electrically, and she proceeded to behave with great mischief.

By the time this highly physical sexagenarian had administered a stupendous *coup de grâce*, I was left exhausted. Then out of the corner of my eye, I noticed a gun pointing at me from the driver's window. I blushed and fidgeted while my naked companion purred, 'Good evening, officer. How can I help you?' A handsome young policeman eyed the two of us cagily, suppressed a smirk, and put away the gun. 'Relax, Al,' he said to his fellow-officer, 'It's only a couple of oldies having a final fling.'

I chased off to Australia to appear in a production of *The Secretary Bird*. Having acquired a delicious Australian blonde as my latest girl-friend, I spent all my autumnal spare time lounging with her in bed. It was then that I made yet another of the classic Macnee blunders. A call came through fromLondon inviting me to take over from Tony Quayle in *Sleuth* in the West End. 'Oh no, darling,' I drawled to my agent, while cuddling the blonde. 'It's not really me, you know.'

If I'd had the sense to take that offer, I'd have played the lead in a West End smash that could well have led to even greater theatrical glory, and a more secure position as an actor. Hypothesis? Perhaps. But I still regret what I consider to have been utterly crass and careless conduct.

On visiting England I saw Mama, who'd just been awarded the British Empire Medal. For fifteen years she had lived in a one-room hut and worked as an official Agony Aunt for the families of British servicemen. Now retired, she was once more on her uppers. The honour apart, the news was not promising. Mama now had nowhere to live and to quote one of her medicine men: 'The old girl's legs are going.' In desperation I called up Colin and Anne Shand, two dear friends who are still madly in love after twenty-five years of marriage! They found Mama a comfortable suite of rooms in a Wiltshire hotel, but as she idled away her days drinking and smoking, it never occurred to me to have strict limitations put upon her bar bills.

Then, for the next few months I went into retreat at Malibu.

I was now forty-nine. I had attained spectacular success, international fame and new wealth, and I was no doubt the envy of more than a few people. But the rewards of a materialistic world meant little to me now. Weary, contemplative, and with many regrets, for the time being I was tired of alternating between the roles of elegant sophisticate and riotous buffoon. The time had come, not to alter my character out of recognition, but just to consider what could be learnt from the different outlooks and options which had attracted me to California.

My son came to live with me briefly and his stay was both edifying and enlightening. He had recently graduated with honours from Princeton and he had the political awareness of his generation. At his age I'd been groomed as an officer and gentleman whose duty to sovereign and country was to lead my men into war and kill. Rupert gave me a different perspective on life. Strolling the beach at Malibu, sometimes with my son, other times alone, I began to appreciate that while I'd never offer any kind of solution to even one of the problems infesting the planet, I was at least slowly shaking off more of the embedded bigotry, insularity and intolerance that had resulted from my upbringing. The further away I grew from Eton, the closer I came to Elysium.

It was perhaps coincidental, or maybe deliberate, that I went on to become an active member of a nudist colony bearing that name. Wandering around the Californian compound called Elysium, I felt no sense of embarrassment at my nakedness. It wasn't long, however, before the Press got wind of my exploits. I was now dubbed as a hippie and a nude nut. I received the wrong kind of headlines, but I didn't care. John Lennon and Yoko Ono had recently been ridiculed for spending a week in bed to publicize peace. I could only wish them well as I crept, not so much towards happiness, as towards contentment and a much longed-for peace of mind. Let the world construe as it wished, but for me, now in middle age, an exciting new life was opening up in many directions. A postscript to the nudist colony story came when, with splendid irony, I was voted the 'Best Dressed Man in the World!'

Tom McGowan, a director friend, called me up. He was driving over to Arizona to see Paul Newman, who was making a movie there, and he needed company for the ride. Tom proved to be tremendous fun, and after we'd left the set the two of us finished up in Palm Springs, where we stopped off for a few days. I went to see John Scott, an accomplished chiropractitioner and one-time physician to President Kennedy. On my first visit to John I'd been a cigarette with a man attached to it, and he had severed that umbilical cord. John approved of my reformed ways, but hinted that I should take it easy with the Scotch. That day, Thursday 17 June 1971, I renounced alcohol. In the event, it was another thirteen years before I finally won the battle.

By now I'd decided to make Palm Springs my base. The town and its inhabitants had become, and were to remain, one of the great love affairs of my life, and with more offers of work coming in from the American market than from anywhere else, it did make a lot of sense to base myself in the United States. If only there was somewhere similar in England where I could stay upon my regular visits home. But that was a treat to come. In the meantime, I bought a delightful Spanish ranch-style house in Palm Springs.

I then found myself faced with one of the greatest challenges of my career. I was again invited to appear as Andrew Wyke, this time in the Broadway production of *Sleuth*. Penned by the ingenious Anthony Shaffer, the play had originally been entitled *Anyone For Tennis?* Tony's more famous twin, Peter, had hawked the play in vain around almost every theatrical and production agency on both sides of the Atlantic. Then Tony Quayle noticed a copy of the script as it lay unwanted on Sir Ralph Richardson's coffee table. The rest became theatrical history.

Although two-thirds of my career had been spent in theatres, in my frequent moments of insecurity I would convince myself that I was not a stage actor. The role of Andrew Wyke would surely be well outside my dramatic range. Such fears were not without foundation given the actors who's previously played the part. It had first been given life by my old chum Tony Quayle, and was then played on screen by Laurence Olivier. Both are blessed with extraordinary versatility and a strong stage and screen presence. They are also highly gifted Shakespearian actors who lent an essential satanic quality to the part.

Tony Quayle had been succeeded on Broadway by Paul Rodgers, and it was now suggested that I should succeed Paul. I went to see the play in Los Angeles. The role was certainly a tempting one, but I was still unsure and, not wanting to risk a hideous mauling from the critics, I decided against it. A letter promptly arrived from Anthony Quayle. 'You must do it, Pat,' he wrote. 'The part is made for you.' Boosted by his insistence, I accepted with a sense of challenge and terror, and also hoped this acceptance would make up for my stupidity in originally declining the offer.

I spent nearly four months studying the part. I also read innumerable books on psychopaths and gained a fair idea about the particular breed of maggots writhing in Andrew Wyke's brain. I opened to a predictable bruising from Clive Barnes, the influential English critic. Then writing for the *New York Times*, he succinctly summed up my performance as 'awful'. But another was kind enough to remark that 'Macnee alone is worth the price of admission', while yet another wrote, 'Macnee communicates an undercurrent of malice and impotent rage necessary to our acceptance of Wyke's scheming'. With Tony Shaffer and a long run of packed houses giving encouragement, I began to relax, and following some extra coaching from David Greene, the mad director of my Toronto days, I grew into the part, and enjoyed sixteen months in *Sleuth*.

Playing Milo Tindle, my intended victim, was Brian Murray, a South African actor. His place was soon taken by Jordie Christopher, who, with his wife Sybil, became two of my closest friends. After her divorce from Richard Burton, Sybil had married Jordie, and when she wasn't rearing her offspring by both gentlemen, Sybil ran a club called Arthur's. One of New York's favoured night spots, it had taken its name from George Harrison, who on being asked what he called his fringed mop, simply replied 'Arthur.'

Away from the bustle and bright lights of Broadway, I played a role quite different from that of Andrew Wyke. I was now a regular visitor to the Christophers' family home, and it was as an adopted uncle that I'd go to Long Island with Jordie, Sybil and their children. There we spent weekends memorable not only for their tranquillity, but for the opportunity they gave me to reassess my views on family life. Given my own upbringing, marital failures and the punishing guilt I'd felt since abandoning my family in 1952, I was cynical about domestic fulfilment. An abandoned child myself, I still believed I'd behaved with similar irresponsibility to my own children, and felt cheated of their love. But thanks to the wise counsel of Honor Blackman, however, I had eventually sought help through psychoanalysis. I now wish I'd seen a psychoanalyst just after the war for, unknown to me at that time, it was then that I badly needed healing.

I felt intense joy during these weekends, joy for the Christophers, joy for all my happily married friends, and joy for myself. Like Jordie and Sybil, many caring chums have welcomed me into their homes with the affection more often reserved for a lost son, brother or uncle.

During my New York sojourn I became something of a regular on the television chat shows. Quelling nerve-racking memories of my quite forgettable debut as a contributor to David Frost's chat show in London, I swotted up on current affairs, memorized chunks out of encyclopaedias, learnt a few stock quips by heart and, putting together a few views of my own, went on the air, miraculously raised a few laughs and was suddenly in demand. It was on the Dick Cavett Show that I casually mentioned I'd been celibate for three years. The television company's switchboard was jammed, and I became the recipient of thousands of letters asking how the hell I'd got by. Several months later, Dick Cavett invited me to make another appearance, to monitor my progress, as it were. There'd been none. I simply no longer wanted casual affairs; perhaps this was a sign that I'd finally matured in at least one respect.

My first *Sleuth* run came to an end, and after a tour of Canada in *The Secretary Bird*, I briefly resumed my blissful partnership with Diana Rigg on a situation comedy series called *Diana*, which she was then doing for American television. After another run of *Sleuth* with Jordie, I was obliged to return urgently to Palm Springs. Not only did I have to complete my contractual obligations on the house I'd bought, but my daughter had arrived unexpectedly in California. Jenny had been working as cook to the Rolling Stones, but she suffered from severe asthma, and had been advised that a dry desert climate was more conducive to her condition. Jenny had come to Palm Springs to seek my help and I was horrified by what greeted me. My giggling bundle of fun had been replaced by an ashen-faced, gasping cripple who could scarcely walk fifty yards without falling over. I immediately had her rushed up to a Santa Monica hospital. She is a girl of rare courage, but she betrayed panic in her voice when she gasped, 'Pa, I can't breathe.'

Mercifully she recovered, but it was essential that she remain in the Californian heat. I owe so much to John Scott for the help and comfort he gave us during those terrible months. The kindness of many people was overwhelming. It was a tragic irony that it should be Jenny's medical condition that gave me the first opportunity in my life to care for her as I should have done when she was a little girl. I wondered whether this trauma wasn't a belated punishment for the desertion of my family in 1952.

Settled comfortably in California, Jenny continued to make a promising recovery and was soon sufficiently well to play a not unimportant part in the re-furbishment of my new home. Having inherited her mother's talent for interior decoration, my daughter helped turn what had previously been a drab place into an elegant but snug ideal of a Spanish ranch house. Soon the gardens blossomed with mimosa, grapefruit and lemon trees.

When Jenny appeared sufficiently well to take care of herself, I returned to Elysium. I also became a responsive pupil of John Scott, who furthered my education in the benefits of healthy living, and spent restful, but highly entertaining evenings with my old chums Mel Torme and his wife Janette Scott, and the effervescent Peter Sellers and his latest wife, Miranda Quarry. I also took long hikes on the beach, especially along the sands of La Jolla's famed Blacks Beach. Such walks had become a vital part of my life, an occasion for quiet contemplation.

Following another tour of *Sleuth*, I seemed to be crossing the Atlantic as many times as David Frost, alternating between working for American and British television networks. I journeyed to San Francisco to work with Robert Vaughn, Peter Falk and Ben Gazzara. One of the sweetest men I've ever met, Bob Vaughn kept pretty much to himself; but Peter and Ben were worried about my drinking, saying 'There's nothing worse than a reformed alcoholic.' I played the captain of a cruise ship that sailed from San Francisco to Acapulco and back; during the trip we hit a force 8 gale and again I succumbed to the bottle. Jenny met me at San Francisco, saying she'd come to take me home since rumour had it I'd been boozing. I was marched back to Palm Springs by my asthmatic daughter, where I found my movements watched until she was satisfied I'd dried out.

Another *Sleuth* tour with Jordie followed, and while I played in Chicago, Diana Rigg returned to New York to do a stage version of *The Misanthrope*. After a quick get-together with her, a surprise and an invitation arrived almost simultaneously. I'd won the 'Straw Hat Award'. Before anyone gets the erroneous idea that this award is the equivalent of an Oscar, it has to be explained that it's given for endurance as opposed to talent. I had won it for my lengthy tours of *Sleuth*. The invitation was from Keith Michell, the then Artistic Director of the Chichester Festival Theatre in England, to do a season with the company. I decided to pick up the award in New York before heading for my homeland where, in that glorious summer of 1975, I would discover England's answer to Palm Springs.

With Diana Rigg conveniently in New York, who else could I possibly invite to accompany me to the award ceremony? Making my entrance with a lady later described by *Time* magazine as Britain's greatest living actress might just inspire a director to cast me as a seasoned Romeo. Along with New York's current mayor, Abe Beame, and the luscious Margaux Hemingway, grand-daughter of Ernest and the latest modelling sensation, Diana and I giggled our way through the lunch preceding the presentation of my award.

The presentation was made by Cary Grant. Not only had Cary done his homework but, being a gentleman of immense kindness he proceeded to quite deliberately mislead the guests with a somewhat innacurate account of my career. He announced that 'The Straw Hat Award' was being given to Patrick Macnee, international star of stage and screen, who in his long and distinguished career had co-starred with Faye Dunaway, Dame Edith Evans, Sir Robert Helpmann, Vivien Leigh, Roger Moore, David Niven (his cousin!), Laurence Olivier and Jean Simmons and many more glittering names. That I'd acted with these notables was not in dispute, but far from being a co-star, I'd more usually been a humble extra. I can only bless Cary Grant for his sense of mischief and desire to imbue me with such a feeling of confidence. I was both thrilled and amused with the award, and I sent it to Mama. It might conceivably alter her views about 'That stew of raga-muffins', as she still persisted in calling members of my profession.

Heading for Chichester I realized that I scarcely knew the county of Sussex. Driving southwards, I was soon confronted by the rolling South Downs where I'd once walked hand in hand with Kate. The heavenly summer of 1975 was soaring towards its zenith. I stopped the car several times and strolled through the hamlets of Didling, Cocking, Harting and Funt-ington. It was in the churchyard at Harting that I marvelled at the shades and inhaled the scents of cowslips, foxgloves, honeysuckle and love-lies-bleeding. Ancient hedgerows ran raggedly alongside this floral spectacular, and behind the green foliage lay a rich spread of corn-coloured fields whose golden streaks complemented the softer tints of lush green meadows. Seated upon a flagstone in front of the church's porch, I gazed in wonder at the countryside of West Sussex. The landscape was totally different from that of my adopted village, Palm Springs. I'd come to Chichester to act in a play, but I'd also come home.

Made in Heaven was a jumble of fantasy and fun penned by the hilarious actor/writer Andrew Sachs. I didn't receive great reviews, but I did spend a season playing to full houses. Offstage I opened Boy Scouts' fetes, further explored the countryside, discovered West Wittering beach, which was so reminiscent of my beloved Blacks Beach in California, and to my joy found that Chichester was inhabited by a nest of enchanting loons.

I was housed in the divinely named 'Dove Cottage' where doves did indeed coo, and the bloody bell, which chimed every fifteen minutes, from the church next door kept me awake half the night. The landlord and landlady of 'Dove Cottage' were an enchanting couple called Willie and May Sauer, who resided at the larger residence of 'Pigeon House'. Willie was a German who had been captured by the British during the last war, and put to work in Sussex fields owned by May's family. Against the wishes of her family, May and Willie married after the war, and a happy marriage it proved to be.

I discovered a couple of gastronomic paradises. The 'Little London', owned by the affable though eccentric Phillip Groud, proved a treasure, and I then discovered the nearby hamlet of Chilgrove. Chilgrove boasts roughly three buildings, a smithy, a house containing an empty coffin, and the 'White Horse', one of England's finest hostelries. It is owned by Barry and Dorothea Phillips. Barry is an inspired madman. He fights to stay out of good restaurant guides, preferring to concentrate his talents and efforts on faithful customers. New arrivals are always welcome, but Barry is likely to greet them with a Highland Fling or a threat to walk on the ceiling.

For the first time in years an unrelenting sun continued to bake an already parched English countryside. Having sweated it out on stage, I'd flee to Cowdray Park to watch the Prince of Wales play polo, or attend race meetings at Goodwood with Lise, a long-standing chum who lived in London. The two of us had already enjoyed a four-year relationship based almost entirely upon correspondence, but now Lise swept into Sussex, creating mayhem wherever the two of us went, and cheerfully all but wrecked the years of good work done by my team of psychoanalysts.

I received an urgent message from Colin and Anne Shand. Mama was playing up and this time it was serious. More than at home in her Wiltshire hotel, she'd been running up bar bills of three hundred pounds a week, had tumbled off a bar stool and cracked a couple of ribs, and to my mortification, displayed the 'Straw Hat Award' in a prominent position at her favourite boozer. Accompanied by Lise, I walked into that hotel bar only to find Mama back on her stool, from where she'd ordered drinks for all in a voice whose volume was remarkable for a female octogenarian. I began to colour.

'My son, Patrick Macnee,' she trumpeted.

That everyone should toast me with drinks I'd be paying for was most kind, but what to do with Mama? I arranged a limit on her bar bills, but before I could make further plans for her well-being, *Made in Heaven* drew to the end of its run, I had to consider a theatrical engagement in America, and my British agent telephoned. Would I be interested in joining Linda Thorsen to make a champagne advertisement for French television?

Of all the *Avengers* girls Linda had been the most popular in France. Upon discovering that I was in England, the directors of Laurent Perrier had immediately made plans for Linda and me to team up as John Steed and Tara King for a television film to advertise their champagne. On my last day at Chichester I left 'Dove Cottage' before dawn and motored to Elstree to film the commercial before tearing back to Chichester for the play's final performance that night. The commercial's producer, a Frenchman called Rudolf Roffi, was a pleasant and plausible gentleman who asked me whether I'd be interested in making another series of *The Avengers*. I shook my head. The series had become something of a television classic. Taking the view that a re-make could not possibly come up to the standards of the original, I gave the matter no further thought.

Up at The 'White Horse', Lise and I struggled through a tearful farewell lunch. She gave me a copy of Graham Greene's book *Lord Rochester's Monkey*, a biography of one of England's most notorious hell-rakes during the reign of Charles the Second. Inside she wrote, 'Thank you, Patrick, for the summer of the doves.' The peace I had enjoyed that summer had been a rarity in my frantic life.

I joined a production of Alan Ayckbourn's play *Absurd Person Singular* that toured Canada and America with a cast including Judy Carne, Sheila Macrae and Betsy von Furstenberg. The critic on *The Toronto Star* was kind enough to describe me as 'the best of an absurdly inept lot', and with this echoing in our ears, we got the hell out of town and headed for the US border. It was when we were playing in Chicago that I was offered another television advertisement scheduled for shooting in New York. The management kindly gave me a couple of days off, and with a competent understudy taking over my role, I travelled east without a care in the world and returned feeling equally at ease and with a plump cheque now in my bank.

Trouble had flared in my absence. During the first act Betsy von Furstenberg had quite accidentally spilled a glass of wine onto Judy Carne's costume. Tragically, Judy has over the years had problems with drugs. Whether or not she was high that night I don't know, but before a packed theatre that included Sheila Macrae's devout Christian Scientist family in the front row, Judy turned on Betsy, accused her of spilling the wine deliberately, and issued a string of startling expletives. Uncertain as to whether this outburst was part of the script, the audience sat numbed. Then a fight broke out and as the two of them rolled across the stage clawing and kicking, Sheila went up to the footlights and, sinking to her knees, invited the audience to join her in prayer. The curtain came down, the two actresses were separated, and refunds given to the many who asked. After that exciting improvization, *Absurd Person Singular* did not run for much longer.

I went back to Los Angeles to play Dr Watson in a Sherlock Holmes television production with Roger Moore. I was looking forward to a Christmas break when a heap of fan mail arrived from England. One of them read,

Dear John Steed,

Just in case you didn't know, the Sex Discrimination Act is about to become law. Although the sufferings of women in Great Britain were first highlighted by Mrs Pankhurst and her brave Suffragettes, you have also done so much to further our emancipation. You treated Mrs Gale, Mrs Peel and Miss King with an unusual degree of intelligence and civilization that is rarely found in men. Women are your equals and not your inferiors. I congratulate you for your vision.

Yours sincerely, an Educated Feminist and Nice Girl.

I wondered how the old bats at Rooksnest would have reacted to the apparent influence being wielded upon the fair sex by 'that terrible boy' whose trousers they'd taken away.

The Avengers was on again, backed by French money and re-named *The New Avengers*. As always I'd been told very little, but I later discovered that the sacking of Steed had been suggested. The French, however, did not want Steed replaced by a new and younger man, and were poised to return to Paris unless given assurance that I would remain in the series. After further meetings it was settled that I would be assisted by a junior team that comprised one female and one male agent.

Once again a search was on, this time for a girl to succeed Honor, Diana and Linda. Of the thousands of hopefuls who aspired to play the role of Charley, the new heroine, it was Joanna Lumley, a delicately boned blonde with the appearance of a Dresden shepherdess, who was chosen. Since Revlon cosmetics had just launched a new perfume called Charley, Joanna suggested Purdey, which happened to be the name of an elegant shotgun. Here proposal was acepted, while Gareth Hunt was cast as Gambit, Purdey's opposite number in the field of combat and the obvious heir apparent to Steed.

I returned to England in the spring of 1976 to begin filming the first series of *The New Avengers*. Frankly, the scripts had reduced my role. I'd all but been put out to grass. Had it not been for the pleasure of working with Joanna and Gareth, and my contractual obligations, I would have walked out. The pleasant and plausible Frenchman, Rudolf Roffi, appeared. He told me not to worry, all would be well, and it went without saying that my part would be re-written to perfection.

Things took a turn for the better when those brilliant directors and old friends Jimmy Hill, Sidney Hayers, Johnny Hough and Bob Fuest returned to work on the show. Such episodes of 'Cat Among the Pigeons' and 'Faces' would have worked brilliantly as individual thrillers. Now feeling more at ease over the series, I spent pleasant weekends either at Beaconsfield or back at Chichester, where I'd rented properties for the duration of this first series.

During that scorching summer of 1976 most of those weekends were spent with Lise, who was back in my life, but among the other chums who came to stay was Diana Rigg. For Diana this was a particularly happy period of her life. She'd just met the gentleman with whom she'd make such a joyous second marriage and, radiantly in love, she'd never looked so happy, relaxed and beautiful.

My visits to Mama, however, were becoming more harrowing, a fact noticed by Lise who, offering to accompany me down to Wiltshire, did what she could to cheer me up during those tortuous journeys. Mama's beady eyes fastened themselves upon Lise. Brushing me aside, she exclaimed, 'Oh, what a vision of loveliness. Do come closer, my dear, that a poor old lady may inspect you further.' As Lise afterwards remarked, she'd been subjected to more than a few unusual proposals during her life, but not one from a lady pushing ninety.

Mama did occasionally attempt a flirtation with a young woman, but from all accounts she had now entered her 'elderly he-man' period. Numerous rugged and well-built old gents were queueing up to take Mama out for rides and afternoon tea, including the late Lord Methuen, whose stately heap, Corsham Court, was a stone's-throw from Mama's hotel. I privately expressed reservations when a misty-eyed Mama informed me of her secret engagement to the peer, but leaving her to revel in her fantasies and chatter away to Lise about her life, I consulted doctors as to what should be done with her.

The medics came bluntly to the point. Get Mama off the fags and booze, or else she'd be a dead woman. Moving her out of the hotel, I placed her in the care of a clergyman who had something of a record for drying out hardened soaks. The cure cost me a fortune, but it did put another few years on Mama's life. Her 'engagement' abruptly called off, Mama denounced men and, after some initial difficulties, settled into her new home where she was eventually weaned off tobacco and alcohol.

When the first series of *The New Avengers* had been completed I flew to Swaziland to film what must surely be the most appalling re-make of *King Solomon's Mines*. Swaziland and South Africa lie next door to each other. A distinguished black actor in the cast was 'one of us' in Swaziland. In South Africa we were issued with directives as to where we could be seen with him!

In 1977 I returned to England to begin the second series of *The New Avengers*, but from day one it was obvious that the show was in deep trouble. The first series had, contrary to the critics' expectations, held up very well, but behind the scenes no one had been paid for about three months. Then quite suddenly francs dried up amid rumours of dark goings-on. To add to these woes, ratings then began to slip. I was not surprised by any of this. I felt that *The New Avengers* had feebly attempted to imitate the then popular American series *Starsky and Hutch*, and had in consequence become a mish-mash. The final blow came with the news that the charming Monsieur Rudolf Roffi had disappeared.

I went on a trip to Singapore and Australia. While I was in Australia, an announcement was made on the television news that Patrick Macnee, star of the British TV series *The Avengers*, had died that night. Members of the Press phoned Jenny, my daughter, who lives in Palm Springs, California, to offer their sympathy on my demise. She was not only shocked by surprised.

'But I was speaking to him on the phone in Australia only, oh, abut twelve minutes ago', she said.

'No,' they replied. 'We're very sorry, but it's the time difference. We're afraid he is dead.'

Jenny immediately telephoned me in Australia to ask if I'd died.

'Not that I know of,' I replied. 'Certainly not since you phoned me.' It was of course dear Patrick Magee, the famous star of *Marat/de Sade* and *The Clockwork Orange*, who had died that night.

Some nights later, lying in bed reading, I was disturbed once again by the ringing of the telephone. This time it was Rupert, my son. 'Pa,' he said, his voice shaking. 'You've got to come home at once.'

'What is it, Roop?'

'Jenny's going to die.'

Jenny's health had improved immeasurably in the dry heat of Palm Springs, though she still remained an asthmatic. She was able to lead a normal life, and felt sufficiently confident to embark upon a course of business studies at a local college. There she made many friends and, putting her superb culinary skills to use, often entertained chums, and chums of chums, to dinner parties and barbeques at my home, which soon became known as Macnee's Chuck Wagon.

It was around this time that I first began to invest heavily in real estate. Having purchased great tracts of desert land, I also bought a plot next door to Walter Annenberg's estate, where I planned to build Jenny a house of her own. My finances, like my life, had fluctuated alarmingly, but at last I'd had the sense to make sound investments, which would make me a wealthy man and enable me to leave my children a decent legacy. Having deserted them as infants, I owed them something. Rupert and Jenny would inherit the financial security I had been denied after Mama's debacle at Rooksnest.

Life continued pleasantly until one evening when, immersed in some homework, Jenny complained that she felt peculiar. There was no physical discomfort or emotional fear. She just felt peculiar. This haze of uncertainty quickly developed into a precise and horrifying form of reality when Jenny stood up. Instead of maintaining her balance, she passed out and crashed into some chairs. Her eyes then receded into their sockets, her jaw contorted and her complexion turned to blue. John Scott, a near neighbour, heard Jenny's panic stricken screams and tore around. After he'd massaged her heart, Jenny came to, but at John's insistence she was taken up to Los Angeles the following morning where she spent several days in hospital undergoing intensive tests.

The nature of my daughter's attack and the contortion of her jaw convinced the doctors that she'd suffered an epileptic fit. She was accordingly treated for this. Shortly afterwards Jenny returned to Palm Springs, but within days it became clear that matters were far from being well. Her mind frequently blurred, she could scarcely move and persistently wanted to vomit. Though the attacks were brief, they were also frightening and embarrassing since they came on suddenly and unexpectedly, whether she was at home or in a supermarket.

Further tests revealed that Jenny had a tumour on her brain. Though not malignant, the tumour would continue to grow and Jenny's doctors wanted it removed at once. Jenny had possibly carried the tumour since childhood. As a doctor explained, they begin as pinpricks but can balloon into tennis balls. He also emphasized that even the vital operation could prove hazardous since in the event of a mishap, the risk of paralysis could arise. But, he stressed, unless that tumour came out, my daughter would die.

Not wishing to burden me with her health problems, a frightened and confused Jenny refused to make contact. Instead, she consulted with other members of the family as to whether or not the operation should go ahead. She was fortunate in having the support of Rupert, her wise brother, who lived and worked in Los Angeles. Having thrashed out all the aspects and likely outcomes of such an operation, Jenny decided to risk it. Only after Rupert had called did she telephone me. That journey back to California was crucifying. Convinced that my daughter would die, I found myself overwhelmed with feelings of guilt. Yet again I felt I was being punished for what I believed was my irresponsible and even callous conduct earlier in life.

The time spent waiting outside the operating theatre ran to nearly four hours. I felt utterly wretched and quite devoid of hope, and could scarcely bring myself to dwell upon what my daughter must be suffering. It didn't matter that she'd feel nothing under an anaesthetic and that a team of America's top neuro-surgeons were exercising their formidable talents to save Jenny's life. If I had not abandoned a tiny blonde moppet of just two years old, God would not be inflicting this upon her to exact such penance from me.

After a tumour the size of a golf ball had been sliced off Jenny's brain, the operation was judged successful. Following a lengthy stay in intensive care, Jenny was allowed to return to Palm Springs.

'It's okay, Pa,' she grinned. 'I feel just great. Don't you realise that I've pulled through?'

I nodded and, managing a tight smile, wondered whether I wasn't becoming obsessed with the notion of betrayal. What none of us then realized was that the worst was still to come.

After a relapse, my daughter endured three further operations, and partial paralysis, before finally recovering. When this nightmare had finally ended, I poured out my soul to Rupert and Jenny. God knows what I actually said, but it was probably a tedious, if sincere, plethora of regrets and apologies that concluded with a recitation of my worldly goods and chattels, chunks of real estate, investments and insurance policies. I'd behaved like a blackguard, I told them, but come the time when their reprobate old Pa tumbled off his perch, they would not starve.

Flinging an arm around my shoulders, Rupert ordered me to stop breast-beating. He took the view that an absent father sending regular money from Canada was preferable to an out-of-work father in England. I was about to argue, but I was silenced when he yawned, 'You are becoming a bore.' Jenny said much the same thing, though I felt that my desertion had affected her more than my son. Still, she begged me to forget the past and look forward to a happy future that we could all share.

With Rupert in Los Angeles, Jenny living with me, and

Barbara, her husband having tragically died, now resident in California, the family was almost one again. But I continued to fester. It was an exasperated Jenny who called me a masochist and blurted out, 'Pa, why can't you see that the two of us really love you?' I didn't know why. Given the way I'd behaved towards my family, perhaps I didn't feel worthy of their love. Unable to speak and not wanting my children to see me in tears, I stumbled into the garden and sat along by the pool, where I wept with gratitude and joy. I was fortunate in having such understanding children. Most of my guilt had now been exorcised.

One of my agents called to say that he'd got me a part in a forthcoming film called *The Sea Wolves*. Directed by Andy McLaglen, son of the late and rumbustious Victor, it was a yarn about some military geriatrics who'd once served sovereign and country in The Calcutta Light Horse. Upon the 1939 declaration of hostilities, these gentlemen felt they should do their bit for Great Britain by throwing fireworks at Brother Boche. I was assigned to play Major 'Yogi' Crossley, a yoga practitioner who at the time of making the film was himself pushing ninety, resident in Bombay, and still practising Yoga.

Along with Gregory Peck, Roger Moore, David Niven, Trevor Howard and many of the British acting profession's notable stalwarts, I headed for Bombay, from where I'd fly on to Goa. Since those notable stalwarts included Terry Longdon and John Standing, I looked forward to reminiscing and boozing with old chums, many of whom I hadn't seen for years. Upon arriving at Heathrow I was greeted by a smiling David Niven who insisted we must enjoy a long chat together once we'd settled down in Goa. It had been nearly twenty-five years since I'd last spoken with him.

A small island situated on India's Malabar Coast, Goa is packed with curiosities, left-overs from hundreds of years of Portugese rule. Among these curiosities are the remains of St

Francis Xavier which, to my disappointment, I couldn't find. It was explained to me that the saint is no longer on public view since a couple of religious maniacs bit off both his big toes. Compensation came when David suggested we take a walk. Given our shared passion for this exercise, plus the discovery of miles of lonely sandy shores, the two of us set off.

I thought I was fit, but I discovered that it was not uncommon for David, now in his seventieth year, to walk up to eighteen miles a day. During the first four miles we'd pass Indians on holiday, the ladies always swimming fully dressed in their saris! Then avoiding countless merchants peddling drugs of all kinds, the two of us would end up in a German-run nudist village complete with a general store and disco. Back at the hotel we'd settle down to enjoy that most sacred of English rituals – tea. As it was election year, alcohol was strictly forbidden. In view of this, David and I poured neat whisky from the teapot and soda out of the milk jug.

Although Jenny continued to make encouraging progress, there was scarcely a moment when she was not out of my mind and, still gravely concerned, I continued to drink. David was a man of great sweetness and sympathy, and his ability to listen rivalled his talent as a superb raconteur. He told me of the experience suffered by one of his adopted daughters, Christina, who'd nearly lost her own life after a car accident in Switzerland. Given the severity of Christina's ensuing head injuries, David, like me, had believed his daughter would surely die. As in my case, David would be lucky. Christina managed to pull through and, though unwell for some time, she too survived to resume her normal life. I wish for the sake of David and his family that the accident had never occurred, but I felt very grateful to a friend who could truly understand my own desperate concern.

I was confused when David told me that he and I were not in fact cousins. Knowing Mama and her antics, I shouldn't have been too surprised, but it was a truth that left me disappointed. Apparently Mama had once enjoyed an affair with David's elder brother, Max. 'This is your Uncle Max, dear,' she'd gushed at me. 'He's the father of your famous cousin, David Niven.' This had been Mama's gracious way of disguising her affair with a man from the ever vigilant Evelyn.

Filming *The Sea Wolves* ended too quickly for me. David had been a marvellous companion, and I realized how desperately I'd miss him. We corresponded regularly until his death, but sadly all subsequent attempts to meet up were thwarted. It was at this time that David finished writing his novel, *Go Slowly, Come Back Quickly*. I was told that one of the characters in the book had been based on me, and felt inordinately proud of this. 'Yes,' David hooted when I asked him about it. 'You're marvellous as Charlie Macnee, the milkman.'

Jenny had much improved, but just looking at her brought me near to tears. Only thirty, this pretty girl now resembled a wizened old woman. Was there nothing that could be done, I asked myself and my friends? I was prepared to spend every dollar I had to have my daughter looking well again. They advised me to hold on to my money and exercise patience. It would be a question of time.

I was also advised to plunge myself into work. If nothing else, it might distract me from torturing myself over Jenny. Since she was well cared for by family and friends, I felt able to leave California with a moderately easy conscience. Keeping in touch with my daughter on a daily basis, I embarked upon a theatrical tour that took me around the world.

I was not at my best myself, however. 'Patrick,' worried friends remonstrated, 'have you looked at yourself in a mirror?' I had, but it was a sight I preferred to ignore. I was still drinking heavily, my weight had ballooned, and I now resembled Tweedle Dee and Tweedle Dum rolled into one. Added to my concern for Jenny, I had to contend with worries over my property speculation. I'd bought more land than I could really afford. The monthly mortgage repayments, coupled with Jenny's huge medical bills – though I didn't grudge her that – had all reduced me to a state of penury. Instead of listening to the brilliant advice of Edgar Gross my business manager, I continued to pay out money, borrow, live beyond my means and drink.

I was momentarily distracted from these woes when Rupert telephoned to say that he'd married Heather Stewart, his long-standing girl-friend. A delicately boned young Canadian, Heather's a girl of marked intelligence and has shown promising flair as a writer. This talent has been invaluable to Rupert in his work as a film producer, and I can only admire his good taste in marrying such a fine girl.

After lecturing on The Liberation of Women during a visit to Saudi Arabia – a reckless topic to have chosen in the circumstances – I returned to Australia to film a television series. Entitled *For The Term Of His Natural Life*, the story was about the sufferings endured by convicts when Australia had been a penal colony. Having studied my script, I found myself appalled by the outrages that had been commited to comparatively recently in a British colony, and by individuals who'd largely come from a similar background to my own.

Given my worries, many of which were still coupled with recurring remnants of guilt over the children, I quickly slid into a state of depression. I masochistically and quite absurdly blamed my ancestors and even myself for the excesses of the British ruling class, past and present. I brooded and continued to increase both my drinking and my weight. Although she was too polite to comment, the sad look in the eyes of my old chum Samantha Eggar, who was playing the part of my wife, said it all. Nevertheless, I went on downing the Scotch.

A friend had given me the run of his London house during a brief stay in London, so I invited Lise for drinks one evening prior to dinner. She arrived in a state of giggles claiming she'd spotted a naked man clambering out of an upstairs window in a house opposite. I glanced across at the house disbelievingly, but she was right. This naked gentleman had by now squeezed himself out of a small window and appeared to be making a courageous if foolhardy assault upon his roof. Furthermore, he was someone I knew, an easy-going American called Boris, and I rushed out to discover what he was up to. He spotted me from where he was now perched between the window ledge and the guttering, waved and drawled, 'Oh, hi Pat.'

I've described Boris as easy-going, and that he needed to be. I believe he hovered somewhere between being the fifth and ninth husband of an American heiress whose delusions of dramatic grandeur and acrobatic talent on casting couches had once long ago landed her some minute film parts. Now a disgruntled drunk who must have been tricky to live with, the lady was lucky to be married to a man who adored her. 'For God's sake, love,' I said. 'What are you doing?'

Boris explained that the two of them had returned from a wedding reception. His wife had hit the champagne with enthusiasm, locked herself in the bathroom and wouldn't come out. For hours Boris had hammered upon the bathroom door, but his repeated cries of 'You okay, Honey?' were not answered. Boris was now poised to clamber on to the roof from where he intended to slip down through the open bathroom window and find out if 'Honey' was okay. I suggested he slip into a dressing-gown. This sweet, if not overly bright, gentleman digested my advice. 'Say,' he drawled, 'you could be right, Pat. It ain't fitting that I should be seen like this in Belgravia – London – England.'

Now in a short bath-robe, Boris climbed back out of the bedroom window, grabbed the guttering, and heaved his hefty frame up on to the roof. The guttering shuddered, and some tiles crashed down onto the pavement. As Boris continued his ascent I averted my eyes and wished he'd worn a longer bath-robe.

Boris made it into the bathroom. Poking his head out of the window he shouted 'You okay, Honey?'

There was no reply.

'Gee! Is that you Honey?'

If it wasn't Honey, I wondered, then who the hell was it? But leaning out of the window, Boris now announced, 'It's Honey.'

I felt relieved.

'Pat, Honey's drunk.'

Dear God, I thought, would my torment never end?

'You listening, Pat?' I nodded. 'Okay. Honey's sprawled out across the john. Her skirt's fallen around her ankles and her hat's over one eye.' I could have done without this graphic description.

'You still there, Pat?'

Since he couldn't avoid seeing me then where did Boris think I was? But to reassure him I waved. 'What shall I do?' he asked.

I advised Boris to leave the bathroom, put Honey to bed, and call her doctor in case she had an attack of alcoholic poisoning. I could only gasp in disbelief when Boris re-emerged from the bathroom window, climbed back on to the roof and clambered down back through the bedroom window. What was he up to now? Boris explained that, following my instructions, he'd left the bathroom, would now put Honey to bed and then call her doctor. But how, I enquired with strained patience, could he put Honey to bed since the bathroom door was still locked and he was now back in the bedroom?

'Hey, you could be right, Pat,' he agreed. And with that he climbed back onto the roof and tumbled down into the bathroom.

Leaving the lunacy of London, I returned to Palm Springs. After a date shake near the Morongo Indian Bingo Hall, I arrived home to learn that Bull Moses had been on the phone requesting further donations. By now I had concluded he must be a charlatan and I fled to Jenny's house, where I laid low. Jenny had recovered from the operations and was feeling in good shape, although her asthma attacks were still horrendous. I reflected upon my current situation. By now I doubted whether I could ever repay the enormous mortgages I'd taken out. Given Edgar's many warnings, I was well aware of my commitments, but rather than act positively, I continued to procrastinate and drink.

One of my agents, a kindly man, told me quite bluntly that unless I lost weight I could only hope to play fat-men parts. He was genuinely concerned for me, and he was right. My belly had so distended that I could no longer see my feet, while my sagging jowels and sad and worried eyes had given my face the appearance of a bloodhound. I was clearly in a state of crisis. Edgar Gross continued to call, but I didn't call back. Instead, I went to see Baba.

A beautiful, warm-hearted, mature Hungarian, Baba had come into my life when we were introduced at one of Palm Springs' many charity functions, for which she works untiringly. Though the two of us had got along famously, I'd regarded her as just a good friend. Now, in this time of desperation, my thoughts returned to Baba. Had I deluded myself or had I been right in thinking that this patient, warm and understanding lady was just waiting for me to approach her? I unashamedly poured out my heart to her, and the response was overwhelming. Not only did she understand, but also longed to help, offering me an affection I had never received from any other woman. I also took her advice to see Edgar. 'About time you showed up,' Edgar grumbled. Then, giving me an optimistic smile, he added, 'It will take time, but if you start listening, then I think we can get you back on your feet.' After years of desolation and loneliness I now believed that matters would right themselves and I began listening to these two marvellous people. But not even they could stop my drinking.

Given my weight, I easily passed as a fat cat when offered the role of Calvin Cromwell, the demonic head of a ball-bearing company, in the television series *Empire*. A satire on American big business, *Empire* offered me the most satisfying part since I'd played Andrew Wyke in *Sleuth*. Cromwell was an appalling chairman of the board whose favourite phrases included 'Anxiety Breeds Excellence' and 'Panic Precipitates Performance'. Was it so surprising that his staff met in the boardroom carrying Oxygen tents, airline barf bags and boxes of Valium?

While seated in this boardroom with several fellow-actors awaiting the next shot, one of them fixed me with a glare and exclaimed: 'Why are you Goddam Limeys always coming over here and taking work away from us Americans?'

I was stunned by the ferocity of this question, but collecting myself, stated quietly that I'd lived in the States for over thirty years. Aware that all the other actors present were now listening intently, my assailant said nothing, but continued to glare.

'And what's more,' I added, 'I do have American citizenship.'

The actor's face flushed as he hissed: 'But you've still got a British accent.'

He said it as though it was an offence and I realized that George the Third and his ministers have much to answer for.

As I dithered over marrying Baba, once more I was plagued by a sense of desolation. My financial affairs were much improved, but I simply couldn't stop drinking. This brought about the most terrible depressions, which in turn induced feelings of self-doubt about my acting ability. What had I done since *The Avengers*? Frankly, not a lot. Yes, I'd never been without offers of work, whether they were playing werewolves or advertising deodorant, but I was no longer the star I'd once been.

I'd fled to La Jolla alone and whiled away weeks just strolling along the beaches and drinking and eating too much. Feeling terrible, I drove back to Palm Springs and saw my

Canadian doctor who gave me a blood test. The result was alarming, since my liver count in three areas was way over the limit. 'Patrick,' he warned, 'you have got to stop drinking.' I took a second and even a third opinion. The first, an eminent Polish gastroenterologist confirmed the diagnosis. The second, an equally eminent American specialist – after asking me whether I was a homosexual or a drug addict – confirmed that indeed I did have chronic liver disease. In his opinion, this deterioration had either been caused by my sexual habits or genetics! I immediately stopped drinking and have since enjoyed excellent health.

Lise telephoned. Did I know that Rooksnest, my old childhood home, was on the market, its contents going under Sotheby's hammer. I'd heard rumours, and asked her whether she'd drive down to see if there was anything I might like to buy. Her subsequent report was gloomy. 'Not only is the place falling down,' she said sadly, 'but it's crammed with junk, while all the decent stuff has been wrecked.' Over the years the drunken old girls had careered through the mansion, vandalizing its contents. Amid this carnage only the wine cellar had remained well-stocked, but that was of no interest to me now.

When next in England I found myself the victim of Eamonn Andrews' *This Is Your Life*. The experience was terrifying, hilarious and, of course, highly emotional. The show's guest of honour was Mama. Now ninety-five, though passing herself off as eighty-seven, her mind was not what it was; but there was still a look of mischief about her. Tossing sticks and medics aside, Mama staggered on to the stage, where she was given a standing ovation. With great dignity she inclined her head and acknowledged the nation. She'd no idea she was appearing on television. As the cheering continued and I clasped one of her hands in my own, I felt an enormous surge of pride. She really was a magnificent old girl.

Ten weeks later, a cable arrived at my Californian home.

Mama had gone to make peace with her Maker. I had felt much bitterness, but also love that had been impossible to express.

A View To A Kill, the latest James Bond film, was due to be made and Roger Moore sweetly asked whether I'd like to play Sir Godfrey Tibbett, a Whitehall Mandarin who during the film would in the interests of national security be down-graded to play 007's chauffeur. The final decision as to whether I should play Tibbett lay with the film's producer, Albert R. 'Cubby' Broccoli. I wasn't sure how Cubby would react, since I had once berated him for stealing Honor Blackman away from *The Avengers* to play Pussy Galore in *Goldfinger*; but he confirmed that the part was mine, and I flew to France to film at the château of Chantilly.

During the course of his adventures the down-graded Sir Godfrey was assigned to care for some magnificent horses. Someone asked whether I knew anything about equestrian matters. Casting a knowledgeable eye over the horses' withers and examining their fetlocks, I found myself reminded of a tiny man, a 'shrimp', I'd seen doing much the same thing fifty years previously. A tiny man who'd taught me all I know about horses. As with Mama, it is to my everlasting regret that I never got to know my father.

Before attending the London premiere of *A View To A Kill* I saw Edgar Gross. Although I had lost a great deal of money, thanks to his financial acumen and genuine concern Edgar had saved me from bankruptcy, and still enabled me to hold on to much of my land. My children would have their inheritance, and with money now in the bank I could start afresh.

Whenever visiting Great Britain I invariably make contact with my former *Avengers* ladies. Honor enjoys a flourishing career in films and on stage, Diana in the New Year became a Commander of the British Empire and is happily married to Archie Stirling, whose uncle David founded the SAS, Joanna is very busy professionally and recently married a conductor, while back in America Linda is poised to become a successful comedienne. All four ladies were not only a delight to work with, but are still among my dearest chums.

Back in California Jenny has made remarkable progress. The wizened old lady is no more, and I now see a smiling young woman with pink cheeks and blonde hair. These days, Christmas is a family occasion. Barbara comes down from Los Angeles, where she's running a successful glassware business, as do Rupert and his wife, Heather, while Jenny drives over to join us from her house in the desert.

EPILOGUE

Strolling the sands of West Wittering Beach upon a fine morning, dressed in old shorts, scuffed walking shoes and a battered sun hat, I pass for an eccentric and lonely British gentleman. In the frayed satchel hanging from one of my shoulders is a selection of English newspapers, a couple of carrots, a polished mauve stone with wondrous propensities (a gift from the psychic Michael Bentine), some lucky frogs, and a bottle of prune juice. Eccentric I may be, but I'm no longer lonely.

Until recently I'd reconciled myself to being alone for the rest of my days, and had it not been for the constant loyalty, kindness, and above all, love of a most remarkable lady, alone I would have remained. Not wishing to be a burden upon her, I had decided against marrying Baba. But when all my troubles were no more, there she was still wanting and waiting for me. Indeed, I finally realized that she had always loved me while I, probably feeling unworthy, had pretended for so long that such emotion was a myth. I am now deeply in love with Baba, and have dispelled the myth by marrying her.

On 25 February of this year, in The Enchanted Garden Chapel, Palm Springs, California, we became man and wife. Two youthful, happy, sixty-six-year-old romantics – married by a lady preacher. Upon leaving the chapel, the Reverend Shirley Fletcher handed us our licence, along with some folders. When we were seated in a restaurant with my daughter Jenny, to celebrate, we opened the folders. They contained tastefully designated methods of birth control! Baba and I looked at each other, and in our joy, laughed uproariously. 'Well,' giggled Baba, 'that lady must really believe in miracles.' But Jenny laughed even more as she drank our health, her distended tummy bouncing against the table as she rocked with mirth. Two months later she was delivered of a fine, healthy baby boy. I was a grandfather. I wonder what Mama would have said to that!

Acknowledgements

We wish to take this opportunity to thank the many friends and kindly people without whose enthusiastic help *Blind In One Ear* would have been more difficult to write. Our gratitude goes to Stephen and Joy Curry, followed (in alphabetical order) by: Paul Almond, Arthur Anstey (Gardener to the British gentry, Retired), Lieutenant Commander Eric Archer RD, RNR, Peter Barnes CB (ex-Sladden's House), 'Phat' Bear, Michael Bentine, Robert Bertrand, Marie Bohan, Patrick Cargill, Brian Clemens, Margaret Courtenay, Francis Cowper (Hon. Bencher and devoted servant of Gray's Inn), Ronald and Uschi Dunn-Jones (alias 'Nature Boy' and 'Mother Earth'), Tom Egerton, Barbara Foulds (nee Macnee/Douglas), the late Albert Fennell, Cameron Gough DSC, Mel Haber, Felix Hope-Nicholson, Heather Holden-Brown (a lady of superlative good taste!), Francis John Clarence Westenra Plantagenet Hastings MA, 15th Earl of Huntingdon, Derek Johns and his equally delightful colleagues (especially Ian Hyde), John, Mary, Angus and Ailsa Johnson, Jerry Juroe, Peter Lawrence (the greatest living authority on Eton), Christopher Lee, Andrew Lownie, Baba Macnee, James Macnee, Jenny Macnee, Rupert Macnee, Jacques Henri Philippe Auguste Montellier (purveyor of rare folios), Barry and Sydney Morse, Emlyn Owen, Rt Rev. Simon Wilton Phipps MC, Nosher Powell, Sir Anthony Quayle CBE, Harry Ranson (Master of Young's Shire horses, Retired), Trish Reynolds, Dave Rogers (world authority on *The Avengers*), Leonard Sachs, Michael Sloan, David Stuart, Vernon Sugden (who swallowed a bee), Rt Rev. Henry Thorold, Rt Hon. Viscount Thurso of Ulbster JP, Edward Underdown, Richard Usborne, Jim Westoll (ex-Sladden's House), Josephine Williams' 'Apple-cheeked' Cousin Jo, John Young and Thomas Young (otherwise known as The Ram Brewery), and finally, Harrap for taking us on!

And if we've left out anyone, they'll probably run us to ground.

Patrick Macnee and Marie Cameron

Index

294

*The authors wish to apologize for the confusion that has arisen over David, King of Scotland. Although one source claimed there had been a King David VII, subsequent checking proved this to be unfounded. However, the following points have been established with regard to the relationship of Patrick Macnee's Huntingdon ancestors and the kings of Scotland.

David I ('The Saint') married Matilda, widow of Simon de Senlis, or St Liz, daughter and heiress of Waltheof, Earl of Huntingdon. Issue of this union included, Henry, Earl of Huntingdon who died on 12 June 1152, and it is through this line that Patrick can claim Robert I 'The Bruce', Mary, Queen of Scots and Charles II of England and I of Scotland among his ancestors.